CHEF JAMIE'S
MODERN COMFORTS

CHEF JAMIE'S
MODERN COMFORTS

Healthy Updates for Traditional Foods

Chef Jamie Gwen
Culinary Institute of America Graduate

and

Dr. Myles Bader
"The Wizard of Food"

FRIEDMAN/FAIRFAX

A FRIEDMAN/FAIRFAX BOOK

© 2002 by Jamie Gwen and Dr. Myles H. Bader

Please visit our website: www.metrobooks.com

Library of Congress Cataloging-in-Publication Data

Gwen, Jamie.
   Chef Jamie's modern comforts : healthy updates for traditional foods / Jamie Gwen and Myles H. Bader.
     p.cm.
   Includes index.
   ISBN 1-58663-191-8(alk. paper)
    1. Low-fat diet—Recipes. I. Bader, Myles. II. Title.

RM237.7. .G944 2001
641.5′638—dc21

2001033621

Editor: Susan Lauzau
Art Director: Jeff Batzli
Designer: Joe Rutt
Production Manager: Michael Vagnetti

Printed in the USA by R.R. Donnelley & Sons

1 3 5 7 9 10 8 6 4 2

Distributed by Sterling Publishing Company, Inc.
387 Park Avenue South
New York, NY 10016
Distributed in Canada by Sterling Publishing
Canadian Manda Group
One Atlantic Avenue, Suite 105
Toronto, Ontario, Canada M6K 3E7
Distributed in Australia by
Capricorn Link (Australia) Pty, Ltd.
P.O. Box 704, Windsor, NSW 2756 Australia

Acknowledgments

M yles, thank you for the incredible opportunity to collaborate with you and to share my recipes with so many people. It is a privilege to work with such a brilliant, kind, and generous man.

To my Mom, Lana, without whom I wouldn't be who I am. This book would not exist if it weren't for your tireless efforts and for always believing that I can do *anything*. You have given me the strength and perseverance to succeed, along with never-ending support and guidance. You are the finest chef I know! Thank you for sharing your talents and love for food with me, and for your endless hours of being my sous-chef, my editor, my researcher, and my dishwasher!

With gratitude to Bruce Lubin, for your support, time, effort, and most especially for believing in this project.

Special thanks to Susan Lauzau, my editor, for your guidance, creativity and hard work.

And to Daryl, Nicole, Phyllis, Jamie D., Loren, David, Andrea, Aunt Joyce, and Aunt Helen, who believed....

Helene, your support and advice is immeasurable...Thank you from the bottom of my heart.

Chef Emeril Lagasse, who has always believed in me and whose kindness, friendship, and fine food has always inspired me.

Chef Octavio Becerra, who started the whole thing for me, thank you for taking in a C.I.A. intern!

Thank you to everyone who donated special recipes for the world to appreciate....

And thanks to my family and friends...who tested and tasted and always understood when I said, "I have to call you back"!

Eat Well,
Jamie

Contents

Introduction

In my culinary career thus far, I have had the privilege of working with incredibly talented chefs and teachers, wonderful cooks, and many food lovers. Of them, I was blessed to have met a gentleman, during my time on the Home & Family television show, who is a brilliant food scientist, but even more importantly, as kind a person as I could ever wish to meet. Working with Dr. Myles H. Bader, the "Wizard of Food," has been an incredible learning experience and a wonderful form of entertainment for both the audience and myself. The greatest blessing came when "The Wizard," who had always believed in my talents, asked me to write a cookbook with him.

This book allows me to share with you my passion for good, simple food, and at the same time, to add to your knowledge of low-fat cooking by giving you valuable tips and nutritional breakdowns from the "Wizard of Food" himself.

During my time working in restaurants, catering, and cooking on television (and on the radio!), I have come to love simplicity in food. Fresh seasonal produce, high-quality meats, and flavorful seasonings make for exciting tastes.

The recipes in this book are childhood memories of mine, and most likely, yours. Old-fashioned foods can mean so many things to so many people. To me, old-style, rich, wonderful foods from every culture and every table are categorized as comfort foods. The foods that made you feel better when you were sick and those you requested for your birthday celebration—those are comfort foods.

I remember sitting on the counter in the kitchen as my mom prepared eight-course meals that began with vichyssoise and baby green salad with homemade pâté, paused for beaujolais granita, continued with succulent meat, poached fish, or roasted chicken, and ended with desserts of almond brioche bread pudding or chocolate soufflé. I grew up eating well!

A passion for food and an appreciation for its beauty were instilled in me from a young age. My mother has always cooked with such love, making the food taste that much sweeter. Today, I pour my heart into every dish, with the hope of bringing joy and great flavors to the incredible culinary adventure so many of us call life!

This cookbook is filled with wonderfully homey comfort foods that I remember eating while growing up. My mother always taught me that food shared around the table with family and friends creates warm and lasting memories. May these recipes create new memories for you and your family, and rekindle old ones you may have left behind.

From my kitchen and my heart to yours....

How to Use This Book

All of the recipes in *Chef Jamie's Modern Comforts* feature soothing favorites from our collective childhood—some of the recipes have been given a deliciously modern twist, while others remain in their cherished traditional form. But, in keeping with the times, each recipe in this book offers you a low-fat alternative that allows you to eat more healthily and still savor the comforts of old-fashioned cuisine.

Tips throughout from "The Wizard of Food," Dr. Myles H. Bader also help you work more efficiently and cook successfully, giving you greater culinary wisdom and insight into the science of food. New low-fat products and healthy tricks of the trade are tools that you can use to create wholesome comfort foods that are good for you.

At the end of each recipe, you will find a complete nutritional breakdown for both the traditional version and the reduced-fat variation, allowing you to evaluate fat, calories, cholesterol, carbohydrates, and other food facts quickly and easily.

Whether you choose to indulge or slim down, you will find recipes that make use of the bounty of every season and that cater to widely varying personal tastes. Of course, you may want to alter some of the recipes to suit your cooking style and your family's preferences—if you remember your mother's borscht tasting very lemony, add a squeeze of fresh lemon juice; substitute parsley in place of mint if you can't find the fresh herb you are looking for. Cooking should be experimental and fun!

There are a few basics to keep in mind while reading the recipes:

- Large eggs are standard
- Unless otherwise specified, sugar in the recipe refers to granulated sugar
- Use unsalted butter, so that you can determine the salt content of your food (Dr. Bader says that unsalted butter reduces sticking too!)
- Season with salt and pepper a few times during the cooking process to create depth and layers of flavor in the dish
- Unless otherwise specified in the recipe, the reduced-fat nutritional information was calculated using all the fat-lowering options discussed in the tip.
- Fill your pantry with good-quality olive oil, aromatic spices, and all your favorite things!

This book has been an incredible learning experience for me, and I hope it is the same for you. May you enjoy the modern comforts of life and always eat well!

A Note from the Wizard

The information regarding nutrients and their relative values were determined as accurately as possible given the unique nature of each recipe and ingredients. The values will vary somewhat depending on the ingredients you actually use and how careful you are when measuring them.

Lowering fat levels in any recipe is critical to maintaining a person's optimum weight. Since fat calories have 9 calories per gram, and protein and carbohydrates only have 4 calories per gram, the total calories in a recipe can be easily reduced with intelligent substitutions. Also, calories from fat may not be as easily broken down and used by the body as carbohydrates calories are. The body requires only a small amount of essential fatty acids to function at optimal levels.

A number of sources were used to determine the relative food values to make the information as accurate as possible. It is extremely difficult to change a recipe into a low-fat recipe and still keep the palatable quality of that recipe intact.

Chef Jamie Gwen has done a miraculous job and has spent hundreds of hours testing and retesting these recipes to be sure that they will all be as satisfying as the original recipes, with all the taste and flavor you could possibly want.

About the Authors

Chef Jamie Gwen is a distinguished graduate of the Culinary Institute of America in Hyde Park, New York. She apprenticed under the tutelage of several renowned chefs, including Wolfgang Puck and Joachim Splichal. After working with Chef Octavio Becerra at Pinot Bistro in Los Angeles, she practiced her craft at several top restaurants in the Los Angeles area.

Jamie is a nationally recognized food expert and chef, and can be seen on Home & Garden Television, The Do It Yourself Network, national news programs, and network talk shows. She is the food producer and stylist for the NBC television show *Emeril*, starring chef Emeril Lagasse. Beyond television, Jamie hosts her own live radio program, entitled "Chef Talk with Chef Jamie Gwen" on Newstalk 870–The New KRLA.

Chef Jamie has been a popular personality on television ever since she brought her culinary expertise to "Home & Family," the flagship show of The Family Channel. As the show's resident chef and food expert, Jamie created, cooked, and presented more that one thousand recipes during the show's three-year run!

Chef Jamie resides in Los Angeles and is accredited to teach the culinary arts by the American Culinary Federation. She also volunteers her culinary talents to at-risk high school students in the Los Angeles school district's Careers Through Culinary Arts Program.

Dr. Myles H. Bader, The Wizard of Food, has been a guest on more than five thousand radio shows and has made more than 130 major television appearances. These included *The Oprah Winfrey Show*, *Crook & Chase*, *America's Talking*, the Discovery Channel's *Home Matters*, *Help at Home*, The Home and Garden Channel's *Smart Solutions*, *The Morning Exchange*, QVC, Trinity Broadcasting, and many more.

Dr. Bader received his Doctoral Degree in Health Science from Loma Linda University, is board certified in preventive care, and has practiced in major clinics in California for more than twenty-two years. He specialized in nutrition, stress management, cardiac rehabilitation, fitness, weight management, and executive health. Dr. Bader has established programs for thirty-five Fortune 500 companies as well as many civic organizations and safety departments. During this period, he lectured extensively throughout the United States and Canada in all area of preventive care, weight control, supplementation, and anti-aging.

Recent books authored by Dr. Bader include: *21ST Century Reference Guide to Cooking Secrets & Helpful Household Hints*; *10,001 Food Facts, Chef's Secrets & Household Hints*; *5,001 Mysteries of Liquids & Cooking Secrets*; *250 Future Food Facts & Predictions for the Millennium*; *To Supplement or Not to Supplement*; and *The Wellness Desk Reference*. Dr. Bader's books have sold more than five hundred thousand copies.

Chapter 1

Wake Up!
It's Breakfast Time

There are few things better than waking up to a delicious breakfast or brunch. Eggs, considered by many to be the perfect food, are incredibly versatile: they puff, fry, bind, enrich, and create creamy texture in dishes ranging from simple to refined.

Whether you enjoy elegantly prepared eggs, perfect pancakes, or morning treats like muffins or coffee cakes, rise and shine. . . it's breakfast time.

Glazed Doughnuts

MAKES 2 DOZEN DOUGHNUTS

History tells us that the first doughnut was made in 1847 when fifteen-year-old Hanson Gregory removed the middle of his mother's small cakes, which had a soggy center that he didn't like.

The first record of a commercial doughnut dates back to 1920 when a New York baker, Adolph Steinberg, invented a machine that made doughnuts, and opened the Broadway Doughnut Shop near Broadway and 42nd Street in New York City.

These homemade doughnuts are a bit more work than running to the corner store, but they're well worth it!

For the doughnuts:
1 cup whole milk, scalded
4 ounces unsalted butter
½ cup sugar
½ teaspoon salt
2 large eggs plus 1 egg yolk, beaten
2 packages (2 tablespoons) active dry yeast

4 cups all-purpose flour, sifted
canola oil, for frying

For the glaze:
1 cup powdered sugar
3 tablespoons water
1 teaspoon vanilla

To make the doughnuts: In a large mixing bowl, pour the scalded milk over the butter, sugar, and salt. Cool slightly, then add the eggs. Mix well to combine. Using a kitchen thermometer, cool to 115°F. Add the yeast and let stand for 5 minutes.

Add the flour a little at a time to create a soft dough. Turn the dough out onto a well-floured board and knead for 2 minutes. Place the kneaded dough in a greased bowl, cover with plastic wrap, and let rise for 1 hour. Punch the dough down and divide it in half. On a floured surface, roll each piece of dough to half-inch thickness. Using a floured doughnut cutter, cut the dough into doughnuts and place on wax paper.

Set in a warm place and allow to rise for 30 minutes.

Heat the oil to 375°F in a large electric skillet. Using a slotted spoon, gently drop each doughnut into the oil. Fry until golden brown, turning once. Drain on paper towels.

To make the glaze: In a small mixing bowl, whisk together the powdered sugar, water, and vanilla. Drizzle over the doughnuts while the doughnuts are still warm.

			PER DOUGHNUT		
STANDARD RECIPE:	CALORIES 412	FAT 33G	PROTEIN 3G	CARBOHYDRATES 26G	CHOL 39MG
REDUCED FAT:	CALORIES 164	FAT 5G	PROTEIN 3G	CARBOHYDRATES 26G	CHOL 39MG

Glazed Doughnuts (continued)

CHEF JAMIE'S LOW-FAT TIP

Doughnuts, while they taste better fried, can be baked to create a much lower-fat breakfast or snack. After allowing the cut doughnuts to rise, place them in a 450°F oven and bake them for 8 to 10 minutes or until golden. Eliminating the frying process makes a huge difference in the total calories and fat content.

HELPFUL HINTS FROM THE WIZARD

- To keep doughnuts from becoming soggy, add one teaspoon of white vinegar to the frying oil.
- Canola oil is the oil of choice because it has a high smoking point.

Old-Fashioned Cinnamon Rolls

MAKES 2 DOZEN CINNAMON ROLLS

Homemade cinnamon buns always get a "Wow!" from an appreciative guest (or child) impressed with your culinary talents! These tempting, scrumptious, gooey rolls are delicious when served the same day or frozen for later use.

For the rolls:

1 package (1 tablespoon) active dry yeast

⅓ cup warm water (110° F)

2 cups whole milk

4 tablespoons unsalted butter, softened

½ cup sugar

1 teaspoon salt

2 large eggs

6½ cups all-purpose flour, sifted

2 tablespoons unsalted butter

4 tablespoons sugar

2 teaspoons ground cinnamon

½ cup walnuts, chopped

½ cup raisins

For the glaze:

1½ cups powdered sugar

3 tablespoons unsalted butter, softened

1 tablespoon heavy cream

1 teaspoon vanilla

To make the cinnamon rolls: In a mixing bowl, dissolve the yeast in the water. In a small saucepan, scald the milk and then stir in the butter, sugar, and salt. Cool to lukewarm and combine the milk mixture with the yeast. Beat in the eggs and combine well. Add half of the flour and stir to combine. Add the remaining flour and stir to form a sticky dough. Turn the dough out onto a floured surface and knead for 10 minutes or until very smooth. Place the dough in a greased bowl, cover with a dry towel, and let rise in a warm place until doubled in size, about 1 hour.

After allowing the dough to rise, remove it from the bowl and roll the dough out to form a ¼-inch-thick rectangle. Spread the dough with the softened butter. Combine the sugar and cinnamon and sprinkle over the butter. Top with the walnuts and raisins. Roll up the dough lengthwise, into a log. Cut the log into one-inch thick slices.

Preheat the oven to 400° F.

Grease a large baking sheet and lay the cinnamon roll slices in a single layer so the rolls are touching. Let the dough rise until the rolls have doubled in size. Bake for 20 minutes or until golden brown.

To make the glaze: In a mixing bowl, whisk together the glaze ingredients. Drizzle the glaze over the warm cinnamon rolls.

			PER ROLL		
STANDARD RECIPE:	CALORIES 276	FAT 9G	PROTEIN 6G	CARBOHYDRATES 43G	CHOL 34MG
REDUCED FAT:	CALORIES 255	FAT 6G	PROTEIN 6G	CARBOHYDRATES 43G	CHOL 26MG

Old-Fashioned Cinnamon Rolls (continued)

CHEF JAMIE'S LOW-FAT TIP

Low-fat milk and "light" (50 percent less-fat) butter work well to create a slightly lighter version of this recipe. Unfortunately, cinnamon rolls were meant to be fattening! To jazz up the less-indulgent low-fat version, make the cinnamon roll spicier with extra cinnamon, nutmeg, or ground ginger.

HELPFUL HINTS FROM THE WIZARD

- Sifting aerates the flour, producing light rolls and biscuits.

Beignets

MAKES ABOUT 25 BEIGNETS

It is thought that Arabs introduced the technique of frying dough in about 1170. The method became popular along the Mediterranean coast, and was eventually carried to France. These rectangular puffs of dough were originally sprinkled with a fine powdered sugar; the filling varied from fruits and vegetables to a mélange of seafood. It was the French of Louisiana who introduced beignets to North America in 1727.

This famous French pastry, especially popular today in New Orleans, tastes like the best puffy doughnut you have ever had! Eater beware: they are extremely addictive and much tastier when eaten hot!

½ cup boiling water
¼ cup sugar
2 tablespoons vegetable shortening
½ teaspoon salt
1 cup heavy cream
½ package (1 ½ teaspoons) dry yeast

½ cup warm water
3¾ cups all-purpose flour
2 large eggs, beaten
vegetable oil, for frying
powdered sugar, for dusting

Pour the boiling water over the shortening, sugar, and salt. Add the cream and let stand until the mixture is just warm, not hot.

In a separate bowl, sprinkle the yeast over the warm water, let stand until dissolved, then add to the shortening mixture. Mix to combine well. Add 2 cups of the flour and the eggs, and beat until well combined. Add just enough of the remaining flour to make a soft dough that holds together and is not sticky.

Turn the dough out onto a lightly floured work surface and pat the dough into a rectangle, about 1 inch thick. Dust the dough with flour and, using a rolling pin, roll out the dough to a ¼-inch thickness. Using a sharp knife, cut the dough into 2-inch-square pieces.

In a large heavy pot or electric skillet, heat the oil to 360°F. Fry the beignets, 2 to 3 at a time, until brown and crispy on all sides. Drain on paper towels, dust liberally with powdered sugar, and serve immediately.

Chef's Note: Do not let the dough rise before frying. You can chill the dough in a greased bowl covered with plastic wrap until ready to use.

CHEF JAMIE'S LOW-FAT TIP

I, Chef Jamie Gwen, cannot bear to disturb the precious beignet by creating a low-fat version of this recipe. Your hips will hate me but your lips will thank me! Splurge!

HELPFUL HINTS FROM THE WIZARD

- Canola oil is the oil of choice for frying because it has a high smoking point.

PER BEIGNET

STANDARD RECIPE: CALORIES 134 FAT 5G PROTEIN 3G CARBOHYDRATES 19G CHOL 30MG

World-Class Pancakes

MAKES 10 PANCAKES

The following pancake recipe is pretty close to the original International House of Pancakes (IHOP) recipe. IHOP was established in 1958 and has boasted ever since that it serves the finest pancakes of any restaurant chain.

1¼ cups all-purpose flour
1 cup buttermilk
¼ cup vegetable oil
¼ cup sugar

¼ cup unsalted butter, melted
1 large egg
1 heaping teaspoon baking powder
1 teaspoon baking soda

In a blender or using an electric mixer, combine all of the ingredients and blend until smooth. Refrigerate the batter for 15 minutes before using.

Preheat a skillet over medium heat. Brush the pan lightly with melted butter. Pour the batter by spoonfuls into the hot pan to form 5-inch circles. When the edges begin to harden and bubbles appear in the center, flip the pancakes. Cook on the other side until golden brown.

CHEF JAMIE'S LOW-FAT TIP

Most pancake recipes are really not too terrible for you; the downfall is the scoop of butter and syrup that they swim in! Try using low-fat buttermilk in the batter and non-stick cooking spray in place of the butter for a really good-for-you version.

HELPFUL HINTS FROM THE WIZARD

- Pancakes can be frozen!
- Turn the pancakes as soon as you see air pockets forming.
- Mix the batter frequently to avoid settling.
- Place a few drops of water on the griddle to see if they bounce. If they bounce, the griddle is hot enough to pour the batter.

		PER PANCAKE			
STANDARD RECIPE:	CALORIES 185	FAT 11G	PROTEIN 3G	CARBOHYDRATES 18G	CHOL 35MG
REDUCED FAT:	CALORIES 138	FAT 6G	PROTEIN 3G	CARBOHYDRATES 18G	CHOL 35MG

German Apple Pancake

MAKES 4 SERVINGS

When I was growing up, my mom made this "Dutch Baby" for breakfast on special mornings. I still love the way the batter crawls up the sides of the pan—and the cloud-like pancake is still a wonderful treat!

4 green apples, peeled and thinly sliced
2 tablespoons lemon juice
2 tablespoons unsalted butter
6 large eggs, beaten

1 cup whole milk
1 cup all-purpose flour
½ teaspoon salt
powdered sugar, for garnish

Preheat the oven to 450°F.

Mix the apples with the lemon juice in a large mixing bowl. Melt the butter in a 12-inch ovenproof sauté pan over medium heat. Add the apples and sauté for 10 minutes, tossing often, until tender and caramelized.

In a separate mixing bowl, combine the eggs, milk, flour, and salt, and whisk to combine.

Pour the batter over the apples and place the pan immediately in the oven. Bake for 20 minutes, then reduce heat to 350°F and bake 10 minutes more until crisp and brown. Dust the puffed pancake liberally with powdered sugar and serve immediately.

CHEF JAMIE'S LOW-FAT TIP

Use low-fat milk in place of whole milk, and substitute reduced-fat butter for the real thing. Also, substitute 3 whole eggs and 4 egg whites for the whole eggs to create a terrifically tasty lower-fat version.

		PER SERVING		
STANDARD RECIPE:	CALORIES 400	FAT 16G	PROTEIN 15G	CARBOHYDRATES 49G	CHOL 344MG
REDUCED FAT:	CALORIES 294	FAT 9G	PROTEIN 10G	CARBOHYDRATES 52G	CHOL 166MG

Homemade Morning Waffles

MAKES 8 WAFFLES

The Chinese invented waffles about two thousand years ago— their batter consisted of rice, soybeans, and curd cheese. Indentations were created by hand and the "waffle" was then cooked in a round shape and called a "pan cake." In 1734, a London chef accidentally hit a pancake with a meat tenderizer—the cake now had small indentations that would hold syrup easily, and it proved a big hit!

The secret to this recipe is the club soda. The carbonation creates a light, airy batter that cooks up crisp on the outside and soft on the inside! Enjoy them with real maple syrup or a shower of fresh fruit.

½ cup unbleached all-purpose flour
2 tablespoons sugar
4 teaspoons double-acting baking powder
½ teaspoon salt

2 large eggs, lightly beaten
4 tablespoons unsalted butter, melted and cooled
1½ cups club soda

Preheat a waffle iron and grease it lightly.

Sift together the dry ingredients in a large bowl. Whisk together the eggs and melted butter in a separate bowl. Pour the egg mixture and club soda into the dry ingredients. Blend just until combined.

Use approximately ¼ cup of batter for each waffle. Cook the batter in the prepared waffle iron until crisp and golden. Serve immediately.

CHEF JAMIE'S LOW-FAT TIP

Substitute egg whites for whole eggs by using 2 egg whites plus 1 tablespoon of water for each whole egg. You can also cut down on the butter by substituting 2 tablespoons of applesauce for two tablespoons of the butter. Don't eliminate the butter completely; the waffles just aren't the same!

HELPFUL HINTS FROM THE WIZARD

- To stop waffles from sticking to the iron, just add 1 teaspoon of white wine to the batter. The taste will not be affected.
- All-purpose flour is a blend of hard and soft wheat flour. It has a balanced protein/starch content, which makes it an excellent choice for waffles. Presifted, all-purpose flour has been milled to a fine texture, is aerated, and is best for waffles.
- Waffles may be frozen and then placed in the toaster.
- The batter should always be mixed between batches of waffles to eliminate settling of ingredients and to keep the batter aerated.

		PER WAFFLE			
STANDARD RECIPE:	CALORIES 168	FAT 7.7G	PROTEIN 4G	CARBOHYDRATES 19G	CHOL 65MG
REDUCED FAT:	CALORIES 129	FAT 3.3G	PROTEIN 4G	CARBOHYDRATES 19G	CHOL 8MG

Belgian Waffles
MAKES 12 WAFFLES

The Belgian waffle first became popular as a dessert, and it wasn't until the early 1900s—when it was introduced in the United States—that it became a breakfast food. In Brussels, it was served with a variety of fresh sliced fruits and topped with cream. The following recipe is for the original Belgian waffle!

The difference between Belgian waffles and the ones we are more familiar with is the yeast in the batter, which yields a lighter waffle with the flavor of fresh-baked bread.

1 package (1 tablespoon) active dry yeast
2 cups whole milk, warmed
2 ¼ cups all-purpose flour
3 tablespoons sugar
1 large egg

3 egg yolks
1 stick unsalted butter, melted and cooled
1 teaspoon vanilla
3 egg whites, beaten to soft peaks

Sprinkle the yeast over ¼ cup of the warm milk in a small bowl and allow it to proof for 5 minutes. (To proof, set the yeast and warm milk aside—it will swell and become bubbly.)

Sift the flour into a large mixing bowl and add the egg, yeast mixture, and sugar. Mix well with a wooden spoon. Add the remaining milk and the egg yolks one at a time, stirring after each addition. Add the melted butter and vanilla, stirring until just combined. Fold the egg whites into the batter, cover with a towel, and allow to rise for 1 hour.

Preheat a waffle iron and grease lightly. Stir down the batter just before baking.

CHEF JAMIE'S LOW-FAT TIP
Use low-fat milk in place of whole milk and look for 50 percent-less-fat butter in your local supermarket. It works great to lower the fat but keep the flavor!

HELPFUL HINTS FROM THE WIZARD
- Allow the butter to soften at room temperature to retain the flavor.

		PER WAFFLE			
STANDARD RECIPE:	CALORIES 172	FAT 7G	PROTEIN 5.5G	CARBOHYDRATES 19.6G	CHOL 107MG
REDUCED FAT:	CALORIES 157	FAT 4G	PROTEIN 5.5G	CARBOHYDRATES 19.6G	CHOL 73MG

Santa Fe French Toast

MAKES 4 SERVINGS

This is the original recipe from the Santa Fe Railroad! French toast was one of the favorite breakfast items in the dining cars of the nineteenth century. This recipe is easy to prepare and comes out crispy and fluffy every time. It tastes best when served with authentic maple syrup.

Use good Italian, French, challah, or raisin bread.

8 (¾-inch-thick) slices bread
3 large eggs
½ cup heavy cream
1½ teaspoons vanilla extract
pinch of salt
dash of nutmeg
6 tablespoons vegetable oil

Preheat the oven to 400°F.

Trim the crusts from the bread. Lightly beat the eggs with the cream. Add the vanilla, salt, and nutmeg, and whisk to combine. Soak the bread, a few pieces at a time, in the egg mixture so they absorb the liquid thoroughly.

Heat 2 tablespoons of oil in a large sauté pan over medium heat. Place two pieces of soaked bread in the pan and fry on both sides until golden brown. Drain on paper towels to absorb any excess oil. Repeat the process using the remaining oil and the remaining soaked bread.

Place the browned French toast on a baking sheet and bake for 3 to 5 minutes or until puffed and crisp. Serve hot with maple syrup.

CHEF JAMIE'S LOW-FAT TIP

Try using liquid egg substitute in place of whole eggs. The standard conversion is ¼ cup of egg substitute to each whole egg. Use whole milk (even low-fat milk works) in place of the heavy cream, and use only 3 tablespoons of oil when frying. Also, an updated version of this recipe might use canola oil in place of vegetable oil. Using canola oil will increase the level of monounsaturated fat, which is preferred by the body.

HELPFUL HINTS FROM THE WIZARD

- The bread will retain its shape and not fall apart if it is 2 days old.
- The eggs should be at room temperature to increase the volume when beaten.
- Spray oil will reduce the amount of oil used by about 85 percent.

		PER SERVING			
STANDARD RECIPE:	CALORIES 521	FAT 41G	PROTEIN 10G	CARBOHYDRATES 37G	CHOL 227MG
REDUCED FAT:	CALORIES 375	FAT 29G	PROTEIN 9G	CARBOHYDRATES 36G	CHOL 42MG

Creamy Cheese Blintzes

MAKES 12 BLINTZES

I remember my grandmother making these blintzes . . . and my mother making these blintzes! They were soooo good served with sour cream and homemade strawberry jam!

For the crepes:

3 large eggs

¾ cup milk

⅓ cup plus 2 tablespoons all-purpose flour

1 teaspoon sugar

pinch of salt

2 tablespoons unsalted butter, melted

For the filling:

8 ounces cream cheese

8 ounces cottage cheese

½ cup sour cream

3 large eggs

⅓ cup sugar

1 teaspoon vanilla

To make the crepes: In a large mixing bowl, beat the eggs and milk until frothy. Sift together the flour, sugar, and salt and gradually beat the dry mixture into the egg mixture until smooth. Strain into a bowl, pressing any lumps of flour through the sieve.

Heat a 6- or 7-inch crepe or sauté pan over medium heat. Brush the pan with a little bit of the melted butter. Pour in 3 tablespoons of batter and tilt the pan from side to side so the batter covers the bottom of the pan. Cook until the sides of the crepe begin to come away from the pan, about 1 minute. Flip the crepe over and cook about 30 seconds more. Turn the crepe out onto a paper towel and repeat the process using the remaining melted butter and crepe batter.

To make the filling: In a large bowl, mix the cream cheese, cottage cheese, and sour cream until well blended. Add the eggs, one at a time, mixing well after each addition. Stir in the sugar and vanilla. Cover and chill until firm.

Place a crepe on a work surface. Place 2 tablespoons of the filling in the center of the crepe, fold in both sides of the crepe to cover the cheese, then roll up the blintz. Place the rolled blintzes, seam side down, on a tray lined with wax paper.

		PER BLINTZ			
STANDARD RECIPE:	CALORIES 198	FAT 14G	PROTEIN 7G	CARBOHYDRATES 118G	CHOL 123MG
REDUCED FAT:	CALORIES 164	FAT 6G	PROTEIN 7G	CARBOHYDRATES 118G	CHOL 110MG

To serve, heat a large non-stick skillet over medium heat. Lightly brush the bottom of the pan with melted butter. Sauté the blintzes, seam side down, in a single layer until golden brown, about 5 minutes. Turn the blintzes over and fry until golden on the bottom side, and heated through (about 5 minutes longer). Serve hot.

CHEF JAMIE'S LOW-FAT TIP

These blintzes taste almost as good when you lighten the filling by substituting low-fat cream cheese, cottage cheese, and/or sour cream. They lose some of their rich flavor but the creamy texture remains. Also, prepare the crepes with low-fat milk and use 1 whole egg and 3 egg whites for a scrumptious lower-fat version!

HELPFUL HINTS FROM THE WIZARD

- If you don't have a non-stick pan, make sure you remove the pan from the heat and rub the inside of the pan with a butter wrapper, or brush some butter on it, in between batches.

Breakfast Casserole

MAKES 6 SERVINGS

This make-ahead casserole is terrific for company or perfect for a breakfast buffet with fresh fruit and morning breads.

8 slices white bread, crusts removed and cubed
1 pound raw sweet Italian sausage meat (casings removed)
½ cup cheddar cheese, shredded
½ cup Swiss or jack cheese, shredded
½ cup mushrooms, sliced
2 cups whole milk
6 large eggs
1 teaspoon dry mustard
1 teaspoon Worcestershire sauce
salt & pepper, to taste

Preheat the oven to 350°F. Grease a 7 × 11-inch baking pan and cover the bottom with the bread cubes.

Brown the sausage in a hot skillet, then drain it well. Sprinkle the cooked sausage over the bread. Top with the shredded cheeses and mushrooms.

In a separate bowl, beat the eggs lightly and add the milk and seasonings. Pour the egg mixture over the ingredients in the pan. Cover and refrigerate overnight.

Bring the casserole to room temperature before baking. Bake for 35 to 40 minutes or until puffed and cooked through. Serve immediately.

CHEF JAMIE'S LOW-FAT TIP

For a lighter version, use chicken or turkey sausage in place of pork sausage. Use low-fat milk and reduced-fat cheese to lower the fat content. You can also use 2 whole eggs and 1 cup of egg substitute in place of the 6 whole eggs without losing the light, puffy quality of this terrific dish.

HELPFUL HINTS FROM THE WIZARD

- Never use potatoes in a casserole if you are going to freeze it—they become mushy.
- Never freeze a casserole that contains a dairy product.

		PER SERVING			
STANDARD RECIPE:	CALORIES 608	FAT 40G	PROTEIN 37G	CARBOHYDRATES 22G	CHOL 400MG
REDUCED FAT:	CALORIES 308	FAT 14G	PROTEIN 34G	CARBOHYDRATES 26G	CHOL 128MG

Creole Eggs

MAKES 6 SERVINGS

The word "Creole" was derived from the Latin "creare," which means to create. Creole cooking combines many different ethinic traditions—this tasty blending of spices and local ingredients originated in New Orleans, Louisiana.

Usually a favorite with "the guys," these Creole eggs bake up great!

2 tablespoons unsalted butter
1 yellow onion, diced
1 cup celery, diced
½ cup green bell pepper, diced
4 cups diced tomatoes
1 bay leaf

salt, pepper, cayenne pepper & Tabasco to taste
1½ cups soft bread crumbs
1 cup frozen peas
2 cups cheddar cheese, shredded
8 large eggs

Preheat the oven to 350°F.

Melt the butter in large sauté pan over medium heat. Add the onion, celery, and green pepper, and sauté until tender. Add the tomatoes and bay leaf, and sauté 5 minutes more. Remove the bay leaf and season to taste with salt, pepper, cayenne pepper, and Tabasco. Add the bread crumbs and the peas, and stir to combine.

Pour half of the tomato mixture into a 2-quart ovenproof casserole dish. Top with half of the shredded cheese. Repeat using the remaining sauce and cheese. Using a tablespoon, make eight wells on the top of the casserole. Break an egg into each of the wells.

Bake for 20 minutes or until the eggs are cooked to your desire. Serve immediately.

CHEF JAMIE'S LOW-FAT TIP

Find your favorite low-fat cheese (experiment with the many on your super-market shelves to find out which ones melt best) and use it in place of whole-milk cheese. Liquid egg substitute also works well in place of whole eggs because of all of the bold flavors in this dish.

HELPFUL HINTS FROM THE WIZARD

- Make sure to use unsalted butter. Salt has a tendency to separate from the butter in the salted variety, making a dish slightly bitter.

		PER SERVING			
STANDARD RECIPE:	CALORIES 611	FAT 39G	PROTEIN 34G	CARBOHYDRATES 38G	CHOL 375MG
REDUCED FAT:	CALORIES 388	FAT 13G	PROTEIN 20G	CARBOHYDRATES 37G	CHOL 166MG

Corned Beef Hash & Eggs

MAKES 8 SERVINGS

Corned beef was named in England during the 1700s, when large grains of salt resembling "corn" were used to preserve the beef. Salt has been used for thousands of years to preserve food by inhibiting bacterial growth. This tends to dry the meat, thus reducing the water content. The more moisture left in stored meat, the faster it will go bad!

This recipe is so Irish. . . so simple. . .yet so good! If you choose to make hash with eggs, you've got breakfast. Take away the eggs, pair it with a great salad, and dinner is served.

6 medium potatoes, peeled
¼ cup unsalted butter
1 yellow onion, diced
1 red bell pepper, diced

1 pound corned beef, shredded
salt & pepper, to taste
8 large eggs

In a large pan, cover the potatoes with water and season with salt. Boil until tender but still firm enough to hold their shape. Drain the potatoes and allow to cool. Shred the potatoes on a box grater (use the coarse side) and set aside.

Melt the butter in a large skillet over medium heat. Add the onion and the red bell pepper and sauté for 5 minutes, stirring often. Add the corned beef, shredded potatoes, and pepper. Cook for 10 to 15 minutes, stirring occasionally, until the mixture browns.

Make 8 wells in the hash and crack an egg into each well. Cover the pan and reduce the heat to low. Cook for three minutes. Serve immediately.

Chef's Note: This recipe only works with whole eggs (not liquid egg substitute) because of the preparation.

CHEF JAMIE'S LOW-FAT TIP

Corned beef can be quite fatty (even the "lean" kind), so try using shredded turkey or chicken. Leftover meat from the previous night's dinner also works well, and should be lower in fat since it has already been cooked once. Also, use only 2 tablespoons of butter (50 percent-reduced-fat butter works fine) and a liberal spray of non-stick vegetable spray in the sauté.

HELPFUL HINTS FROM THE WIZARD

- Corned beef is prepared by poaching the beef.
- Lean ground turkey works great.

			PER SERVING		
STANDARD RECIPE:	CALORIES 447	FAT 30G	PROTEIN 24G	CARBOHYDRATES 23G	CHOL 345MG
REDUCED FAT:	CALORIES 290	FAT 15G	PROTEIN 25G	CARBOHYDRATES 23G	CHOL 253MG

Blueberry Buckle Cake

MAKES 12 SERVINGS

This recipe came from a television fan who is a great cook! I have adjusted the measurements slightly to suit my taste (and my love for blueberries), and since the recipe always gets rave reviews, I continue to prepare it with homage to its author!

For the cake:
2 cups all-purpose flour
½ cup sugar
2½ teaspoons baking powder
½ teaspoon salt
¼ cup vegetable shortening
¾ cup whole milk
2 large eggs
3 cups fresh or frozen blueberries

For the crumb topping:
½ cup sugar
⅓ cup all-purpose flour
2 tablespoons unsalted butter, softened
1 teaspoon cinnamon

Preheat the oven to 375°F. Grease a 9 × 9 × 2-inch pan or use a round 9 × 1 × ½-inch pan.

To make the cake: In a large bowl, blend together the flour, sugar, baking powder, salt, shortening, milk, and eggs. Beat for 2 minutes. Carefully stir in the blueberries until just combined.

To make the crumb topping: In a separate bowl, combine the crumb topping ingredients. Blend with a fork until crumbs form.

Pour the batter into the prepared pan and sprinkle the top with the crumb-topping mixture. Bake for 45 to 50 minutes or until golden brown and a cake tester inserted in the middle of the cake comes out clean.

CHEF JAMIE'S LOW-FAT TIP

Try using low-fat milk in place of whole milk, liquid egg substitute instead of the eggs, and canola oil in place of the shortening. But, don't count on the texture remaining as flaky and light as the original recipe. For the crumb topping, 50 percent-less-fat butter works just fine.

HELPFUL HINTS FROM THE WIZARD

• Save your butter wrappers to grease pans.

		PER SLICE			
STANDARD RECIPE:	CALORIES 282	FAT 10G	PROTEIN 4G	CARBOHYDRATES 45G	CHOL 49MG
REDUCED FAT:	CALORIES 194	FAT 6G	PROTEIN 3.5G	CARBOHYDRATES 46G	CHOL 6MG

Healthy Breakfast Apple Cake

MAKES 9 SERVINGS

This recipe hails from my mother's repertoire. Serve the cake warm, right out of the oven, with a great cup of coffee for the perfect breakfast!

1¾ cups oat bran
¾ cup all-purpose flour
1 teaspoon cinnamon
1 teaspoon baking powder
¾ teaspoon baking soda
½ teaspoon salt
¼ teaspoon nutmeg
2 large green apples, peeled, cored & diced

½ cup fresh orange juice
½ cup buttermilk
3 tablespoons molasses
2 large eggs
3 tablespoons vegetable oil
1 teaspoon vanilla

Preheat the oven to 375°F. Lightly grease an 8-inch-square baking pan.

In a large mixing bowl, combine the oat bran, flour, cinnamon, baking powder, baking soda, salt, and nutmeg. Stir to combine well. Add the apples and toss to coat.

In another bowl, whisk together the orange juice, buttermilk, molasses, eggs, oil, and vanilla.

With a wooden spoon, stir the juice mixture into the dry ingredients until just combined.

Pour the batter into the prepared pan and bake for 35 minutes or until a cake tester inserted into the center of the cake comes out dry. If the cake browns too quickly, cover lightly with foil during baking.

Allow the cake to cool in the pan for 30 minutes before removing, then invert onto a cooling rack to cool completely.

			PER SERVING		
STANDARD RECIPE:	CALORIES 198	FAT 7G	PROTEIN 6G	CARBOHYDRATES 31G	CHOL 43MG
REDUCED FAT:	CALORIES 156	FAT 3G	PROTEIN 6G	CARBOHYDRATES 39G	CHOL 0.5MG

Healthy Breakfast Apple Cake *(continued)*

CHEF JAMIE'S LOW-FAT TIP

This delicious cake is actually quite healthy as is. Substitute smooth apple-sauce for the vegetable oil and use 3 egg whites in place of the 2 whole eggs. Do be sure to store the cake in the refrigerator, tightly wrapped, to preserve freshness.

HELPFUL HINTS FROM THE WIZARD

- Baking powder is a combination of acids, bases, and a starch. When combined, they produce a gas that creates minute air pockets that make the dish lighter.
- Always combine wet and dry ingredients separately.

Crumb Cake

MAKES 10 SERVINGS

Crumb cake is an old English favorite and has been made by bakers for hundreds of years. In the old days, children were called in when the time came to make the cake's delicious topping. They would gather around the table and, using their hands, crumble the mixture that was to be used for the "crumb" topping.

An old family favorite, this quick and easy recipe is a great last-minute breakfast or tea cake. . . and it freezes beautifully too!

For the cake:
1¾ cups all-purpose flour
2½ teaspoons baking powder
½ teaspoon salt
⅓ cup vegetable shortening
¾ cup whole milk
1 large egg
2 teaspoons vanilla

For the crumb topping:
2 cups all-purpose flour
1½ teaspoons cinnamon
1 cup sugar
¾ cup unsalted butter, melted
pinch of salt

Preheat the oven to 350°F. Grease and flour a 9 × 13-inch baking pan.

To make the cake: Mix together the flour, baking powder, and salt in a large mixing bowl. Cut in the shortening using a pastry blender or a fork until well combined.

In a separate bowl, whisk together the milk, egg, and vanilla. Add the wet mixture to the dry ingredients and mix gently just until blended. Spread the batter into the prepared pan.

To make the crumb topping: In a small bowl, mix together the flour, sugar, salt, and cinnamon. Pour the melted butter over the flour mixture and mix with a fork or your hands until small crumbs form.

Sprinkle the crumb topping evenly over the batter. Bake the cake for 25 to 30 minutes or until a cake tester inserted in the center of the cake comes out clean.

CHEF JAMIE'S LOW-FAT TIP

To lower the calories and fat in this delicious cake, use low-fat milk in place of whole milk and non-diet, tub-style margarine in place of the shortening. To lower the fat in the topping, use ¾ cup of 50 percent-less-fat butter in place of whole butter.

HELPFUL HINTS FROM THE WIZARD

• Make sure the baking powder is very fresh for the best results.

			PER SERVING		
STANDARD RECIPE:	CALORIES 514	FAT 23G	PROTEIN 6G	CARBOHYDRATES 73G	CHOL 63MG
REDUCED FAT:	CALORIES 399	FAT 14G	PROTEIN 6G	CARBOHYDRATES 73G	CHOL 40MG

Sour Cream Coffee Cake

MAKES 10 SERVINGS

I love the texture of a cake with sour cream. A chef mentor once told me that every cake, brownie, and baked good should have a bit of sour cream or cream cheese in it, just for texture!

1 cup sugar
½ cup unsalted butter
2 large eggs
1 teaspoon vanilla extract
2 cups all-purpose flour
1 teaspoon baking soda

1 teaspoon baking powder
½ teaspoon salt
1 cup sour cream
½ cup walnuts, chopped
⅓ cup brown sugar
1 teaspoon cinnamon

Preheat the oven to 350°F. Grease a 9-inch cake pan.

In a large mixing bowl, cream the sugar and butter until light and fluffy. Beat in the eggs and vanilla and combine well.

In a separate bowl, sift together the flour, baking powder, baking soda, and salt. Add the dry mixture to the butter mixture, incorporating small amounts at a time and adding small amounts of the sour cream alternately, until well combined.

In a separate bowl, mix together the walnuts, brown sugar, and cinnamon.

Spoon half of the batter into the prepared pan. Sprinkle the batter with half of the walnut filling. Spoon the remaining batter over the filling. Top with the remaining walnut filling.

Bake the cake for 45 minutes, or until a cake tester inserted into the center of the cake comes out clean.

CHEF JAMIE'S LOW-FAT TIP

Low-fat sour cream is actually one of the best low-fat products available on the market today. The texture is terrifically smooth and it works well in baked goods. This coffee cake shows almost no effect from the substitution! Eliminate the walnuts and use reduced-fat butter to lower the calories and fat. You'll create a healthier version without altering the taste.

HELPFUL HINTS FROM THE WIZARD

- Baking powder only retains its potency for about six months.
- Date all boxes of baking powder and baking soda when you purchase them. After six months, use them to freshen your refrigerator.

			PER SLICE		
STANDARD RECIPE:	CALORIES 341	FAT 18G	PROTEIN 6G	CARBOHYDRATES 41G	CHOL 64MG
REDUCED FAT:	CALORIES 194	FAT 9G	PROTEIN 3G	CARBOHYDRATES 35G	CHOL 34MG

Date and Nut Bread

MAKES 8 SERVINGS

This old-fashioned recipe, passed down from generation to generation, is one of my favorites. It's especially delicious when spread with cream cheese!

1 cup pitted dates, chopped
1 cup boiling water
1 teaspoon baking soda
1¼ cup sugar

½ cup vegetable shortening
2 tablespoons molasses
1¾ cups all-purpose flour
1 cup chopped walnuts

Preheat the oven to 350°F. Grease a 9-inch loaf pan.

In a mixing bowl, combine the dates, boiling water, and baking soda. Let stand for 15 minutes.

In a large mixing bowl, cream the sugar and shortening until smooth. Add the molasses and mix to combine.

In a separate bowl, toss the nuts with the flour.

To mix the batter, combine the dates (with the soaking liquid), the shortening mixture, and the flour mixture alternately, stirring with a wooden spoon until well combined. Pour the batter into the prepared pan. Bake 1 hour or until a cake tester inserted in the middle of the cake comes out clean.

CHEF JAMIE'S LOW-FAT TIP

This recipe is so delicious as is; I hate to change it! However, you can use ¼ cup of shortening and ¼ cup of smooth applesauce to lighten it.

HELPFUL HINTS FROM THE WIZARD

- The only difference canola oil would make over a vegetable shortening is the type of fat that is absorbed by the body, for example, a polyunsaturated compared to a monounsaturated. Seeing that it does not affect the nutritional analysis, I recommend that you use Chef Jamie's suggestion and follow the traditional recipe.

			PER SLICE		
STANDARD RECIPE:	CALORIES 503	FAT 29G	PROTEIN 10G	CARBOHYDRATES 48G	CHOL 0MG
REDUCED FAT:	CALORIES 394	FAT 17G	PROTEIN 8G	CARBOHYDRATES 53G	CHOL 0MG

Chapter 2

Delicious Soups, Salads & Starters

*P*lato once said that *"the beginning is the most
important part of the work,"* and the beginning
of a meal is no different from the start of any other
great endeavor. A scrumptious first course sets the
stage and builds anticipation for what is yet to come.

Serve these soups, salads, and starters to kick off
a meal, or prepare a big pot of soup or a bountiful
salad as the main course and allow the dish to have
the spotlight all to itself.

Borscht

MAKES 6 SERVINGS

Eastern European peasants, who used wild beets to infuse flavor and color into foods, created borscht.

This cold beet soup is traditionally served topped with a dollop of sour cream. The Russian version is sometimes served hot. . .it's your choice!

1 (14-ounce) can julienne beets, with the juice
2 cups beef broth
1 cup water
½ cup yellow onion, diced
1 tablespoon sugar

2 teaspoons lemon juice
1 teaspoon lemon zest
salt & pepper, to taste
1 cup sour cream
sour cream, for serving
chopped chives, for garnish

In a large saucepan combine the beets, 1 cup of the beet juice from the can, beef broth, water, onion, sugar, lemon zest, lemon juice, salt, and pepper. Bring to a boil, and then reduce the heat to low and simmer for 20 minutes. Allow to cool slightly.

Working in batches, transfer the soup to an electric blender. Blend with the 1 cup sour cream until smooth. Place the blended mixture in a clean pan or storage container and refrigerate until thoroughly chilled. Serve with a dollop of sour cream and chopped chives.

CHEF JAMIE'S LOW-FAT TIP

Low-fat, even fat-free, sour cream works well in this borscht. The soup is light and healthy!

HELPFUL HINTS FROM THE WIZARD

- The sour cream will help the beets retain their color.

		PER SERVING			
STANDARD RECIPE:	CALORIES 130	FAT 9.3G	PROTEIN 3G	CARBOHYDRATES 18G	CHOL 6MG
REDUCED FAT:	CALORIES 101	FAT 2.7G	PROTEIN 3G	CARBOHYDRATES 18G	CHOL 0MG

Sweet & Sour Cabbage Soup
MAKES 6 SERVINGS

This is my all-time favorite soup. With a piece of fresh, buttered rye bread, there is nothing better.

1 (28-ounce) can diced tomatoes, in their juice
12 cups water
3 pounds beef brisket
2 soup bones (ask your butcher!), optional

2 pounds green cabbage, coarsely shredded
¾ cup sugar
1 (6 ounce) can tomato paste
juice of 2 lemons (or to taste)
salt & pepper, to taste

Combine the tomatoes (with their juice) and the water in a large stockpot; bring to a boil. Remove all but a thin layer of fat from the beef and cut the meat into large chunks.

Add the beef, soup bones (optional), cabbage, sugar, tomato paste, and lemon juice. Simmer, partially covered, for 2 to 2½ hours or until the meat is very tender.

Remove the brisket from the soup and shred the meat. Add the shredded meat back to the soup. Remove the soup bones and season with salt and pepper before stirring.

Remove the bones before serving.

CHEF JAMIE'S LOW-FAT TIP
Sweet & Sour Cabbage Soup is often prepared in the vegetarian manner, by excluding the meat and using a rich vegetable broth in place of the beef broth. By removing the brisket from the recipe, you make the soup practically fat-free.

HELPFUL HINTS FROM THE WIZARD
- Cooking cabbage is beneficial because it destroys the enzyme thiaminase, which reduces the potency of B vitamins.
- Red cabbage may change color from red to purple, depending on the acidity level of the liquid it is cooked in.

		PER SERVING			
STANDARD RECIPE:	CALORIES 675	FAT 23G	PROTEIN 70G	CARBOHYDRATES 46G	CHOL 222MG
REDUCED FAT:	CALORIES 184	FAT 1.5G	PROTEIN 3.5G	CARBOHYDRATES 46G	CHOL 0MG

Onion Soup Gratinée

MAKES 6 SERVINGS

This recipe is prepared with Parmesan cheese, in the traditional French manner, and is absolutely delicious!

3 tablespoons unsalted butter
6 yellow onions, sliced thinly
2 tablespoons flour
8 cups beef broth
1 cup dry white wine

1 tablespoon cognac
salt & pepper, to taste
12 slices French bread, toasted
2 cups freshly grated Parmesan
   cheese

In a large saucepan, melt the butter over medium heat. Add the onions and sauté, stirring often until the onions are tender and golden brown, about 20 to 25 minutes.

Add the flour to the sautéed onions and stir to coat. Add the beef broth and use a wire whisk to combine well. Add the wine and simmer the soup for half an hour. Remove from the heat and stir in the cognac. Season with salt and pepper, to taste.

To serve, place 2 slices of toasted French bread in each of 6 ovenproof bowls. Sprinkle the bread liberally with Parmesan cheese. Ladle the soup into the bowls and top with more Parmesan cheese. Place the bowls under the broiler until the cheese melts and forms a golden brown crust. Serve immediately.

CHEF JAMIE'S LOW-FAT TIP

Aside from the minimal amount of butter and the Parmesan cheese, which happens to be rather low in fat compared with other cheeses, this soup isn't too bad for you. For a lighter version, sauté the onions in non-stick cooking spray or a teaspoon of olive oil instead of butter, but be sure to stir constantly so the onions don't burn. Also, try reducing the Parmesan cheese by half to lower your cheese consumption.

HELPFUL HINTS FROM THE WIZARD

- Parmesan cheese will have a richer flavor if purchased in bulk and grated just before it's used.
- De-fatted beef broth will reduce the fat in this dish even more.

			PER SERVING		
STANDARD RECIPE:	CALORIES 92	FAT 8G	PROTEIN 6G	CARBOHYDRATES 19G	CHOL 19MG
REDUCED FAT:	CALORIES 53	FAT 3G	PROTEIN 3G	CARBOHYDRATES 18G	CHOL 14MG

Autumn Pumpkin Soup

MAKES 8 SERVINGS

This hearty soup is wonderful on a cold day with crusty bread! Create an elegant presentation by serving the soup in a pumpkin shell (see Chef's Note below).

6 cups chicken broth
2 pounds (about 5 cups) pumpkin, peeled and cut into 1-inch cubes
2 yellow onions, chopped
1 small baking potato, peeled and cut into 1-inch cubes

1 garlic clove, minced
salt & pepper, to taste
1 teaspoon fresh thyme, minced
1 teaspoon fresh sage, minced
½ cup crème fraiche (see *Chef's Note* on page 160) *or* sour cream

In a large saucepan, bring the chicken broth, pumpkin, onions, potato, and garlic to a boil over medium heat. Reduce the heat and simmer, partially covered, until the pumpkin and potato are very tender, about 30 minutes. Season with salt and pepper. Allow to cool slightly.

Puree the soup in batches in a blender or food processor and return to the pan.

Over medium heat, bring the pureed soup back to a boil. Add the thyme and sage, and reduce the heat. Simmer for 5 minutes.

Remove from the heat and stir in the crème fraiche or sour cream. Adjust the seasoning. If using sour cream, do not reheat the soup, as the sour cream will curdle.

Chef's Note: To serve the soup in a pumpkin shell, you will need a 5- to 6-pound pumpkin and 1 tablespoon of vegetable oil. Wash and dry the pumpkin and cut off the top about a quarter of the way down from the stem. Clean out any seeds and fibers from inside the pumpkin. Rub the outside of the pumpkin with the oil and roast at 350°F for 30 minutes or until tender. Let shell cool and ladle the soup into the shell immediately before serving.

	PER SERVING				
STANDARD RECIPE:	CALORIES 127	FAT 4G	PROTEIN 6G	CARBOHYDRATES 28G	CHOL 3MG
REDUCED FAT:	CALORIES 120	FAT .4G	PROTEIN 7G	CARBOHYDRATES 28G	CHOL .1MG

CHEF JAMIE'S LOW-FAT TIP

To lighten the soup, omit the sour cream or crème fraiche stirred in at the end, and instead add 4 ounces of non-fat cream cheese when pureeing the soup, making sure to blend until smooth. The cream cheese adds incredible texture and richness with no fat!

HELPFUL HINTS FROM THE WIZARD

- Be sure the potato does not have any green areas. This may affect the flavor due to a chemical called solanine.

Vichyssoise

MAKES 6 SERVINGS

Cold potato soup was invented as a result of King Louis XV of France's fear that he was being poisoned. He insisted that his servants taste all of his food before he ate it. When hot soup was passed around one day, it grew cold before it reached him. It is said that he enjoyed the cold soup so much that this variant recipe gained acceptance, and vichyssoise was born!

This recipe has certainly stood the test of time. It is creamy, rich, and a sure crowd-pleaser!

4 tablespoons (2 ounces) unsalted butter
2 leeks (white part only), chopped
½ cup yellow onion, chopped
2 cups water
2 cups chicken broth
1 tablespoon all-purpose flour

2 large baking potatoes, peeled and diced (or try Yukon Gold potatoes for great flavor)
½ cup heavy cream
1 cup half & half
salt & white pepper, to taste
chopped chives, for garnish

In a large saucepan, melt 2 tablespoons of the butter over medium heat. Add the leeks and onion and sauté, stirring often, until tender but not browned, about 10 minutes. Add the water and chicken broth and bring to a boil.

In a small mixing bowl, knead the flour with the remaining 2 tablespoons of butter to form a paste. Using a whisk, stir the paste into the boiling mixture and blend well. Add the diced potatoes, then reduce the heat and allow the soup to simmer gently until the potatoes are tender, about 20 minutes. Allow to cool slightly.

Puree the soup in a blender or food processor, working in batches. Transfer the pureed soup to a clean pan and stir in the cream and half & half. Season with salt and pepper to taste.

Refrigerate the soup until thoroughly chilled. Serve cold, garnished with chopped chives.

CHEF JAMIE'S LOW-FAT TIP

Did you know that fat-free half & half is now available? I know, it sounds crazy, but it tastes pretty good. You might try using it in this cream-based soup, or substitute regular half & half for the heavy cream to create a slightly lighter version that still tastes wonderfully rich.

HELPFUL HINTS FROM THE WIZARD

- Make sure that there is no hint of green on the potatoes you use for the soup. The green part contains the chemical solanine, a naturally occurring toxin.

		PER SERVING			
STANDARD RECIPE:	CALORIES 231	FAT 19G	PROTEIN 4G	CARBOHYDRATES 11G	CHOL 61MG
REDUCED FAT:	CALORIES 130	FAT 7G	PROTEIN 4G	CARBOHYDRATES 11G	CHOL 49MG

My Grandma's Split Pea Soup

MAKES 6 SERVINGS

Growing up, I remember sitting on the counter in the kitchen and watching my mother prepare this soup. There is still no better comfort food than a big bowl of split pea soup with a few homemade croutons floating on top.

2 cups dried green split peas
8 cups water
1 ham hock
2 celery stalks, with tops and leaves, chopped
2 large carrots, chopped
1 yellow onion, peeled and cut in half
2 garlic cloves, peeled
fresh herbs, tied in a bundle (such as fresh parsley & thyme)
salt & pepper, to taste

Place the split peas and water in a large stockpot. Bring to a boil, uncovered, then skim the top of any foam. Add the ham hock, celery, carrots, onion, garlic, and the bundle of herbs.

Cover and simmer for 2 hours. Be sure to keep the flame low and stir often, as the soup scorches easily. When the soup is finished cooking, remove it from the heat and let cool slightly.

Remove the ham hock and herb bundle and discard them. In a blender or food processor, puree the soup in batches until very smooth. Season generously with salt and pepper and serve hot.

CHEF JAMIE'S LOW-FAT TIP

This soup, minus the ham hock, is practically fat-free! It's a great hearty snack or meal that's low in fat!

PER SERVING

	CALORIES	FAT	PROTEIN	CARBOHYDRATES	CHOL
STANDARD RECIPE:	CALORIES 149	FAT 4G	PROTEIN 14G	CARBOHYDRATES 19G	CHOL 33MG
REDUCED FAT:	CALORIES 99	FAT .5G	PROTEIN 6G	CARBOHYDRATES 19G	CHOL 0MG

New England Clam Chowder

MAKES 6 SERVINGS

This recipe comes from a retired sea captain who, in 1892, opened a restaurant near Boston Harbor. The restaurant is still standing, the recipes have rarely changed, and the food is still Boston's best.

1 tablespoon unsalted butter
1 large baking potato, peeled and cut into ½-inch cubes
1 yellow onion, diced
1 cup bottled clam juice

2 cups chopped fresh clams
or 4 (6-ounce) cans chopped clams, liquid drained and reserved
1 cup heavy whipping cream
3 tablespoons chopped fresh dill
salt & pepper, to taste

Melt the butter in a heavy stockpot over medium heat. Add the potato and onion and sauté, stirring often, until the onion is tender, about 10 minutes.

Add enough bottled clam juice to the reserved clam juice to measure 2 cups. Add the clam juice to the pot. Cover and cook until the potato is tender, about 10 minutes more.

Add the chopped clams, heavy cream, and dill. Bring to a simmer, season to taste with salt and pepper, and serve.

CHEF JAMIE'S LOW-FAT TIP
Clam chowder should be creamy! Try using half & half in place of the heavy cream or, for a much lighter version, use low-fat milk, but keep in mind the soup will lose some of its body.

HELPFUL HINTS FROM THE WIZARD
- Always add clams to chowder just before serving or they may become tough.

	PER SERVING				
STANDARD RECIPE:	CALORIES 244	FAT 18G	PROTEIN 12G	CARBOHYDRATES 10G	CHOL 12MG
REDUCED FAT:	CALORIES 159	FAT 7G	PROTEIN 12G	CARBOHYDRATES 10G	CHOL 7MG

Cucumber Bisque

MAKES 6 SERVINGS

This beautifully rich, refreshing cold soup is lovely topped with a dollop of sour cream.

6 tablespoons (3 ounces) unsalted butter

2 yellow onions, finely chopped

2 large cucumber, peeled, seeded and diced

4 cups chicken broth

2 tablespoons all-purpose flour

2 large egg yolks

½ cup heavy cream

salt, to taste

1 large cucumber, seeded, peeled and diced, for garnish

2 tablespoons chopped chives

In a large saucepan, melt 4 tablespoons of the butter over medium heat. Add the onions and sauté, stirring often, for 5 minutes or until tender. Add the cucumbers and sauté 1 minute. Add the chicken broth and bring to a boil. Reduce the heat to a simmer and cook uncovered for 20 to 30 minutes, or until the vegetables are very tender.

Remove the soup from the heat, and allow to cool slightly. In a blender or food processor, working in batches, puree the soup until very smooth.

Meanwhile, melt the remaining 2 tablespoons of butter in a large saucepan. Add the flour and cook for 1 minute, stirring constantly. Pour in the pureed soup and whisk to combine. Cook over medium heat for 3 to 5 minutes, whisking constantly, until thickened slightly.

In a medium-sized mixing bowl, combine the egg yolks and cream. Slowly add ½ cup of the hot soup to the cream mixture, while whisking constantly. Return the cream mixture to the pan, still whisking constantly. Reduce the heat to low and cook for 5 minutes, being sure not to let the soup come back to a boil. Remove from the heat and let cool to room temperature. Season with salt, to taste.

Refrigerate the soup until well chilled, at least 3 hours. Stir the diced raw cucumber and chives into the soup before serving.

PER SERVING

STANDARD RECIPE:	CALORIES 364	FAT 33G	PROTEIN 7.5G	CARBOHYDRATES 11.5G	CHOL 92MG
REDUCED FAT:	CALORIES 202	FAT 13G	PROTEIN 8G	CARBOHYDRATES 12G	CHOL 67MG

Cucumber Bisque (continued)

CHEF JAMIE'S LOW-FAT TIP
Low-fat bisque can be prepared by using reduced-fat (50 percent-less-fat) butter, 1 whole egg in place of the 2 egg yolks, and half & half in place of the heavy cream.

HELPFUL HINTS FROM THE WIZARD
- Use fat-free chicken or turkey broth.

Iowa Corn Chowder

MAKES 6 SERVINGS

True chowder is categorized as a very thick, chunky, hearty soup. The majority of chowders are prepared with shellfish, fish, or vegetables or a combination of all three, and most recipes call for the addition of potatoes, milk, or cream to aid in thickening.

This recipe came from a friend whose childhood in the cornfields of Iowa is still most memorable.

6 slices of bacon, cut into ½-inch pieces
2 tablespoons unsalted butter
1 yellow onion, diced
1 green bell pepper, diced
2 ribs of celery, diced

4 cups fresh corn kernels (cut from about 6 large ears)
1 cup cooked ham, diced
3 cups heavy cream
2 cups milk
salt & pepper, to taste
4 scallions, chopped

In a large saucepan, cook the bacon over medium heat until the fat is rendered and the bacon is crisp. Remove with a slotted spoon to paper towels. Pour off all but 2 tablespoons of the bacon grease in the pan and add the butter.

Add the onion, bell pepper, and celery, and sauté over medium heat, stirring often, for 15 minutes or until the onion is very tender. Add the corn and ham and sauté 5 minutes longer. Add the cream and milk and bring to a simmer, then reduce the heat and simmer for 10 minutes.

Season with with salt and pepper. Serve the soup garnished with crumbled bacon and chopped scallions.

CHEF JAMIE'S LOW-FAT TIP

This rich soup needs a lot of trimming to be considered reduced-fat! I hate to remove the bacon from the recipe because its smoky flavor adds so much to the soup. So, cook the bacon in the microwave until crisp and blot it well with paper towels, or use turkey bacon for an even better-for-you version. Or use the crumbled bacon only as a garnish instead of as a main ingredient. Using milk alone (instead of cream and milk) reduces the fat even more, and low-fat milk would work fine.

		PER SERVING		
STANDARD RECIPE:	CALORIES 937	FAT 47G	PROTEIN 22G	CARBOHYDRATES 39G	CHOL 124MG
REDUCED FAT:	CALORIES 710	FAT 18G	PROTEIN 21G	CARBOHYDRATES 39G	CHOL 115MG

Minestrone Soup

MAKES 6 SERVINGS

If you are feeling innovative, try adding a bunch of fresh asparagus and cooked orzo pasta to this classic Italian soup.

¼ cup olive oil
1 tablespoon unsalted butter
1 yellow onion, chopped
1 garlic clove, chopped
1 tablespoon tomato paste
10 cups water
1 head cauliflower, cut into small florets
1 head broccoli, cut into small florets
½ head green cabbage, shredded
½ pound green beans, cut into 1-inch pieces

2 zucchini, halved lengthwise & sliced
2 yellow squash, halved lengthwise & sliced
1 (14-ounce) can cannellini beans
1 (11-ounce) can corn kernels, drained
salt & pepper, to taste
¼ cup fresh parsley, chopped
freshly grated Parmesan cheese

Heat the oil and butter in a large stockpot over medium heat. Add the onion and garlic and sauté, stirring often, until the onion is tender. Add the tomato paste and mix to combine. Add water and all of the vegetables, except the cannellini beans, corn, and parsley. Season with a dash of salt and pepper.

Bring the soup to a boil, reduce to a simmer, and allow it to cook for 1 hour. Stir in the cannellini beans, corn, and parsley. Adjust seasonings to taste.

Serve the soup garnished with Parmesan cheese.

CHEF JAMIE'S LOW-FAT TIP

Minestrone is a wonderful way to eat all your vegetables! Eliminate the butter and substitute 2 tablespoons of olive oil to reduce the cholesterol and saturated fat content. Also, for the brightest flavor, be sure to use only the freshest vegetables.

HELPFUL HINTS FROM THE WIZARD

- Make sure that the cauliflower has no rust areas and the bottom is all white.
- The broccoli florets should be closed and not yellowed.

		PER SERVING			
STANDARD RECIPE:	CALORIES 181	FAT 11G	PROTEIN 1G	CARBOHYDRATES 17G	CHOL 6MG
REDUCED FAT:	CALORIES 123	FAT 5G	PROTEIN 1G	CARBOHYDRATES 17G	CHOL 0MG

Mushroom and Barley Soup

MAKES 6 SERVINGS

The combination of mushrooms and grains has been popular in England for hundreds of years. This soup is a favorite of mine and it tends to taste even better the second and third day after you make it.

1 pound white mushrooms
3 tablespoons unsalted butter
2 carrots, peeled and diced
1 yellow onion, diced
1 leek (pale green and white parts only), diced

8 cups chicken broth
1 pound (2 large) baking potatoes, peeled & diced
½ cup pearl barley
2 bay leaves
salt & pepper, to taste

Separate the mushroom stems from the caps. Slice the caps and chop the stems; set aside.

In a large stockpot, melt the butter over medium heat. Add the chopped mushroom stems, carrots, onion, and leek and sauté until tender, about 10 minutes. Add the chicken broth, potatoes, carrots, barley, and bay leaves. Season with a dash of salt and pepper. Cover the pot and simmer on low heat for 30 minutes.

Uncover the pot and add the sliced mushrooms. Continue cooking over low heat, keeping the soup at a slow simmer, until the vegetables are very tender, about 30 minutes. Adjust the seasonings to taste and serve.

CHEF JAMIE'S LOW-FAT TIP
This soup is quite low in fat as is, but reduce the butter by half, or try using 2 teaspoons of olive oil in its place for an even healthier version.

		PER SERVING			
STANDARD RECIPE:	CALORIES 148	FAT 6G	PROTEIN 8G	CARBOHYDRATES 20G	CHOL 7MG
REDUCED FAT:	CALORIES 127	FAT 3G	PROTEIN 8G	CARBOHYDRATES 20G	CHOL 5MG

White Bean, Spinach & Sausage Soup

MAKES 8 SERVINGS

This delicious Tuscan-style soup is a hearty meal when served with crusty bread and a simple salad. Using pre-cooked or canned beans makes it easy to prepare.

1 pound hot or sweet Italian sausage
1 yellow onion, diced
2 garlic cloves, minced
2 yellow squash, sliced
½ teaspoon nutmeg
½ teaspoon dried sage

1 pound fresh spinach leaves
8 cups chicken broth
2 cups cooked *or* canned white
   beans, drained
salt & pepper, to taste
chopped fresh parsley, for garnish

In a large stockpot, brown the sausage until golden brown and cooked through. Slice the cooked sausage into ¼-inch pieces and set aside.

In the same pot, using the rendered fat from the sausage, add the onion and sauté until tender, about 10 minutes. Stir in the squash, garlic, nutmeg, and sage. Sauté for 2 minutes, stirring often. Add the spinach and cook just until wilted. Add the chicken broth, white beans, and salt and pepper to taste.

Bring the soup to a boil, then reduce the heat and simmer for 5 minutes. Add the sausage and serve the soup hot, garnished with parsley.

CHEF JAMIE'S LOW-FAT TIP

Turkey sausage is a terrific alternative to pork-based sausage. If you can find raw turkey sausages, sauté them according to the directions above. Discard any fat left in the pan and use just 1 tablespoon of olive oil and some non-stick cooking spray to sauté the vegetables. If you can only find smoked/cooked sausages, add the sausage to the soup just before serving.

HELPFUL HINTS FROM THE WIZARD

• Store dried herbs in a cool, dry place.

		PER SERVING			
STANDARD RECIPE:	CALORIES 231	FAT 16G	PROTEIN 17G	CARBOHYDRATES 20G	CHOL 38MG
REDUCED FAT:	CALORIES 162	FAT 8G	PROTEIN 17G	CARBOHYDRATES 20G	CHOL 18MG

Egg Drop Corn Soup

MAKES 6 SERVINGS

It is said that Chinese egg drop soup was invented when a cook was about to add scrambled eggs to an assortment of vegetables while preparing Egg Foo Yung. However, he accidentally dropped the mixture into a pot of boiling water that was next to the pot. The eggs cooked immediately, and thus egg drop soup was born!

This simple Chinese soup is full of flavor!

4 cups chicken broth
3 teaspoons dry sherry
1 cup whole-kernel corn, fresh or
   canned

2 large eggs, beaten
2 tablespoons cornstarch
3 tablespoons water
salt & pepper, to taste

In a large saucepan, combine the chicken broth and sherry. Bring to a boil. Add the corn and simmer 5 minutes.

With the soup slowly simmering, add the eggs in a steady stream, stirring to create a ribbon effect.

In a separate bowl, combine the cornstarch and water, stirring to dissolve. Stir the cornstarch into the soup and cook 1 minute longer, stirring gently. Season with salt and pepper.

Serve at once.

CHEF JAMIE'S LOW-FAT TIP

You will find that most Asian dishes are low in fat and full of flavor. Egg whites work great in place of whole eggs in this recipe, creating an almost cholesterol-free result!

HELPFUL HINTS FROM THE WIZARD

- Cornstarch should be mixed slowly to avoid lumps. Dissolve the cornstarch in the water before adding it to any hot liquid.

	PER SERVING				
STANDARD RECIPE:	CALORIES 89	FAT 3G	PROTEIN 6G	CARBOHYDRATES 10G	CHOL 88MG
REDUCED FAT:	CALORIES 69	FAT 1G	PROTEIN 5G	CARBOHYDRATES 10G	CHOL 5MG

Caesar Salad

MAKES 6 SERVINGS

¼ cup olive oil
1 clove garlic, minced
4 slices day-old bread, cubed
6 anchovy fillets, mashed
1 garlic clove, minced
1 whole large egg, coddled (see *Chef's Note* below)
1 tablespoon Dijon mustard
juice of 2 lemons
1 teaspoon Worcestershire sauce
ground pepper, to taste
⅓ cup olive oil
2 heads romaine lettuce, washed and torn into bite-size pieces
½ cup freshly grated Parmesan cheese

In a large sauté pan, heat the ¼ cup of olive oil over medium heat. Add the garlic and bread cubes and sauté, stirring often, until croutons are golden brown. Drain on paper towels and set aside.

In a blender or food processor, combine the anchovies, garlic, and coddled egg. Add the mustard, lemon juice, Worcestershire sauce, and pepper. With the blender or processor running, slowly drizzle in the ⅓ cup of olive oil to create a thick, creamy dressing.

When ready to serve, toss the lettuce, croutons, and enough dressing to coat. Top with Parmesan cheese and serve.

Chef's Note: Coddling the egg reduces the bacteria associated with raw eggs. To coddle an egg, first bring the egg to room temperature. Bring a small pan of water to a boil and lower the egg into the water. Turn off the heat, cover the pan, and let the egg sit 1 minute, no longer! Immediately break the egg into a bowl. The egg should be very runny with just a bit of the white coagulated.

		PER SERVING			
STANDARD RECIPE:	CALORIES 218	FAT 19G	PROTEIN 5G	CARBOHYDRATES 8G	CHOL 38MG
REDUCED FAT:	CALORIES 130	FAT 8G	PROTEIN 5G	CARBOHYDRATES 10G	CHOL 3MG

CHEF JAMIE'S LOW-FAT TIP

To lower the fat in the croutons, I recommend that you brush the bread cubes with 1 tablespoon of olive oil and bake them in a 350°F oven until golden, instead of frying! The ingredient highest in fat is the ⅓ cup of olive oil, so use only 2 tablespoons of olive oil for a low-fat version and add 2 tablespoons of reduced-fat mayonnaise for creaminess.

HELPFUL HINTS FROM THE WIZARD

- The best olive oil is extra virgin, cold pressed.
- To get the maximum amount of juice from a lemon, place it in the microwave on high for about 15 seconds before juicing.

Spinach Salad with Warm Bacon Dressing

When I was growing up, this "dinner party salad" was always a hit at our house! The warm, creamy dressing coats the spinach leaves so wonderfully, and the flavors and textures complement each other so well. This salad is a perfect marriage of tart and sweet, crisp and velvety!

4 slices bacon
2 tablespoons vegetable oil
2 tablespoons red wine vinegar
1 tablespoon sugar
1 garlic clove, minced

pepper, to taste
1 pound spinach leaves, washed thoroughly
½ pound fresh mushrooms, sliced

Sauté the bacon until crisp. Crumble and set aside. Do not discard the bacon grease.

Using the same pan, add the oil, vinegar, sugar, and garlic to the bacon grease left in the pan. Whisk to combine over low heat for 1 minute. Season to taste with freshly ground pepper.

Place the spinach leaves, sliced mushrooms, and crumbled bacon in a large salad bowl. Add the warm dressing and toss to coat. Serve immediately.

CHEF JAMIE'S LOW-FAT TIP
Oh, what I would give for a substitute for bacon grease! This dressing gets its velvety texture and great flavor from the bacon grease, so don't eliminate it completely. For a lighter version, use only 1 teaspoon of bacon grease and discard the rest. As for the crumbled bacon, use only a little bit on each serving as a garnish.

HELPFUL HINTS FROM THE WIZARD
• Microwaving the bacon, first covering it with paper towels, reduces some of the fat—and some of the mess.

			PER SERVING		
STANDARD RECIPE:	CALORIES 211	FAT 22G	PROTEIN 3G	CARBOHYDRATES 6G	CHOL 15MG
REDUCED FAT:	CALORIES 109	FAT 8G	PROTEIN 5G	CARBOHYDRATES 6G	CHOL 2.5MG

Summer Tomato Bread Salad

MAKES 6 SERVINGS

A traditional Italian favorite modernized, this salad is best prepared with day-old bread to soak up the dressing. This dish is a great way to use summer's sweet tomato crop!

1 small loaf crusty French or sourdough bread, cut into cubes
4 large or 8 small tomatoes, cut into bite-sized pieces
1 large cucumber, seeded and sliced
1 small red onion, diced
¼ cup fresh basil leaves, cut into thin strips

½ cup pitted kalamata or green olives, halved
¼ cup chopped fresh parsley
¼ cup red wine vinegar
1 tablespoon lemon juice
1 large clove garlic, minced
½ cup olive oil
salt & pepper, to taste
freshly shaved Parmesan cheese

In a large salad bowl combine the bread, tomatoes, cucumber, onion, basil, olives, and parsley.

In a separate bowl, combine the garlic, lemon juice, and vinegar. Slowly whisk in the olive oil to make a vinaigrette, and season to taste with salt and pepper.

Pour the vinaigrette over the bread mixture and toss well. Cover with plastic wrap and allow to sit at room temperature for at least 30 minutes, or up to 3 hours.

When ready to serve, garnish with shavings of Parmesan cheese.

CHEF JAMIE'S LOW-FAT TIP

Reducing the amount of olive oil in the salad will reduce your fat intake. Prepare the vinaigrette with only a few tablespoons of olive oil and add half a packet of no-calorie sweetener (such as Equal) or 1 teaspoon of sugar (only 16 calories) to tone down the pungency of the vinegar. (This is a great trick for creating lower-fat salad dressings. . .the addition of sugar balances the tart flavor!)

HELPFUL HINTS FROM THE WIZARD

• Parsley can be easily snipped with scissors.

			PER SERVING		
STANDARD RECIPE:	CALORIES 301	FAT 13G	PROTEIN 7G	CARBOHYDRATES 37G	CHOL 1.3MG
REDUCED FAT:	CALORIES 262	FAT 7G	PROTEIN 7G	CARBOHYDRATES 37G	CHOL 1.3MG

Pineapple Molded Salad

MAKES 10 SERVINGS

This classic Jell-O mold is exactly what my mother remembers her mother making!

1 (3-ounce) package lime Jell-O
1 (3-ounce) package lemon Jell-O
¾ cup boiling water
1 (20-ounce) can crushed pineapple, drained, 1 cup of the juice reserved

1 (13-ounce) can evaporated milk
1 cup cottage cheese
1 cup mayonnaise
½ cup walnuts, chopped
½ cup celery, chopped

Oil a bundt or ring mold and it set aside.

Mix both packages of Jell-O with the boiling water and stir until completely dissolved. Stir in the reserved pineapple juice. Refrigerate until partially set.

Add the remaining ingredients and stir to combine. Place in the prepared pan and refrigerate until firm. Unmold onto a serving plate just before serving.

CHEF JAMIE'S LOW-FAT TIP

This molded salad can easily be "thinned out" by substituting low-fat or even fat-free cottage cheese, low-fat evaporated milk and light mayonnaise. Also, use only ¼ cup of walnuts for a lower-fat version. These simple substitutions will bring you similar results when it comes to flavor, and much better results when it comes to your figure!

		PER SERVING			
STANDARD RECIPE:	CALORIES 249	FAT 18G	PROTEIN 8G	CARBOHYDRATES 22G	CHOL 6MG
REDUCED FAT:	CALORIES 132	FAT 9G	PROTEIN 5G	CARBOHYDRATES 15G	CHOL .5MG

Green Goddess Salad

MAKES 6 SERVINGS

Green Goddess Salad dressing was first created in 1922 to honor an actor who was performing in a play called The Green Goddess. *The play was a big success, and so was the new salad dressing!*

1 head iceberg lettuce, cut into bite-size pieces
1 bunch watercress, chopped
2 large tomatoes, sliced
1 small yellow onion, thinly sliced
12 medium shrimp, cooked and chilled
½ cup mayonnaise
¼ cup sour cream

4 anchovy fillets
1 tablespoon fresh parsley, finely chopped
1½ teaspoons red wine vinegar
1½ teaspoons lemon juice
1 teaspoon fresh tarragon, finely chopped
salt & pepper, to taste

Arrange the iceberg lettuce in a large salad bowl. Top with the watercress, tomatoes, and onion. Arrange the shrimp on top. Cover and refrigerate until ready to serve.

To prepare the dressing, in a food processor, blend the mayonnaise, sour cream, anchovies, vinegar, lemon juice, parsley, and tarragon until smooth. Season to taste with salt and pepper.

To serve, pour the dressing over the chilled salad.

CHEF JAMIE'S LOW-FAT TIP

Light mayonnaise and low-fat sour cream are terrific alternatives to the higher-fat versions. Both light products retain the delicious creamy texture that so many low-fat foods lack.

HELPFUL HINTS FROM THE WIZARD

- Keep tomatoes at room temperature—never refrigerate—for the best flavor.

			PER SERVING		
STANDARD RECIPE:	CALORIES 137	FAT 9G	PROTEIN 5G	CARBOHYDRATES 10G	CHOL 9MG
REDUCED FAT:	CALORIES 85	FAT 5G	PROTEIN 5G	CARBOHYDRATES 12G	CHOL 6MG

Waldorf Salad

MAKES 4 SERVINGS

The original Waldorf Salad was created in 1893 by "Oscar of the Waldorf," the first chef at the famous Waldorf Astoria Hotel in New York City. The original salad used only apples, celery, and mayonnaise and was considered just another salad until walnuts were added in 1895—this addition made the salad famous and it is now recognized worldwide as the Waldorf Salad.

2 sweet red apples, cored and diced
1 cup red grapes
½ cup celery, chopped
¼ cup raisins
¼ cup walnuts, chopped

1 tablespoon lemon juice
½ cup mayonnaise
1 tablespoon sugar
1½ teaspoons apple cider vinegar
⅛ teaspoon celery salt

In a large mixing bowl, combine the apples, grapes, celery, raisins, walnuts, and lemon juice.

In a separate bowl, whisk together the mayonnaise, sugar, vinegar, and celery salt. Add the dressing to the apple mixture and toss to coat. Refrigerate for 2 hours before serving.

CHEF JAMIE'S LOW-FAT TIP

I love a good Waldorf Salad. . .and this is it! Low-fat or even fat-free mayonnaise makes it the perfect low-fat side dish or accompaniment to a picnic, a brunch, or even your favorite meat dish. Do be aware, though, that mixing low-fat or non-fat sour cream with any acid might cause a curdling effect. The look changes but the great taste remains!

HELPFUL HINTS FROM THE WIZARD

• Make sure the apple cider vinegar is fresh for the best results.

PER SERVING

STANDARD RECIPE:	CALORIES 336	FAT 18G	PROTEIN 6G	CARBOHYDRATES 48G	CHOL 8MG
REDUCED FAT:	CALORIES 287	FAT 8G	PROTEIN 6G	CARBOHYDRATES 48G	CHOL 5MG

Ambrosia Salad

MAKES 6 SERVINGS

This simple, sweet salad is one of my favorites! Variations include adding nuts, maraschino cherries, or anything else that pleases your palate. Ambrosia salad originated in Italy and was served by the Peligrino family in the mid-1800s at a family barbecue.

1 cup miniature marshmallows
1 cup shredded coconut
1 cup canned sliced peaches, drained
1 cup canned pineapple chunks, drained
1 cup canned mandarin oranges
1 cup sour cream
1 cup fresh sliced bananas
1 teaspoon lemon juice

In a large mixing bowl, combine the marshmallows, coconut, canned fruits, and sour cream.

Toss well to combine, cover tightly with plastic wrap and refrigerate overnight.

Before serving, gently toss the bananas with the lemon juice to minimize discoloration. Stir the bananas into the salad and serve immediately.

CHEF JAMIE'S LOW-FAT TIP

Try using low-fat vanilla yogurt in place of the sour cream for a healthier version. The coconut does add to the fat and sugar in this recipe, so if you really want to cut calories, eliminate the sweet stuff!

		PER SERVING		
STANDARD RECIPE:	CALORIES 246	FAT 12G	PROTEIN 5G	CARBOHYDRATES 36G	CHOL 13MG
REDUCED FAT:	CALORIES 149	FAT 4G	PROTEIN 5G	CARBOHYDRATES 34G	CHOL 8MG

Five-Bean Salad

MAKES 8 SERVINGS

Colorful and tasty, this hearty salad is perfect for alfresco summer dining. If you are feeling adventurous, and have some extra time on your hands, cook dried beans instead of using canned. The difference is incredible!

1 (15-ounce) can cut green beans
1 (15-ounce) can yellow wax beans
1 (15-ounce) can red kidney beans
1 (15-ounce) can garbanzo beans
1 (15-ounce) can lima beans
1 (15-ounce) can pitted black olives
½ cup celery, diced

½ cup Spanish onion, diced
½ cup green bell pepper, diced
¼ cup pimentos, chopped
⅓ cup apple cider vinegar
¾ cup sugar
⅓ cup vegetable oil
1 teaspoon paprika

Drain each can of beans well. In a large mixing bowl, combine the beans, olives, celery, onion, green pepper, and pimentos.

To make the dressing, in a separate bowl, whisk together the vinegar, sugar, oil, and paprika. Pour the mixture over the beans and toss gently to coat. Cover and refrigerate overnight before serving.

CHEF JAMIE'S LOW-FAT TIP

Reduce the oil to a few tablespoons (use olive oil for greater flavor) for the ultimate low-fat salad. The beans are high in protein and are very filling.

HELPFUL HINTS FROM THE WIZARD

- The fresher the canned beans, the better the flavor. Beans tend to lose flavor over a period of time.
- Bell peppers in a variety of colors may be used to brighten the dish and add even more nutrients.

			PER SERVING		
STANDARD RECIPE:	CALORIES 258	FAT 18G	PROTEIN 4G	CARBOHYDRATES 34G	CHOL 0MG
REDUCED FAT:	CALORIES133	FAT 4G	PROTEIN 4G	CARBOHYDRATES 34G	CHOL 0MG

Chicken Jewel Salad Ring

MAKES 10 SERVINGS

This recipe was a favorite of the first lady, Mamie Eisenhower, and was often served at luncheons in the White House. Set on a buffet along with a tossed salad, this ring mold was a favorite with the "ladies who lunch."

For the cranberry layer:
1 envelope unflavored gelatin
1 cup cranberry juice
1 (16-ounce) can whole cranberry sauce
2 tablespoons lemon juice

For the chicken layer:
1 envelope unflavored gelatin
¾ cup cold water
1 tablespoon soy sauce
1 cup mayonnaise
1½ cups cooked chicken, diced
¼ cup almonds, coarsely chopped and toasted
½ cup celery, diced

To make the cranberry layer: Sprinkle the gelatin over the cranberry juice in a small saucepan. Over low heat, stir constantly until the gelatin is dissolved. Break up the cranberry sauce and stir in the gelatin mixture and the lemon juice. Pour into a 6-cup ring mold. Chill until almost firm.

To make the chicken layer: Sprinkle the gelatin over the cold water in a saucepan, then, over low heat, stir constantly until gelatin is dissolved. Remove from heat and stir in the soy sauce. Cool slightly, then stir in the mayonnaise until well blended. Mix in the remaining ingredients. Spoon on top of the almost firm cranberry layer. Chill until firm. Unmold and serve on greens.

CHEF JAMIE'S LOW-FAT TIP

Jell-O has always been fat-free! Use non-fat yogurt with a touch of honey in place of the mayonnaise. Garnish with a few sliced almonds instead of mixing chopped almonds into the salad.

HELPFUL HINTS FROM THE WIZARD

• To reduce sodium, use light soy sauce.

		PER SERVING			
STANDARD RECIPE:	CALORIES 245	FAT 14G	PROTEIN 7G	CARBOHYDRATES 23G	CHOL 16MG
REDUCED FAT:	CALORIES 179	FAT 6G	PROTEIN 8G	CARBOHYDRATES 22G	CHOL 7MG

Fruit Salad Dressing

MAKES ABOUT 2 ½ CUPS

This dressing is a great dipping sauce for fresh fruit or a creamy dressing for a fruit salad. So pretty in pink!

1 cup mayonnaise
1 cup sour cream
⅓ cup maraschino cherry juice
¼ cup pineapple juice

2 tablespoons honey
2 tablespoons powdered sugar
1 teaspoon lemon juice

In a large mixing bowl, whisk all ingredients together until smooth. Chill well before serving.

CHEF JAMIE'S LOW-FAT TIP

For a lower-calorie version, replace the mayonnaise with light or fat-free vanilla yogurt. To duplicate the creaminess of the sour cream, substitute ¾ cup of non-fat ricotta cheese for the sour cream. Blend the ricotta in a food processor until silky smooth before using.

	PER SERVING (2 TABLESPOONS)				
STANDARD RECIPE:	CALORIES 114	FAT 8.4G	PROTEIN .6G	CARBOHYDRATES 10G	CHOL 10MG
REDUCED FAT:	CALORIES 47	FAT 0G	PROTEIN 1.6G	CARBOHYDRATES 9G	CHOL 7MG

Thousand Island Dressing

MAKES 1 ¾ CUPS

This famous dressing was created in upstate New York in the small resort village of Clayton. In 1910, a fishing guide named George LaLonde Jr. took small groups of fishermen on outings in the waters of the nearby 1000 Islands area. He made an unusual dressing for the fish they caught and cooked. On one of the trips, May Irwin, a New York actress who was also a renowned chef, was most impressed with the dressing. She named the dressing "Thousand Island," and went on to make it famous.

This dressing is my Mom's FAVORITE! Use it as a salad dressing, a seafood dressing, a spread for sandwiches, or a dip for French fries. . . She puts it on just about anything!

1¼ cups mayonnaise
¼ cup ketchup
¼ cup chili sauce

2 teaspoons chopped pickle relish
salt & pepper, to taste

In a mixing bowl, blend together the mayonnaise, ketchup, and chili sauce until well combined. Stir in the pickle relish. Season to taste with salt and pepper. Cover and refrigerate until chilled through.

CHEF JAMIE'S LOW-FAT TIP

Low-fat Thousand Island dressing is almost as good as the full-fat version. Non-fat mayonnaise actually works great here because the bold flavors of the other ingredients mask any shortcomings the light mayonnaise has!

HELPFUL HINTS FROM THE WIZARD

• Use a major brand of non-fat mayonnaise for a high-quality product.

	PER SERVING (2 TABLESPOONS)				
STANDARD RECIPE:	CALORIES 128	FAT 13G	PROTEIN .2G	CARBOHYDRATES 7G	CHOL 8MG
REDUCED FAT:	CALORIES 114	FAT 0G	PROTEIN .2G	CARBOHYDRATES 5G	CHOL 0MG

Creamy Bleu Cheese Dressing
MAKES ABOUT 2 CUPS

Bleu cheese was created in 1854 in France and was originally called "bleu d'Auvergne." Milk used to produce "bleu cheese" is allowed to stand for about eight hours before processing. A mold, similar to the penicillin mold derived from wheat bread, is introduced into the cheese by a process that punctures the cheese, allowing oxygen to assist in the growth of the bacteria. As the bacteria grow, the oxygen allows the bacteria to send blue streaks throughout the cheese.

Who doesn't love thick, creamy bleu cheese dressing as a dip for crudités, an escape from the heat of hot wings, or the perfect complement to a simple salad of vine-ripened tomatoes and red onion? This dressing is an old diner recipe.

2 tablespoons cider vinegar
1 tablespoon sugar
1 teaspoon Worcestershire sauce
1 cup mayonnaise

½ cup sour cream
½ cup bleu cheese, crumbled
salt & pepper, to taste

In a mixing bowl, whisk together the vinegar and sugar until the sugar is completely dissolved. Stir in the mayonnaise, sour cream, and Worcestershire sauce. Blend well to combine. Stir in the crumbled bleu cheese and season to taste with salt and pepper.

Cover and refrigerate at least 1 hour before using.

CHEF JAMIE'S LOW-FAT TIP
Unfortunately, some of the greatest cheeses, like bleu and goat, do not have a low-fat alternative. I can recommend that you try using half of the bleu cheese called for in the recipe, but prepare the dressing a few days before serving it, allowing it to rest in the refrigerator. During that time, the flavor of the bleu cheese penetrates the dressing, creating a bolder flavor with less fat. You can also reduce the fat calories by using low-fat versions of the sour cream and mayonnaise.

PER SERVING (2 TABLESPOONS)

STANDARD RECIPE:	CALORIES 157	FAT 13G	PROTEIN 3G	CARBOHYDRATES 15G	CHOL 19MG
REDUCED FAT:	CALORIES 89	FAT 3G	PROTEIN 1G	CARBOHYDRATES 12G	CHOL 9MG

Old-Style French Dressing

MAKES ABOUT 2 ½ CUPS

This is the traditional tomato-based French dressing. . .so hard to find nowadays!

1 (10-ounce) can condensed tomato soup
¾ cup sugar
¼ cup cider vinegar
1 tablespoon dry mustard

1 tablespoon celery seed
1½ teaspoons paprika
¼ teaspoon garlic powder
1 cup vegetable oil
salt & pepper, to taste

Using an electric mixer or blender, combine the tomato soup, sugar, garlic powder, vinegar, dry mustard, celery seed, and paprika. Blend until well combined.

In a saucepan, heat the vegetable oil to lukewarm. Remove the oil from the heat and, with the blender running on low, slowly add the warm oil. Blend until smooth. Season with salt and pepper.

Cover and refrigerate until well chilled before serving.

CHEF JAMIE'S LOW-FAT TIP

Try using reduced-fat tomato soup in this scrumptious tomato-based dressing, and cut the oil down to ½ cup in the preparation. Add a few tablespoons of water to the dressing, if necessary, to reduce any sharp flavor from the vinegar.

HELPFUL HINTS FROM THE WIZARD

- Canola oil is high in monounsaturated oil, and would be a healthy alternative in this dressing.

PER SERVING (2 TABLESPOONS)

	CALORIES	FAT	PROTEIN	CARBOHYDRATES	CHOL
STANDARD RECIPE:	CALORIES 69	FAT 6 G	PROTEIN .12G	CARBOHYDRATES 4.75G	CHOL 0MG
REDUCED FAT:	CALORIES 23	FAT 2G	PROTEIN .12G	CARBOHYDRATES 4.75G	CHOL 0MG

Honey Mustard Dressing

MAKES ABOUT 2 CUPS

This sweet-tangy dressing is wonderful with all kinds of salads and cold pasta. It's a great dipper for vegetables and chicken too!

6 tablespoons cider vinegar
6 tablespoons honey
½ cup mayonnaise
3 tablespoons fresh parsley, chopped
2 tablespoons Dijon mustard

2 tablespoons yellow onion, finely
    chopped
salt & pepper, to taste
1½ cups vegetable oil

In a small saucepan, heat the vinegar and honey together over low heat, stirring until the honey dissolves. Pour into a mixing bowl and let cool.

Add the mayonnaise, parsley, mustard, onion, salt, and pepper. Whisk to combine well. Gradually whisk in the oil.

Cover and chill until ready to serve.

CHEF JAMIE'S LOW-FAT TIP

The health benefits of tofu are tremendous. . .and it happens to be a great substitute in some recipes. You can achieve the same creamy finish in this dressing by using 1 cup of soft tofu in place of the mayonnaise and 1 cup of the oil.

HELPFUL HINTS FROM THE WIZARD

- If tofu is stored, the water it sits in needs to be changed daily to keep it fresh.
- Tofu will only last for 3 to 5 days from the "sell date." It can be frozen for up to 2 months at 0°F.

	PER SERVING (2 TABLESPOONS)				
STANDARD RECIPE:	CALORIES 384	FAT 38G	PROTEIN .1G	CARBOHYDRATES 14G	CHOL 3MG
REDUCED FAT:	CALORIES 67	FAT 2G	PROTEIN 2G	CARBOHYDRATES 12G	CHOL 1MG

Poppy Seed Dressing

MAKES ABOUT 2 CUPS

This dressing is still one of my favorites! It is particularly good on a spinach salad or as a dip for crudités.

1 coddled egg (see *Chef's Note* on page 42)
¼ cup red wine vinegar
2 tablespoons sugar

1 teaspoon Dijon mustard
salt & pepper, to taste
1 cup vegetable oil
2 tablespoons poppy seeds

Combine the egg, vinegar, sugar, mustard, and salt and pepper in the bowl of a food processor or blender. Process for 1 minute.

With the motor running, slowly drizzle in the oil in a steady stream to form an emulsified dressing. When the all of the oil is incorporated, shut off the processor, so as not to "break" the dressing. (Breaking occurs when an emulsified sauce separates, forcing the oil and vinegar emulsion to "break" apart.)

Adjust the seasonings with salt and pepper and stir in the poppy seeds. Cover and refrigerate until ready to serve.

CHEF JAMIE'S LOW-FAT TIP

Create an incredible low-fat Poppy Seed Dressing by eliminating the egg and substituting 1 cup of low-fat or non-fat plain yogurt for the vegetable oil. Add a teaspoon of honey to counter out the tartness of the yogurt. Whisk the low-fat dressing ingredients together in a mixing bowl and refrigerate until ready to serve.

		PER SERVING (2 TABLESPOONS)			
STANDARD RECIPE:	CALORIES 130	FAT 14G	PROTEIN .3G	CARBOHYDRATES 1.6G	CHOL 13MG
REDUCED FAT:	CALORIES 22	FAT .3G	PROTEIN .1G	CARBOHYDRATES .3G	CHOL 13MG

Chutney Dip

Before chutney was sold in a bottle, great home cooks slaved for hours to combine dried fruits and seasonings for incredible homemade chutneys. Today, the bottled kind is delicious and a great shortcut! I remember my mom, a truly great cook, quickly spooning bottled chutney over a brick of cream cheese and serving it to last-minute dinner guests as a quick hors d'oeuvre. Her guests were always wowed by this simple treat! This dip, a variation on my mom's, is an easy-to-prepare hors d'oeuvre or a perfect party finger food. Serve the dip with apple wedges or crackers.

1 cup ricotta cheese (or cottage cheese, pureed until smooth)
4 tablespoons cream cheese, softened
¼ teaspoon curry powder
5 to 6 tablespoons prepared chutney
pinch of salt

In the bowl of a food processor, combine the ricotta and the cream cheese. Process until very smooth. Add the curry powder and salt and blend thoroughly.

Transfer to a mixing bowl and stir in the chutney by hand, just until combined, leaving streaks of white and pink. Serve at room temperature.

CHEF JAMIE'S LOW-FAT TIP

For an incredible, flavorful treat for the low-fat eater, use part-skim or even non-fat ricotta cheese and light cream cheese.

	PER SERVING (¼ CUP)				
STANDARD RECIPE:	CALORIES 143	FAT 10G	PROTEIN 8G	CARBOHYDRATES 4G	CHOL 19MG
REDUCED FAT:	CALORIES 110	FAT 2G	PROTEIN 9G	CARBOHYDRATES 4G	CHOL 15MG

Grandma's Famous Shrimp Dip

MAKES 4 SERVINGS

It's "famous" because everyone seems to love it. . .and because everyone seems to have her own famous family version! This delicious dip is so simple to make.

½ cup whipped cream cheese
4 tablespoons chili sauce
2 tablespoons sour cream
1 scallion, chopped finely
1 large celery stalk, sliced thinly

1 garlic clove, chopped finely
½ pound cooked shrimp, cut into
   ½-inch pieces
salt & pepper, to taste

In a mixing bowl, combine the cream cheese, chili sauce, sour cream, scallion, celery, and garlic. Stir in the shrimp and season to taste with salt and pepper. Refrigerate for at least two hours. Serve chilled with crackers.

CHEF JAMIE'S LOW-FAT TIP

Non-fat cream cheese, when blended with other flavors, is a terrific invention. (Alone, it tends to taste chalky and a bit grainy!) Since the non-fat version does not come whipped, blend it yourself in a food processor until light and airy, for better consistency. Low-fat sour cream works well in the dip also.

HELPFUL HINTS FROM THE WIZARD

- For more volume, whip the cream cheese in a very cold, stainless-steel bowl.

		PER SERVING		
STANDARD RECIPE:	CALORIES 270	FAT 15G	PROTEIN 20G	CARBOHYDRATES 10G	CHOL 215MG
REDUCED FAT:	CALORIES 215	FAT 2.5G	PROTEIN 20G	CARBOHYDRATES 10G	CHOL 190MG

Mom's Clam Dip

MAKES ABOUT 2 CUPS

A friend's mom has made this dish for company for more years than she is willing to admit. It is the traditional hors d'oeuvre in her family. . .and soon to be in yours!

16 ounces cream cheese, softened
2 (6-ounce) cans minced clams
3 tablespoons yellow onion, finely
    grated

2 tablespoons Worcestershire sauce
juice of 1 lemon

Drain the clams, reserving 2 tablespoons of their juice. In a small mixing bowl, blend the above ingredients with the reserved clam juice. Chill thoroughly before serving.

Serve with chips or crackers.

CHEF JAMIE'S LOW-FAT TIP

Use low-fat cream cheese instead of the whole-fat version. I find that non-fat cream cheese distorts the flavor and texture of this dish.

HELPFUL HINTS FROM THE WIZARD

- To keep this treat low in fat, look for baked chips and low-fat crackers to serve with the dip.

PER SERVING (¼ CUP)					
STANDARD RECIPE:	CALORIES 89	FAT 8G	PROTEIN 3G	CARBOHYDRATES 1.6G	CHOL 28MG
REDUCED FAT:	CALORIES 59	FAT 4G	PROTEIN 3G	CARBOHYDRATES 1.6G	CHOL 18MG

Salmon Mousse

MAKES 12 SERVINGS

Serve this airy mousse on toasts, black bread, or crackers for a wonderful hors d'oeuvre or as a first course with a simple salad of watercress or arugula.

1 envelope unflavored gelatin
¼ cup cold water
½ cup boiling water
½ cup mayonnaise
2 tablespoons fresh lemon juice
2 tablespoons fresh dill, finely chopped

1 tablespoon yellow onion, finely grated
dash of Tabasco
2 cups poached fresh or canned salmon, bones and skin removed and flaked
1 cup heavy cream

In a large mixing bowl, soften the gelatin in the cold water. Whisk in the boiling water and mix until the gelatin dissolves completely. Cool to room temperature.

Add the mayonnaise, lemon juice, dill, onion, and Tabasco to the cooled gelatin mixture and mix thoroughly. Refrigerate for 30 minutes or until it begins to thicken slightly.

Fold in the flaked salmon and mix well.

In a separate bowl, using an electric mixer, whip the cream until thick and fluffy. Fold the whipped cream into the salmon mixture and blend well.

Transfer to a 6-cup serving bowl. Cover and chill the mousse for 4 hours or until well chilled.

CHEF JAMIE'S LOW-FAT TIP

Using low-fat mayonnaise and only ¼ cup of whipped cream will significantly lower the fat in this mousse. The consistency will be a bit heavier but the calories and fat will be lighter!

HELPFUL HINTS FROM THE WIZARD

- Whipping cream in a copper bowl will create more volume. Also, if all the whipping utensils and the bowl are cold, it will speed up the process.

		PER SERVING		
STANDARD RECIPE:	CALORIES 129	FAT 10G	PROTEIN 7G	CARBOHYDRATES 3G	CHOL 28MG
REDUCED FAT:	CALORIES122	FAT 4G	PROTEIN 7G	CARBOHYDRATES 3G	CHOL 14MG

Who Doesn't Love Crab Cakes
MAKES 8 CRAB CAKES

Blue crab from the Chesapeake Bay is traditionally used in crab cakes, but Dungeness or Alaskan work just fine, too. The secret to perfect crab cakes is an airy consistency, plenty of crab, and great spice!

1 pound fresh or frozen lump
    crabmeat, cartilage and shells
    removed
½ cup yellow onion, finely diced
¼ cup celery, finely diced
¾ cup mayonnaise
1 tablespoon Dijon mustard
1 teaspoon Old Bay seasoning
pinch of cayenne pepper

1 egg, lightly beaten
½ cup saltine cracker crumbs *or*
    bread crumbs, divided
salt & pepper, to taste
2 tablespoons olive oil
2 tablespoons unsalted butter
Homemade Tartar Sauce (see recipe
    on page 195)

Combine the crabmeat, onion, and celery in a large mixing bowl and toss well.

In a separate bowl, combine the mayonnaise, mustard, Old Bay seasoning, and cayenne pepper. Stir the mayonnaise mixture into the crab mixture and blend well. Gently stir in the egg and ¼ cup of the cracker or bread crumbs. Season with salt and pepper.

Form into eight patties. Carefully coat the patties with the remaining cracker or bread crumbs and refrigerate for at least 30 minutes but no longer than 2 hours.

Heat 1 tablespoon of oil and 1 tablespoon of butter in a large sauté pan. Sauté the crab cakes in batches over medium heat until golden brown on both sides and cooked through, about 3 to 4 minutes per side. Add more oil and butter to the pan as needed.

Serve immediately with tartar sauce.

CHEF JAMIE'S LOW-FAT TIP
The trick to low-fat crab cakes is to broil them until golden brown instead of frying them, eliminating the oil and butter. Use low-fat mayonnaise for an even lighter verson.

HELPFUL HINTS FROM THE WIZARD
- Imitation crabmeat made from pollack will work in this recipe.

		PER SERVING (2 CRAB CAKES)		
STANDARD RECIPE:	CALORIES 409	FAT 30G	PROTEIN 23G	CARBOHYDRATES 15G	CHOL 128MG
REDUCED FAT:	CALORIES 241	FAT 8G	PROTEIN 23G	CARBOHYDRATES 13G	CHOL 54MG

Marinated Shrimp

MAKES 6 SERVINGS

This recipe dates back twenty-five years! Today, we start with raw shrimp and call it ceviche! The shrimp are delicious as an hors d'oeuvre for a cocktail party or as a first course for dinner.

2 pounds medium shrimp, cooked
　　and peeled
1 large red onion, cut into thin rings
1¼ cups olive oil
½ cup red wine vinegar
¼ cup lemon juice

¼ cup parsley, chopped
3 tablespoons sugar
1 teaspoon Worcestershire sauce
1 clove garlic, minced
Tabasco sauce, to taste
salt & pepper, to taste

In a large, non-reactive bowl, place the shrimp and onion rings in alternate layers. Whisk together the remaining ingredients and pour over the shrimp. Allow the shrimp to marinate in the refrigerator for 1 to 2 days.

To serve, drain the marinade and place the shrimp and onions on a serving platter. Garnish with parsley.

CHEF JAMIE'S LOW-FAT TIP

If you like, cut down on the olive oil, but be aware that the acid in the vinegar and lemon juice will make the shrimp very pungent. A teaspoon of sugar will smooth out the tartness.

HELPFUL HINTS FROM THE WIZARD

- Devein the shrimp easily with an ice pick by running the pick down the back of the shrimp to remove the vein.
- Make sure to drain the olive oil well to reduce the fat and calories, perhaps even patting the shrimp with a paper towel to remove excess oil.

		PER SERVING		
STANDARD RECIPE:	CALORIES 596	FAT 21G	PROTEIN 31G	CARBOHYDRATES 6G	CHOL 232MG
REDUCED FAT:	CALORIES 298	FAT 5G	PROTEIN 31G	CARBOHYDRATES 6G	CHOL 232MG

Caponata

MAKES ABOUT 5 CUPS

Caponata, native to Sicily, is a mixture of eggplant, onions, red peppers, and celery, punctuated with green olives and capers. The trick to this dish is to season it to taste with salt and pepper at each addition. Serve the caponata as an hors d'oeuvre with crackers or toast points, or use it as a delicious topping for fish.

½ cup extra-virgin olive oil
2 yellow onions, halved and thinly sliced
2 red bell peppers, thinly sliced
6 celery ribs (taken from the heart), thinly sliced
6 garlic cloves, thinly sliced
1 bunch fresh thyme
½ bunch fresh parsley, stems and leaves intact

1 (16-ounce) can crushed tomatoes
1 large eggplant, cut into 1-inch pieces
½ cup red wine vinegar
3 tablespoons sugar
1 cup Italian green olives, pitted and chopped
¼ cup drained capers, rinsed
salt & pepper, to taste

In a large, non-reactive pan, heat ¼ cup of the olive oil over medium heat. Add the onions and sauté, stirring often, until translucent and tender, about 5 minutes. Add the peppers and celery and sauté, stirring often, until softened, about 10 minutes. Season to taste with salt and pepper. Add the garlic and cook until fragrant, about 2 minutes.

Tie the thyme sprigs and parsley together with kitchen twine. Add the tomatoes and the herb bundle to the pan and cover the pan with a lid. Allow to simmer, stirring from time to time, for about 15 minutes.

In a separate skillet, heat the remaining ¼ cup olive oil over medium-high heat. Add the eggplant, and season with salt and pepper. Cook until lightly brown on all sides, about 8 minutes. Add the sautéed eggplant to the tomato mixture. Cover and cook 20 minutes.

Meanwhile, in a small bowl, combine the vinegar and sugar and stir to dissolve the sugar completely.

Remove the vegetables from the heat and discard the herb bundle. Stir in the vinegar mixture, olives, and capers. Adjust the seasoning. Transfer to a serving bowl to cool. Serve warm or at room temperature.

	PER SERVING (¼ CUP)				
STANDARD RECIPE:	CALORIES 78	FAT 6G	PROTEIN .35G	CARBOHYDRATES 5.25G	CHOL 0MG
REDUCED FAT:	CALORIES 20	FAT 3G	PROTEIN .35G	CARBOHYDRATES 5.25G	CHOL 0MG

Traditionally, caponata swims in oil. To reduce the fat, drain the vegetables on paper towels after cooking to absorb any excess oil. Or, use half the oil called for and add some spray oil to the pan each time you begin to sauté a new vegetable.

HELPFUL HINTS FROM THE WIZARD

- Although eggplant is fat-free, it absorbs fat like a sponge, making it very high in fat when it's fried or sauteed.

Western Cocktail Franks

MAKES 8 SERVINGS

Cocktail franks are a fun old-style appetizer! Be careful though, these are a bit spicy—and more than a bit addictive!

1 cup pineapple juice
½ cup chili sauce
2 tablespoons white wine vinegar
2 tablespoons soy sauce
1 tablespoon onion, minced
1 teaspoon dry mustard

½ teaspoon garlic powder
1 teaspoon dried red pepper flakes
1 tablespoon molasses
2 (12-ounce) packages cocktail franks
salt & pepper, to taste

Preheat the oven to 350°F.

In a large saucepan, combine the pineapple juice, chili sauce, vinegar, soy sauce, onion, dry mustard, garlic powder, and red pepper flakes. Bring to a boil, then whisk in the molasses until it dissolves. Reduce the heat to simmer and cook over low heat for 15 minutes.

Place the cocktail franks in a shallow baking pan. Pour the sauce over the franks and bake, uncovered, for 30 minutes. Baste often during cooking. Serve hot.

CHEF JAMIE'S LOW-FAT TIP

Hot dogs are seldom considered low fat . . . until today! A non-fat version of the cocktail frank is available in many supermarkets and they are quite good. Made with turkey instead of pork, they substitute impressively for the real ones. The rest of the ingredients are low-fat on their own, so eat away!

HELPFUL HINTS FROM THE WIZARD

• If you're concerned about salt, use light or low-salt soy sauce.

	PER 3 FRANKS				
STANDARD RECIPE:	CALORIES 186	FAT 13G	PROTEIN 5G	CARBOHYDRATES 12G	CHOL 38MG
REDUCED FAT:	CALORIES 100	FAT 7G	PROTEIN 6G	CARBOHYDRATES 11G	CHOL 26MG

Italian Stuffed Rice Balls

MAKES ABOUT 12

This recipe is a terrific way to use leftover rice! This traditional Italian dish can be served as an appetizer or as an accompaniment to meat, fish, or chicken. The rice balls taste delicious dipped in homemade tomato sauce.

3 large eggs, beaten
2 cups cold cooked rice
6 ounces mozzarella cheese, cut into
    1-inch cubes

canola oil, for frying
1 cup bread crumbs

In a mixing bowl, stir together the beaten eggs and rice. Stir to combine well, but do not mash. Scoop one tablespoon of rice into your hand and place a cube of mozzarella in the middle. Top with another tablespoon of rice and press together to form a ball, enclosing the cheese. Drop the ball into the bread crumbs and toss gently to coat. Place rice balls on a wax paper–lined cookie sheet. Refrigerate for 1 hour.

Heat the oil in a deep fryer or heavy skillet to 375°F. Fry a few of the balls at a time for about 5 minutes or until golden brown. Drain on paper towels. Serve hot.

CHEF JAMIE'S LOW-FAT TIP

This dish can be made lower in fat by using part-skim mozzarella cheese and liquid egg substitute. Unfortunately, there is no substitute for frying in this recipe!

HELPFUL HINTS FROM THE WIZARD

- Canola oil has a very high smoking point and does not break down into dangerous fat as easily as some other oils do.

		PER RICE BALL		
STANDARD RECIPE:	CALORIES 146	FAT 6G	PROTEIN 6G	CARBOHYDRATES 16G	CHOL 53MG
REDUCED FAT:	CALORIES 121	FAT 4G	PROTEIN 7G	CARBOHYDRATES 16G	CHOL 0.4MG

Crab-Stuffed Cherry Tomatoes

MAKES ABOUT 65

My mother says the trendiest thing to do, when she was growing up, was to stuff cherry tomatoes! Pretty to look at and delicious to eat, this is truly an elegant hors d'oeuvre!

½ pound lump crabmeat (cleaned well)
8 black Greek olives, pitted and chopped
2 tablespoons sour cream
2 tablespoons mayonnaise

2 tablespoons roasted red pepper (or pimento), drained and chopped
2 tablespoons fresh parsley, chopped
2 teaspoons fresh lemon juice
salt & pepper, to taste
65 cherry tomatoes (approximately)

In a mixing bowl, combine the crabmeat, olives, sour cream, mayonnaise, roasted red pepper, parsley, and lemon juice. Season to taste with salt and pepper.

To prepare the tomatoes, cut ¼ inch from the stem end of each tomato and scoop out the seeds. Sprinkle the tomatoes lightly with salt. Stuff the tomato shells with the crab mixture and chill before serving.

CHEF JAMIE'S LOW-FAT TIP

Use low-fat sour cream and light mayonnaise to retain the flavor and texture the crab mixture deserves.

			PER TOMATO		
STANDARD RECIPE:	CALORIES 15	FAT 4G	PROTEIN 2G	CARBOHYDRATES .5G	CHOL 6MG
REDUCED FAT:	CALORIES 9	FAT 1G	PROTEIN 2G	CARBOHYDRATES .2G	CHOL 6MG

Sweet & Sour Cocktail Meatballs

MAKES ABOUT 35 HORS D'OEUVRES

I remember eating these tasty treats at my mom's dinner parties, sitting in front of the hors d'oeuvre table armed with my toothpick. The tomatoes, apples, and raisins give the sauce a wonderful sweetness and the meat acquires tremendous moisture.

1 (16-ounce) can whole tomatoes in juice
1 (16 ounce) can crushed tomatoes in juice
1 (8-ounce) can tomato sauce
3 green apples, cored, peeled and diced
½ cup golden raisins

juice of 1 lemon
salt & pepper, to taste
½ cup sugar
2 pounds ground beef
2 slices white bread, soaked in water
3 large eggs
2 tablespoons vegetable oil (if frying)
salt & pepper, to taste

In a large, non-reactive pan, combine the whole tomatoes, crushed tomatoes, tomato sauce, apples, raisins, and lemon juice. Stir in the sugar, and season with salt and pepper. Bring to a boil over medium heat. Reduce the heat to low and simmer, stirring often, for 1 hour.

Meanwhile, in a mixing bowl, combine the ground beef, soaked bread, eggs, and salt and pepper. Form about 35 small meatballs. Brown the meatballs under the broiler until just cooked through, or sauté in a frying pan using 2 tablespoons vegetable oil. Gently add the cooked meatballs to the finished sauce and cook over low heat for 15 minutes. Serve warm.

CHEF JAMIE'S LOW-FAT TIP

Using a lower-fat meat is always a good way to lessen the fat in a recipe. Ground beef with 7 percent fat is the leanest way to go, or you could use ground turkey. Reducing the fat content in the meat will result in a firmer meatball, but still a tasty one!

		PER MEATBALL			
STANDARD RECIPE:	CALORIES 119	FAT 6G	PROTEIN 7G	CARBOHYDRATES 10G	CHOL 43MG
REDUCED FAT:	CALORIES 97	FAT 3.5G	PROTEIN 7G	CARBOHYDRATES 10G	CHOL 30MG

Crab Rangoon

MAKES 30 HORS D'OEUVRES

½ pound lump crabmeat, cleaned of any shell fragments and chopped finely

8 ounces cream cheese, softened

1 teaspoon A-1 or other steak sauce

¼ teaspoon garlic powder

2 ½ to 3 dozen round won ton wrappers

1 large egg, well beaten

canola oil, as needed for frying

Chinese-style hot mustard, for dipping

In a mixing bowl, combine the crabmeat, cream cheese, A-1 steak sauce, and garlic powder. Mix to combine well. Place a heaping teaspoon of the crab filling in the center of each wonton wrapper. Gather the four corners of the wonton together at the top. Moisten the edges with a little bit of the beaten egg. Pinch or twist the top of the wonton together to seal.

Heat the oil in a deep fryer or heavy skillet to 375°F. Fry the won tons in batches until golden brown, about 3 minutes. Drain on paper towels.

Serve with hot mustard for dipping.

CHEF JAMIE'S LOW-FAT TIP

I'm happy to say that these fried "crab pockets" are truly delicious. . .and they taste almost as good when baked! Use low-fat cream cheese and, instead of frying the wontons, eliminate the oil completely by placing them on a baking sheet sprayed with non-stick cooking spray. Bake them at 375°F until golden brown and crisp.

HELPFUL HINTS FROM THE WIZARD

• Make sure you use garlic powder, not garlic salt.

		PER WON TON			
STANDARD RECIPE:	CALORIES 57	FAT 4G	PROTEIN 5G	CARBOHYDRATES .2G	CHOL 26MG
REDUCED FAT:	CALORIES 39	FAT 1G	PROTEIN 5G	CARBOHYDRATES .4G	CHOL 24MG

Mini Quiches

MAKES 16 (2-INCH) MINI QUICHES OR 1 (10-INCH) QUICHE

These buttery, custardy, cheesy surprises are always a cocktail favorite. To create a large tart that can be sliced and served, use the entire recipe to a fill a large 10-inch tart mold. Add your favorite fillings to this basic recipe—try sautéed mushrooms, ham, crabmeat, or smoked salmon!

For the crust:
1½ cups all-purpose flour
¼ teaspoon salt
pinch of sugar
5 tablespoons unsalted butter, cut into small pieces and chilled
3 tablespoons vegetable shortening, chilled
¼ cup ice water

For the custard:
1 cup heavy cream
2 large eggs
¼ teaspoon grated nutmeg
salt & pepper, to taste

For the filling:
8 ounces Gruyere cheese
¼ cup Parmesan cheese

To make the crust: Place the flour, salt, and sugar in the bowl of a food processor and pulse to combine. Add the chilled butter and shortening, and pulse just until the mixture resembles coarse meal, about 6 pulses. With the processor running, add just enough ice water to make a workable dough. Do not over mix.

Turn the dough onto a floured work surface and knead a few times to blend thoroughly. Scrape the dough up from the work surface and form a ball. Wrap in plastic wrap and refrigerate for at least 2 hours. (At this point, you can freeze the dough, then defrost it when needed.)

After the dough has chilled, unwrap it and place it on a floured work surface. Pound the dough a few times with your rolling pin to soften it, then roll the dough to ⅛ inch thick. Cut the dough into 4-inch rounds and fit the dough into mini tart shells (2 inches in diameter) or leave the dough whole and fit the dough into a 10-inch tart pan. Trim off any excess dough. Refrigerate the tart shells for 30 minutes.

Preheat the oven to 400°F. Remove the chilled shells from the refrigerator and prick the bottom and sides with a fork. If you are preparing a 10-inch quiche, line the dough with foil and fill with pie weights or dried beans. Bake the crusts for 8 to 10 minutes or until just beginning to color. Cool the crusts slightly before filling. If you are making mini quiches, unmold the crusts and place them on a cookie sheet before filling. Reduce the oven temperature to 375°F.

	PER SERVING				
STANDARD RECIPE:	CALORIES 431	FAT 31G	PROTEIN 16G	CARBOHYDRATES 19G	CHOL 136MG
REDUCED FAT:	CALORIES 362	FAT 23G	PROTEIN 16G	CARBOHYDRATES 19G	CHOL 835MG

Mini Quiches *(continued)*

To make the custard: In a large mixing bowl, whisk together the cream, eggs, and seasonings.

To assemble the quiches: Place a spoonful of Gruyere cheese in each mini crust or sprinkle all of the cheese in the large crust. Spoon the custard mixture over the cheese in the crusts, filling to just below the edge of the tart shell.

For mini quiches, bake 10 to 15 minutes or until filling is puffed and lightly browned. For a large quiche, bake for 25 minutes or until puffed and golden brown.

CHEF JAMIE'S LOW-FAT TIP

I developed this low-fat quiche recipe for a ladies luncheon and it was very well received! Use my Lower-Fat Pie Crust recipe (see page 245), but add only a pinch of sugar for flavor. For the custard, substitute evaporated skim milk for the cream, and use 1 whole egg and 2 egg whites instead of the 2 eggs. Slim the quiche down even more by substituting a low-fat cheese that melts well.

HELPFUL HINTS FROM THE WIZARD

- If you want the ultimate flaky crust and don't mind splurging on fat and calories, use lard instead of shortening in the crust. Lard has larger fat crystals and produces a flakier crust.

Bread-and-Butter Pickles

MAKES APPROXIMATELY 8 PINTS

Sweet and crisp, these time-honored pickles are great snacks!

12 medium cucumbers, sliced
8 white onions, thinly sliced
1 red bell pepper, cut into thin strips
1 green bell pepper, cut into thin strips
½ cup kosher salt
crushed ice

5 cups sugar
5 cups apple cider vinegar
2 tablespoons mustard seeds
2 teaspoons celery seed
1 teaspoon tumeric
½ teaspoon ground cloves

Place the cucumbers, onions, and red and green bell peppers in a large, non-reactive pan, arranging in a single layer. Add the salt and cover with crushed ice. Let stand at room temperature for 3 hours.

Drain through a colander, removing any remaining ice. Place the vegetables in a 12-quart non-reactive stockpot. Combine the remaining ingredients and pour over the vegetables. Bring to a full boil, then remove from the heat. Preserve the pickles in sterilized jars. Store the pickles in the refrigerator for up to a year.

CHEF JAMIE'S LOW-FAT TIP

While the sodium and sugar content of these pickles is high, they are fat-free!

HELPFUL HINTS FROM THE WIZARD

- To remove the bitterness from a cucumber, just cut one inch off each end and rub the two exposed surfaces together in a circular motion. Then pull them apart creating a small amount of suction. This will neutralize the chemical that causes bitterness in the whole cucumber.

PER PINT

STANDARD RECIPE: CALORIES 632   FAT 0G   PROTEIN 5G   CARBOHYDRATES 163G   CHOL 0MG

Chapter 3

Fantastic Fondue

*F*ondue is not only a delicious meal or starter, it's also a great social event. Its name is French, from the word fonder which means to melt, but the Swiss claim the credit for having originated fondue.

A few tips will help you prepare fondue like a pro: aged cheeses tend to become less stringy when melted and are also popular because they become highly aromatic when heated. Also note that diced cheese melts more smoothly than grated cheese. The best alcohol to use in a classic fondue is kirsch, though you may substitute brandy if you like. Serve a dry white wine as an accompaniment to fondue—the classic combination of wine and cheese is a winning one. Modern recipes generally call for Italian or French bread, which is crusty on the outside and soft on the inside. When you cut the bread, try to leave each chunk with a crusty side!

The peasant custom of eating out of the same pot is practiced in many countries and in many different forms. An evening of good food shared with friends is a truly enjoyable event!

Simple Cheddar Fondue

MAKES 4 SERVINGS

Cheese fondue was first served in the United States by French Chef Jean-Baptiste-Gilbert dis Julien. The dish was served in a small restaurant on the corner of Milk and Congress Streets in Boston in the early 1800s.

This simple fondue recipe incorporates milk for creaminess and dry mustard for heightened flavor. The preparation is slightly different than the classic method.

1 tablespoon dry mustard
2 tablespoons water
3 tablespoons (1½ ounces) unsalted butter
3 tablespoons all-purpose flour
salt & pepper, to taste
1 cup whole milk
2 cups cheddar cheese, diced
1 loaf French bread, cubed

Combine the dry mustard and water in a small mixing bowl and let stand for 15 minutes while preparing the other ingredients. Melt the butter in a fondue pot or cooking pot. Add the flour and stir to create a roux. Slowly whisk in the milk to create a thick, creamy mixture. Add the diced cheese and stir constantly until melted. Add the mustard mixture and blend to combine. Season with salt and pepper to taste. Use the bread cubes for dipping.

CHEF JAMIE'S LOW-FAT TIP
Use low-fat milk and reduced-fat cheese for a lighter version. The dry mustard in this fondue will hide any flaws the low-fat ingredients create.

	PER SERVING				
STANDARD RECIPE:	CALORIES 846	FAT 49G	PROTEIN 39G	CARBOHYDRATES 66G	CHOL 120MG
REDUCED FAT:	CALORIES 701	FAT 30G	PROTEIN 40G	CARBOHYDRATES 66G	CHOL 100MG

Classic Cheese Fondue

MAKES 6 SERVINGS

Emmentaler cheese is produced by more than sixteen hundred dairies in the Emmental Valley in Switzerland. The cheese has a mild, nutty flavor and may resemble Swiss cheese because of the large holes that are formed by pockets of gas that develop during the fermentation process. This cheese is usually lower in fat than many Swiss cheeses since the milk used is partially skimmed.

½ pound Emmentaler cheese
½ pound Gruyere cheese
3 tablespoons all-purpose flour
1 whole garlic clove
2 cups dry white wine

3 tablespoons kirsch
1 tablespoon lemon juice
nutmeg and paprika, to taste
1 loaf French bread, cubed

Dice the cheeses and toss them with the flour. Set aside. Rub the fondue dish or cooking pot with the garlic clove, then discard it. Pour the wine into the pot. Heat until warm. Add the cheese and stir until melted. Add the kirsch, lemon juice, and seasoning, and stir to combine. Keep the heat low once the fondue is combined. Serve with the bread cubes for dipping.

CHEF JAMIE'S LOW-FAT TIP

Finding low-fat cheeses that melt well can be difficult. When it really comes down to it, low-fat fondue is tough! You might experiment with some of the low-fat cheeses at your local supermarket to see which ones work best in this recipe.

HELPFUL HINTS FROM THE WIZARD

- Remember, French bread does not contain any fat and has a very short shelf life.

		PER SERVING			
STANDARD RECIPE:	CALORIES 456	FAT 24G	PROTEIN 26G	CARBOHYDRATES 35G	CHOL 72MG
REDUCED FAT:	CALORIES 387	FAT 14G	PROTEIN 25G	CARBOHYDRATES 35G	CHOL 70MG

Baked Fondue

MAKES 7 SERVINGS

This "casserole" of sorts makes a lovely side dish with meat or a terrific first course when served with a small green salad.

unsalted butter, as needed
10 slices French bread
6 large eggs
2 cups half & half
½ cup dry white wine
1 tablespoon yellow onion, minced
½ teaspoon Worcestershire sauce
½ teaspoon dry mustard
1¾ pounds Swiss or cheddar cheese, grated
salt & pepper, to taste

Preheat the oven to 300°F.

Butter the bread slices, then dice the bread into small cubes and set aside. In a large mixing bowl, beat together the eggs, half & half, wine, onion, Worcestershire sauce, dry mustard, and salt and pepper.

Butter a casserole dish and arrange a single layer of bread cubes on the bottom. Add a layer of cheese, another layer of bread, and then top with the remaining cheese. Pour the egg mixture over the layers. Bake for about 1 hour or until set. Serve hot.

CHEF JAMIE'S LOW-FAT TIP

To make this casserole lower in fat, use 2 whole eggs and 1 cup of egg substitute. Also, use ½ cup of half & half and 1½ cups of low fat milk instead of 2 cups of half & half. The casserole will certainly not be as rich and fluffy, but it will still work!

HELPFUL HINTS FROM THE WIZARD

- The alcohol content of the wine will dissipate during cooking but will leave the flavor.

			PER SERVING		
STANDARD RECIPE:	CALORIES 693	FAT 54G	PROTEIN 20G	CARBOHYDRATES 29G	CHOL 324MG
REDUCED FAT:	CALORIES 518	FAT 36G	PROTEIN 19G	CARBOHYDRATES 29G	CHOL 127MG

Crab Fondue

MAKES 6 SERVINGS

This fondue incorporates the rich flavor of crab-meat and the bite of sharp cheddar cheese.

1 stick unsalted butter
2 yellow onions, diced
1 pound sharp cheddar cheese, diced
1 teaspoon ketchup

3 tablespoons Worcestershire sauce
¼ cup dry sherry
salt & pepper, to taste
3 cups crabmeat
1 loaf French bread, cubed

Melt the butter in the fondue pot or cooking pot, and add the onions. Sauté the onions until tender, about 8 minutes. Add the cheese, ketchup, Worcestershire sauce, sherry, salt, and pepper. Stir constantly until smooth. Add the crabmeat and blend well. Use the bread cubes for dipping.

CHEF JAMIE'S LOW-FAT TIP
Use non-stick cooking spray in place of the butter to sauté the onions. Also, low-fat cheddar cheese tends to taste the best when compared to other light cheeses. The bold flavor masks what you lose in the texture!

HELPFUL HINTS FROM THE WIZARD
- Fresh crabmeat really makes a difference in the taste of this recipe.
- If you're taking the low-fat route, use butter-flavored non-stick cooking spray.

		PER SERVING			
STANDARD RECIPE:	CALORIES 721	FAT 37G	PROTEIN 51G	CARBOHYDRATES 48G	CHOL 155MG
REDUCED FAT:	CALORIES 581	FAT 28G	PROTEIN 51G	CARBOHYDRATES 48G	CHOL 80MG

Fondue Bourguignonne

MAKES 4 SERVINGS

The basic elements of meat fondues are lean beef cubes, oil, and dipping sauces. A heavy cast-iron fondue pot or pan is generally used to help retain the heat of the oil and cook the meat evenly. I serve my classic meat fondue with a wonderfully rich béarnaise sauce, the recipe for which follows.

For the fondue:
2 pounds very tender beef, filet, or tenderloin
2 cups peanut oil
2 sticks (16 ounces) unsalted butter

For the béarnaise sauce:
¼ cup tarragon or white wine vinegar
¼ cup dry white wine
2 shallots, minced
2 sprigs fresh tarragon
3 egg yolks
1 tablespoon cream
½ cup unsalted butter, melted
salt, pepper, and cayenne pepper, to taste

To make the fondue: Cut the beef into 1-inch cubes. Combine the oil and butter in a large, deep, cast-iron or copper pot and place over high heat. Heat the oil and butter until very hot; it should be sizzling. Spear the beef pieces on fondue forks or skewers and place them in the hot oil to cook, about 2 minutes for rare. Remove the meat from the oil and drain slightly.

To make the béarnaise sauce: In a small saucepan, combine the vinegar, wine, shallots, and tarragon. Bring to a boil over medium heat and cook until the liquid is reduced to 1 tablespoon, about 3 minutes. Cool and strain into a heatproof mixing bowl.

Add the egg yolks and cream to the cooled vinegar reduction. Place the bowl on top of a pan of simmering water to create a double boiler (the water should not touch the bottom of the bowl), and stir constantly with a wire whisk until the sauce is creamy. Gradually whisk in the melted butter. Continue beating until the sauce is thickened. Season to taste with salt, pepper, and cayenne. Dip the cooked meat in warm béarnaise sauce and enjoy.

CHEF JAMIE'S LOW-FAT TIP

Because the beef is fried, it is difficult to make this recipe low-fat! The béarnaise though, can be prepared with good results using butter that has 50 percent less fat.

		PER SERVING		
STANDARD RECIPE:	CALORIES 1,346	FAT 132G	PROTEIN 74G	CARBOHYDRATES 2.5G	CHOL 528MG
REDUCED FAT:	CALORIES 1,202	FAT 116G	PROTEIN 74G	CARBOHYDRATES 2.5G	CHOL 493MG

Fondue Au Chocolat

SERVES 4 TO 6 (OR SOMETIMES JUST ONE!)

Chocolate fondue is an American invention, and a good one at that!

There are many variations; my favorites include adding crushed almonds, instant coffee, or ground cinnamon.

1 pound bittersweet chocolate
1 cup heavy cream
1 teaspoon vanilla extract
fresh fruit (such as strawberries, bananas, peaches, and pears), cut into chunks

angel food cake or pound cake, cut into chunks
marshmallows, for dipping

Combine the chocolate and cream in a fondue pot or saucepan. Stir over low heat until smooth. Stir in the vanilla just before serving.

Invite each guest to skewer fruit, cake, and/or marshmallows on fondue forks or skewers. Dip the dessert bites in the warm chocolate and savor each bite!

CHEF JAMIE'S LOW-FAT TIP

When someone finds a low-fat alternative for chocolate, please call me first! This fondue is meant to be an indulgence! I have tried using fat-free half & half and cocoa powder, but it just doesn't work the same way. Enjoy it for a special occasion and just remember, "everything in moderation"!

HELPFUL HINTS FROM THE WIZARD

- To stop the cut fruit from becoming brown, just mix some powdered vitamin C and water in a spray bottle, and give the fruit a little squirt or two after you peel, slice, or cube it. (This trick works for vegetables as well.)

PER SERVING

STANDARD RECIPE: CALORIES 869   FAT 21G   PROTEIN 1G   CARBOHYDRATES 71G   CHOL 42MG

Chapter 4

Ultimate Sandwiches

To me, sandwiches are the ultimate comfort food! Many of us have childhood memories of coming home to a bowl of tomato soup and a grilled cheese sandwich, lovingly prepared by Mom. When it comes to sandwiches, everyone has his or her favorites, some of them interesting combinations (a mayonnaise, radish, and bread-and-butter pickle sandwich is one I have heard of, but not tasted!), others tried-and-true pairings (like the sirloin and American cheese featured in the well-loved Philly Cheese Steak). In this chapter, you'll find an ample selection of sandwich classics. . . .

Chef Jamie's Favorite Grilled Cheese

MAKES 2 SERVINGS

This is my version of the ultimate old-fashioned grilled cheese sandwich. I like the bread crisp and the cheese oozing. The bread is key here; it must be thinly sliced, like cocktail bread. (Cocktail bread should be available in the bread section of your local supermarket.) Try dipping the grilled cheese in spicy brown mustard to complete the entire taste sensation!

unsalted butter, softened

8 slices white bread, thinly sliced

6 slices American cheese

Butter the slices of bread on both sides and lay them in a row. Top the first slice of bread with a slice of cheese. Then place the next slice of bread on top of the cheese. Repeat, using four slices of bread and three slices of cheese, ending with a piece of bread on top. Repeat the process to create a second sandwich.

Heat a large sauté pan over medium heat until the pan is warm. Add the sandwiches to the pan and place a heatproof plate on top of the sandwiches; the goal here is to weigh the sandwiches down and capture the heat in the pan by enclosing the pan as if it had a lid on it. (You could also place a brick or another sauté pan on top of the sandwiches to duplicate the effect.)

Cook for 3 to 4 minutes or until golden brown on the underside. Remove the weight and carefully turn the sandwiches over. Cook 2 to 3 minutes more or until the bottom side is golden brown.

Remove the sandwiches from the pan, cut in half and enjoy!

CHEF JAMIE'S LOW-FAT TIP

This sandwich works quite well with reduced-fat slices of American cheese. Instead of buttering the bread, spray the pan liberally with non-stick cooking spray before placing the sandwiches in the pan and again right before turning the sandwiches over.

		PER SERVING			
STANDARD RECIPE:	CALORIES 659	FAT 41G	PROTEIN 33G	CARBOHYDRATES 47G	CHOL 78MG
REDUCED FAT:	CALORIES 606	FAT 16G	PROTEIN 32G	CARBOHYDRATES 47G	CHOL 28MG

Croque Monsieur
MAKES 2 SERVINGS

The best Croque Monsieur I have ever had was in a small bistro in Paris right on the Champs Élysées. The word "croque" means crunch, and the sandwich should be crisp and crunchy! This famous French sandwich is delicious as a meal and also wonderful as an hors d'oeuvre when cut into bite-sized squares.

unsalted butter, softened
4 slices French bread
4 slices Gruyere or Swiss cheese
4 slices ham, thinly sliced

1 large egg, beaten
2 tablespoons whole milk
4 tablespoons (2 ounces) unsalted butter

Butter the bread slices on both sides. Top one slice of bread with a slice of cheese, a slice of ham, another slice of cheese, and a final piece of bread. Repeat to create a second sandwich.

In a shallow mixing bowl, beat together the egg and milk until foamy. Dip each sandwich in the egg batter to coat both sides.

Place 2 tablespoons of the butter in a large sauté pan over medium heat. When the butter is just melted, add the sandwiches to the pan and sauté over medium heat until golden on the underside. Add the remaining butter to the pan, flip the sandwiches, and continue cooking until golden brown.

CHEF JAMIE'S LOW-FAT TIP
To lower the fat, eliminate buttering the bread and try using a low-fat cheese. Spray the pan liberally with non-stick cooking spray before placing the sandwiches in the pan and right before turning the sandwiches over to finish cooking. The sandwiches won't be as crisp or taste quite as scrumptious. . . but I'm hoping the French will forgive me!

HELPFUL HINTS FROM THE WIZARD
- Using unsalted butter is not only healthier for you, it also reduces the risk of foods sticking to the pan.

		PER SERVING			
STANDARD RECIPE:	CALORIES 808	FAT 68G	PROTEIN 42G	CARBOHYDRATE 25G	CHOL 223MG
REDUCED FAT:	CALORIES 464	FAT 33G	PROTEIN 40G	CARBOHYDRATE 23G	CHOL 208MG

Diner Patty Melt

MAKES 4 SERVINGS

A great patty melt should be a bit greasy; crisp bread and sweet grilled onions are most important!

1 pound lean ground beef
salt & pepper
1 tablespoon unsalted butter
1 tablespoon vegetable oil

large yellow onion, thinly sliced
unsalted butter, softened
8 slices rye bread
8 slices Monterey Jack cheese

In a mixing bowl, combine the ground beef with salt and pepper. (You can add any other ingredients or spices you like!) Shape the meat into 4 patties.

In a large skillet, fry the patties until golden brown on both sides and cooked to just under your desired doneness (the meat will continue to cook slightly when placed under the broiler). Remove the patties from the skillet and set aside.

Add the butter and oil to the same pan and heat over medium heat. Add the onion and sauté over medium heat until golden brown and tender. Remove the onions and set aside.

Butter each slice of rye bread and, using the same skillet, toast the bread on both sides until golden brown. Preheat the broiler to high heat.

To assemble the sandwiches, top each of 4 slices of the toasted bread with the sautéed onions, a beef patty, and two slices of cheese. Place the open-faced sandwiches under the broiler, about 5 inches away from the heat. Broil for 2 minutes or until the cheese melts. Top the sandwiches with the remaining toasted bread.

CHEF JAMIE'S LOW-FAT TIP
Using ground turkey and low-fat cheese will reduce your fat intake significantly. Also, caramelize the onions using non-stick cooking spray instead of butter, but be sure to cook the onions over very low heat to avoid burning.

HELPFUL HINTS FROM THE WIZARD
• Salted butter may cause the bread to burn too easily.

PER SERVING

STANDARD RECIPE:	CALORIES 675	FAT 43G	PROTEIN 36G	CARBOHYDRATES 28G	CHOL 138MG
REDUCED FAT:	CALORIES 546	FAT 27G	PROTEIN 35G	CARBOHYDRATES 28G	CHOL 106MG

Lana's Favorite Tuna Melt

MAKES 2 SERVINGS

A tuna melt is a very personal thing. . .each cook's tuna salad is slightly different, depending, of course, on how his or her mother made it. This is my mother's tuna recipe and her favorite sandwich!

1 (9-ounce) can Albacore tuna, drained well
⅓ cup mayonnaise
¼ cup celery, minced
1 tablespoon sweet pickle relish

2 teaspoons lemon juice
4 slices sourdough bread (or your bread of choice)
4 slices Muenster cheese (or your cheese of choice)

In a mixing bowl, flake the tuna with a fork. Add the mayonnaise, celery, relish, and lemon juice, and mix until well blended.

Toast the bread slices until golden. Preheat the broiler to high heat.

Top four slices of toasted bread with a scoop of tuna salad and spread the tuna to cover the bread. Top the tuna with 2 slices of cheese. Place the open-faced sandwiches under the broiler, about 5 inches from the heat, and broil until the cheese has melted. Top each sandwich with the remaining toasted bread.

CHEF JAMIE'S LOW-FAT TIP

Light mayonnaise substitutes beautifully for the full-of-fat version in my mom's tuna salad. Low-fat Muenster cheese is also quite tasty, and it too will aid in reducing the fat in this delicious sandwich.

HELPFUL HINTS FROM THE WIZARD

• Be sure to purchase tuna packed in water.

		PER SERVING			
STANDARD RECIPE:	CALORIES 949	FAT 37G	PROTEIN 54G	CARBOHYDRATES 74G	CHOL 66MG
REDUCED FAT:	CALORIES 680	FAT 21G	PROTEIN 53G	CARBOHYDRATES 74G	CHOL 45MG

B.L.T. Sandwich or B.L.T.A. or B.L.T.C. or B.L.T.S.

MAKES 4 SERVINGS

Everyone loves a bacon, lettuce & tomato sandwich. Today, many chefs have updated the sandwich to include avocado, chicken, or shrimp. Be creative and experiment to create your own special style!

12 slices bacon
8 slices sourdough bread
¼ cup mayonnaise

8 lettuce leaves
2 large tomatoes, sliced

In a heavy skillet, fry the bacon until crisp. Drain on paper towels and set aside.

Toast the bread slices until golden. Spread one side of each of the toasted bread slices with the mayonnaise. Top four of the slices with a lettuce leaf. Place slices of tomato on top of the lettuce, then top each with 3 slices of bacon. Top the bacon with a leaf of lettuce and the remaining bread slices, mayonnaise side down.

CHEF JAMIE'S LOW-FAT TIP

Turkey bacon is very acceptable in flavor and is a good substitute in this recipe. I am a great fan of light mayonnaise, as I don't think it compromises the flavor.

		PER SERVING		
STANDARD RECIPE:	CALORIES 338	FAT 19G	PROTEIN 11G	CARBOHYDRATES 32G	CHOL 52MG
REDUCED FAT:	CALORIES 255	FAT 10G	PROTEIN 11G	CARBOHYDRATES 32G	CHOL 40MG

Philly Cheese Steak

MAKES 4 SERVINGS

The first Philly cheese steak sandwich was served at Pat's Steaks in South Philadelphia in 1929! Some say there is nothing better than leaning over (to keep any drippings from hitting your lap!) to eat melted cheese, fried meat, and onions glistening with oil, all settled on a large, warm roll!

3 tablespoons vegetable oil
1 pound beef sirloin, sliced paper thin (have your butcher slice it for you)
salt & pepper, to taste

2 large yellow onions, thinly sliced
4 (6-inch) French rolls
8 slices American cheese
hot sauce

Preheat the oven to 250°F.

Heat the oil in a large, heavy skillet over high heat. Season the beef slices with salt and pepper, and add them to the skillet. Fry the steak quickly, stirring often. Remove the meat when it begins to brown. Set aside and keep warm.

Add the onions to the same skillet and sauté until golden brown. Meanwhile, place the French rolls in the oven for 5 minutes to warm.

To assemble the sandwiches, slice the rolls in half lengthwise, cutting only three-quarters of the way through, keeping one side of the roll just attached. Place slices of sirloin in each roll, and place one slice of cheese on top of the warm meat. Then top each sandwich with a spoonful of onions. Top each sandwich with a final slice of cheese. Serve hot with a few shakes of hot sauce, if desired.

CHEF JAMIE'S LOW-FAT TIP

Cheese steaks are meant to be greasy, however, by using a low-fat or non-fat cheese you *can* lower the fat content. Substituting chicken for beef is commonly done to reduce fat as well. Sirloin is actually very lean meat—just be sure to cut off any visible fat.

HELPFUL HINTS FROM THE WIZARD

• If you freeze the meat it will make it easier to slice.

	PER SERVING				
STANDARD RECIPE:	CALORIES 751	FAT 49G	PROTEIN 38G	CARBOHYDRATES 37G	CHOL 165MG
REDUCED FAT:	CALORIES 566	FAT 25G	PROTEIN 41G	CARBOHYDRATES 37G	CHOL 79MG

A REUBENesque Sandwich

MAKES 4 SERVINGS

The original Reuben sandwich was invented in 1914 at Reuben's Deli in New York City for Annette Seelos, the leading lady in a Charlie Chaplin film that was being filmed in the city. In 1955, the sandwich appeared at a poker game in Omaha, Nebraska, where a local grocer named Reuben Kay claimed to have invented it. Mr. Kay then entered the sandwich in a national contest and won first place, giving the claim to fame to Reuben, the grocer!

1 cup sauerkraut, well drained
½ teaspoon caraway seeds
⅛ teaspoon garlic powder
½ cup Thousand Island dressing
   (see recipe on page 53)

8 slices rye bread
1 pound corned beef, sliced thin
8 slices Swiss cheese
3 tablespoons (1½ ounces) unsalted
   butter, melted

In a mixing bowl, combine the sauerkraut, caraway seeds, and garlic powder.

Spread the Thousand Island dressing on one side of each slice of rye bread. Top 4 slices of bread with a slice of the cheese. Top the cheese with corned beef, a spoonful of sauerkraut, and another slice of cheese. Cover the sandwiches with the remaining slices of bread, dressing side down.

Brush the tops of the sandwiches with melted butter. Heat a large sauté pan over medium heat. When the pan is just warm, add the sandwiches, butter side down, and cook until golden brown. Flip the sandwiches over and continue cooking until the cheese has melted and the bread is lightly browned.

CHEF JAMIE'S LOW-FAT TIP

Corned beef tends to be scrumptiously fatty, so make a turkey Reuben for a low-fat sandwich alternative. Thousand Island dressing can be prepared in a low-fat way, too! (See the low-fat tip on page 53.)

		PER SERVING			
STANDARD RECIPE:	CALORIES 763	FAT 55G	PROTEIN 38G	CARBOHYDRATES 32G	CHOL 255MG
REDUCED FAT:	CALORIES 605	FAT 24G	PROTEIN 42G	CARBOHYDRATES 32G	CHOL 111MG

Mom's Meat Loaf Sandwich
MAKES 4 SERVINGS

You have to love leftovers to love this sandwich.
Some people say that cold meat loaf is even better than hot!

2 pounds ground beef
1½ cups seasoned bread crumbs
¾ cup ketchup
½ cup yellow onion, minced
2 large eggs, beaten

1 tablespoon Worcestershire sauce
salt & pepper, to taste
8 slices sourdough bread
ketchup and/or mustard and/or
   mayonnaise

Preheat the oven to 350°F.

To prepare the meat loaf: In a large mixing bowl, combine the ground beef, bread crumbs, ketchup, onion, eggs, and Worcestershire sauce. Season with salt and pepper, and blend thoroughly. Pack the meat mixture into a large loaf pan. Bake 1 hour. Remove from the oven and allow to cool. Cut the meat loaf into ¾-inch slices.

To assemble the sandwiches, toast the sourdough bread slices lightly and spread them with your favorite condiment. Top four of the slices with a slice of meat loaf and top with the remaining slices of bread.

CHEF JAMIE'S LOW-FAT TIP

Meat loaf can be prepared with your health in mind. Use super-lean ground beef or ground turkey, and, during the cooking process, remove the meat loaf from the oven periodically to drain the fat from around the loaf, thus eliminating the absorption of fat into the meat. Also, ½ cup of egg substitute in place of the whole eggs will bind the meat loaf.

HELPFUL HINTS FROM THE WIZARD

- Ground turkey should be lean/white meat.
- Place the meat loaf on 3 or 4 firm celery stalks to create a rack that keeps the loaf away from the fat that has drained off.

		PER SERVING			
STANDARD RECIPE:	CALORIES 871	FAT 34G	PROTEIN 77G	CARBOHYDRATES 23G	CHOL 352MG
REDUCED FAT:	CALORIES 503	FAT 16G	PROTEIN 54G	CARBOHYDRATES 23G	CHOL 131MG

Really Great Egg Salad

SERVES 4

Truly great egg salad is a combination of creamy yellow and chunky white. To me, rye bread and crisp iceberg lettuce make a perfect match. I also like to serve egg salad with Ritz crackers or thin pumpernickel.

6 hard-boiled eggs
¼ cup mayonnaise
1 teaspoon Dijon mustard
salt & pepper, to taste

8 slices rye, white, or sourdough bread
mayonnaise, for spreading
iceberg lettuce leaves
1 medium tomato, sliced

First, carefully separate the hard-boiled eggs by removing the cooked white from the yolks and placing each in separate bowls. Using a fork, mash the yolks until smooth. Add the mayonnaise and the mustard to the yolks and blend well. Season with salt and pepper and blend well.

Place the egg whites on a cutting board and chop them into ½-inch chunks. Do not over chop the whites or they will loose their lovely firm texture!

Add the chopped whites to the yolk mixture and stir to combine well. If possible, refrigerate for 1 hour before serving.

To assemble the sandwiches, use fresh or toasted bread slices. Spread the bottom slice with a thin layer of mayonnaise, top with a scoop of egg salad, lettuce leaf, and a slice of tomato. Spread the underside of the top piece of bread with a thin layer of mayonnaise, assemble the sandwich, and dig in!

CHEF JAMIE'S LOW-FAT TIP

Since the yolks have all of the fat and cholesterol contained in an egg, omitting the yolks is an effective way of reducing the fat, though it certainly changes the look, flavor, and texture of the salad. Light mayonnaise and the other flavorful ingredients, mixed with chopped egg white, create a mock egg salad. You could also use all of the egg whites and only half of the yolks for a lighter but more traditional egg salad. If you're a tofu lover, try substituting tofu for the eggs and adding ¼ teaspoon of curry powder for flavor.

HELPFUL HINTS FROM THE WIZARD

- When choosing iceberg lettuce, be sure that there is no brown ring around the bottom core. This is a sure sign that the lettuce is old.

	PER SERVING				
STANDARD RECIPE:	CALORIES 327	FAT 16G	PROTEIN 14G	CARBOHYDRATES 30G	CHOL 325MG
REDUCED FAT: (Mock Egg Salad)	CALORIES 198	FAT 4G	PROTEIN 10G	CARBOHYDRATES 26G	CHOL 3MG

Beef Barbecue Sandwich

MAKES 8 SERVINGS

This is a great recipe for a busy day, since the sweet and tangy beef practically cooks itself.

2 tablespoons vegetable oil
1 (5-pound) brisket of beef, rolled and tied
salt & pepper, to taste
2 celery stalks, chopped
2 yellow onions, diced
3 garlic cloves, minced
1 cup ketchup
2 (16-ounce) cans diced tomatoes, in their juice

½ cup cider vinegar
⅓ cup light brown sugar
1 teaspoon dried basil
1 teaspoon chili powder
½ teaspoon cinnamon
½ teaspoon oregano leaves
½ teaspoon Liquid Smoke or barbecue sauce
8 crusty sandwich rolls

Preheat the oven to 325°F.

Heat the oil in a large stockpot or Dutch oven. Season the brisket with salt and pepper, and brown the meat on all sides. Remove and set aside.

In the same pot, add the garlic, celery, and onions, and sauté until the onions are tender, about 10 minutes. Add the remaining ingredients except the rolls and mix well.

Return the browned brisket to the pot and spoon the sauce over the roast. Cover and place in the oven. Bake the beef for 3 hours, or until the meat is very tender.

Remove and slice thinly. Return the beef to the pot and stir to coat with the sauce. Return to the oven and bake, uncovered, 45 minutes longer.

Serve the sliced brisket, smothered with sauce on warmed rolls.

CHEF JAMIE'S LOW-FAT TIP

Unfortunately, brisket is not lean meat; that must be why it tastes so good! Use a turkey breast in place of the beef and sear the meat in non-stick cooking spray instead of oil.

		PER SERVING			
STANDARD RECIPE:	CALORIES 790	FAT 33G	PROTEIN 89G	CARBOHYDRATES 29G	CHOL 267MG
REDUCED FAT:	CALORIES 615	FAT 14G	PROTEIN 89G	CARBOHYDRATES 29G	CHOL 198MG

Monte Cristo Sandwich

MAKES 2 SERVINGS

I love a good Monte Cristo, purely because of my sweet tooth!

This sandwich, in its low-fat form, is one of my favorite "light" recipes.

4 slices French or sourdough bread
2 teaspoons unsalted butter, room temperature
3 teaspoons boysenberry preserves
2 slices ham
2 slices turkey

2 slices mozzarella cheese
1 large egg
2 teaspoons whole milk
½ teaspoon vanilla extract
2 teaspoons powdered sugar

Spread the bread slices with butter on one side. Spread the other sides of all four slices with a thin layer of preserves, and layer the ham, turkey, and cheese between the slices, creating two sandwiches.

In a shallow bowl, beat together the egg, milk, and vanilla. Dip each sandwich, on both sides, into the egg mixture.

Heat a large, non-stick sauté pan over medium heat. Spray the pan with non-stick cooking spray and sauté the sandwiches over medium heat, until golden on both sides, cooking about 4 minutes on each side.

Spread the top of the sandwich with additional preserves and sprinkle the sandwiches with powdered sugar. Cut in half and serve hot.

CHEF JAMIE'S LOW-FAT TIP

Create incredible tasting low-fat Monte Cristo sandwiches with all the flavor of the real thing by using turkey ham instead of real ham, or simply substituting sliced tukey in the sandwiches. A low-fat cheese that melts well is a great substitute for the full-of-fat kind, and when it comes to the batter, use 2 egg whites and 2 teaspoons of non-fat milk.

HELPFUL HINTS FROM THE WIZARD

• Make sure the powdered sugar is 10X. This is the "finest" powdered sugar you can buy.

			PER SERVING		
STANDARD RECIPE:	CALORIES 852	FAT 30G	PROTEIN 62G	CARBOHYDRATES 38G	CHOL 171MG
REDUCED FAT:	CALORIES 766	FAT 16G	PROTEIN 71G	CARBOHYDRATES 78G	CHOL 150MG

Chapter 5

Grandma's Casseroles & Pastas

W elcoming, comforting, and nourishing, these hearty one-dish meals always conjure up fond childhood memories. The down-home recipes in this chapter are ideal for family dinners, but don't forget to consider them for casual entertaining, too—your guests will appreciate the simple, wholesome fare. Serve these bubbly casseroles and flavorful pastas with a crisp green salad for the perfect Sunday dinner.

Sunday Macaroni & Cheese

MAKES 4 SERVINGS

Good old macaroni and cheese doesn't get any better than this. I transformed the standard American recipe to include four types of cheese, resulting in an irresistibly elegant dish, rich in flavor. If you are a creature of habit and prefer it to taste the way it did when you were growing up, use only sharp cheddar.

5 tablespoons unsalted butter
3 tablespoons all-purpose flour
2 cups milk
4 ounces sharp cheddar cheese, shredded
4 ounces fontina cheese, shredded
4 ounces mozzarella cheese, cut into ¼-inch cubes

4 ounces Parmesan cheese, grated
1 teaspoon Dijon mustard
pinch of cayenne pepper
salt & pepper, to taste
¾ pound elbow macaroni, cooked and well drained
1 cup bread crumbs

Preheat the oven to 350°F. Grease a 1 ½ quart baking dish.

In a large sauté pan, melt 3 tablespoons of the butter over medium heat. Add the flour and cook, whisking constantly, for 1 minute. Slowly whisk in the milk, whisking constantly to avoid lumps. Continue cooking over medium heat and bring to a boil, whisking often. Reduce the heat and allow to simmer 5 minutes, stirring occasionally.

Remove from the heat and stir in all four cheeses, the mustard, cayenne, salt and pepper. Whisk the sauce until completely smooth.

Combine the cooked macaroni and the cheese sauce and transfer to the prepared baking dish.

Melt the remaining 2 tablespoons of butter and combine it with the bread crumbs. Sprinkle the bread crumbs over the macaroni. Bake the casserole until brown and bubbly, about 30 minutes.

CHEF JAMIE'S LOW-FAT TIP

To enjoy this classic favorite without feeling guilty, use 1 percent low-fat milk and reduced-fat sharp cheddar cheese. Reduce the butter to 3 tablespoons, using 2 tablespoons for the cream sauce and 1 tablespoon with the bread crumbs.

HELPFUL HINTS FROM THE WIZARD

• Always use a warm colander when draining pasta. A cold colander will cause the pasta to stick together.

		PER SERVING		
STANDARD RECIPE:	CALORIES 853	FAT 61G	PROTEIN 39G	CARBOHYDRATES 46G	CHOL 138MG
REDUCED FAT:	CALORIES 608	FAT 35G	PROTEIN 36G	CARBOHYDRATES 46G	CHOL 80MG

Tuna Casserole #1

The best tuna is "albacore white" packed in water. Keep in mind that the darker the color of the tuna, the lower the quality and flavor.

This is an old favorite that most everyone remembers from childhood—a simple version of the classic.

1 tablespoon vegetable oil
1 yellow onion, sliced
2 tablespoons flour
2 cups chicken broth
¼ cup jack cheese, shredded
¼ cup cheddar cheese, shredded
¼ cup frozen peas, thawed or
    blanched

1 (12-ounce) can tuna, drained
½ cup bread crumbs
8 ounces thin egg noodles, cooked
    and well drained

Preheat the oven to 350°F. Grease a 2-quart casserole dish.

In a large sauté pan, heat the oil. Add the onion and sauté until tender and lightly golden, about 10 minutes. Add the flour and stir well. Pour in the chicken broth and mix well using a wire whisk. Remove the pan from the heat and transfer to a large mixing bowl.

Add the cheeses, peas, tuna, ¼ cup of the bread crumbs, and the noodles and stir to combine well.

Place in the prepared casserole dish. Top with the remaining bread crumbs. Bake the casserole, uncovered, for 45 minutes or until golden and bubbly.

CHEF JAMIE'S LOW-FAT TIP

Mozzarella cheese is a nice complement to tuna, and replacing the jack and cheddar cheeses with part-skim mozzarella works well in this recipe to reduce the fat. Use non-stick cooking spray in place of the oil to lighten the recipe even more.

HELPFUL HINTS FROM THE WIZARD

- Onions can be placed in the freezer for 5 minutes before slicing to reduce fumes and tearing.

			PER SERVING		
STANDARD RECIPE:	CALORIES 410	FAT 18G	PROTEIN 32G	CARBOHYDRATES 29G	CHOL 68MG
REDUCED FAT:	CALORIES 338	FAT 11G	PROTEIN 30G	CARBOHYDRATES 28G	CHOL 52MG

Tuna Casserole #2

MAKES 6 SERVINGS

I believe that this particular recipe originated in the 1940s. It varied as much as the cooks who made it! Some added hard-boiled eggs, olives, and even chiles. . .so do add your favorite ingredient if you wish.

1 (10-ounce) can cream of
    mushroom soup
½ cup whole milk
½ cup mayonnaise
1 (12-ounce) can tuna, drained
1 (10-ounce) package frozen peas,
    thawed

1 cup celery, diced
2 tablespoons fresh parsley, chopped
3 tablespoons (1½ ounces) unsalted
    butter, melted
½ cup crushed potato chips
⅓ cup cheddar cheese, shredded

Preheat the oven to 375°F.

In a large mixing bowl, combine the soup, milk, and mayonnaise; mix well.

Break the tuna into pieces and fold it into the soup mixture, along with the peas, celery, and parsley.

Grease a 2-quart casserole dish with 1 tablespoon of the butter. Pour the tuna mixture into the casserole dish. Top with the crushed potato chips and drizzle with the remaining butter. Sprinkle the top with the cheese. Bake 20 to 25 minutes or until the top is brown and is bubbly.

CHEF JAMIE'S LOW-FAT TIP

Low-fat canned soup will give this recipe the same flavor and texture, and the difference in fat grams is unbelievable. Use non-fat milk, low-fat cheese, and baked potato chips to further lighten the casserole.

HELPFUL HINTS FROM THE WIZARD

• Tuna packed in water is preferred.

	PER SERVING				
STANDARD RECIPE:	CALORIES 434	FAT 23G	PROTEIN 25G	CARBOHYDRATES 23G	CHOL 49MG
REDUCED FAT:	CALORIES 321	FAT 8G	PROTEIN 23G	CARBOHYDRATES 27G	CHOL 36MG

Shrimp Amandine Casserole

MAKES 4 SERVINGS

This casserole is a great company dish! You can prepare the casserole before your guests arrive, set it in the oven as they come through the door, and have nothing to do but enjoy the conversation.

2 pounds raw shrimp
¾ cup raw white rice
2 tablespoons (1 ounce) unsalted
    butter
¼ cup green pepper, diced
¼ cup yellow onion, diced

1 (10-ounce) can condensed
    tomato soup
1 cup half & half
½ cup sherry
½ cup sliced almonds
salt & pepper, to taste

Preheat the oven to 350°F. Grease a 2-quart casserole dish.

Shell and devein the shrimp. Boil the shrimp in salted water for 1 minute, then remove from the water and drop the shrimp into ice water to stop the cooking process. Split the shrimp down the back for presentation purposes, and set aside.

Prepare the rice according to package directions and set aside.

In a large sauté pan, melt the butter over medium heat. Add the green pepper and onion, and sauté until tender, about 5 minutes. Add the condensed soup, half & half, sherry, ¼ cup of the almonds, and salt and pepper. Stir to combine. Heat almost to simmering.

Remove the pan from the heat and stir in the shrimp and the rice. Season to taste with salt and pepper.

Pour into the prepared casserole dish and bake for 30 minutes.

Top with the remaining ¼ cup of almonds and bake 10 minutes more, or until the casserole is bubbly.

CHEF JAMIE'S LOW-FAT TIP

Substitute either whole milk or 2 percent milk for the half & half; both perform well in this recipe. Cut the almonds to ¼ cup and use them only as garnish if you really want to skimp.

HELPFUL HINTS FROM THE WIZARD

- Devein the shrimp by running an ice pick down the spine.

		PER SERVING			
STANDARD RECIPE:	CALORIES 568	FAT 27G	PROTEIN 32G	CARBOHYDRATES 41G	CHOL 184MG
REDUCED FAT:	CALORIES 460	FAT 17G	PROTEIN 29G	CARBOHYDRATES 39G	CHOL 175MG

Creamy Chicken Casserole

MAKES 4 SERVINGS

This casserole is true comfort food. Create an elegant version by adding exotic mushrooms and a touch of white wine. (See Chef's Note below!)

1 cup wild rice
1 stick (4 ounces) unsalted butter
1 yellow onion, diced
½ cup mushrooms, sliced
¼ cup all-purpose flour
1½ cups chicken broth

1½ cups half & half
3 cups cooked chicken, diced
¼ cup roasted red peppers or diced pimentos
3 tablespoons fresh parsley, chopped
salt & pepper, to taste

Preheat the oven to 350°F. Grease a 2-quart casserole dish.

Prepare the rice according to package directions and set aside.

In a large sauté pan, melt the butter over medium heat. Add the onion and mushrooms; sauté until tender, about 5 minutes. Stir in the flour and cook 1 minute more, stirring constantly. Gradually stir in the chicken broth, using a wire whisk to create a smooth sauce. Add the half & half and continue to stir over medium heat until thickened.

Remove from the heat and stir in the rice, chicken, roasted red peppers, and parsley. Season to taste with salt and pepper.

Pour into the prepared casserole dish. Bake for 25 to 30 minutes or until bubbly.

Chef's Note: Use a mix of shiitake, crimini, and oyster mushrooms in place of the white mushrooms for a woodsier mushroom flavor. You can also substitute ½ cup of wine for ½ cup of the chicken broth for added complexity.

CHEF JAMIE'S LOW-FAT TIP

Try using 50 percent-less-fat butter and whole milk or 2 percent milk. You will need to cook the cream sauce a little bit longer to get it to thicken, as the lower-fat butter has a higher water content.

HELPFUL HINTS FROM THE WIZARD

- Parsley can be easily sniped with scissors or kitchen shears.
- Place the onion in the freezer for 5 minutes before slicing to reduce tearing.

	PER SERVING				
STANDARD RECIPE:	CALORIES 543	FAT 38G	PROTEIN 22G	CARBOHYDRATES 30G	CHOL 109MG
REDUCED FAT:	CALORIES 406	FAT 19G	PROTEIN 22G	CARBOHYDRATES 30G	CHOL 79MG

Layered Tex-Mex Casserole

This casserole is the perfect party food, since it can be assembled a day ahead and refrigerated.

3 pounds ground beef
2 tablespoons olive oil
2 medium yellow onions, chopped
2 garlic cloves, minced
2 tablespoons chili powder
1 teaspoon sugar
4 cups red enchilada sauce
1 cup black olives, sliced
2 (4-ounce) cans diced green chilies, drained

16 corn tortillas
vegetable oil, for frying
32 ounces (4 cups) small-curd cottage cheese
2 large eggs, beaten
12 ounces jack cheese, thinly sliced
1½ cups cheddar cheese, grated
¾ cup sour cream
½ cup green onions, chopped
salt & pepper, to taste

Preheat the oven to 350°F.

Using a large frying pan, brown the meat in batches over high heat. (Do not put too much meat in the pan at once; it will cause the temperature of the pan to drop significantly and the meat will turn gray instead of brown.) Remove the browned meat and set aside.

Using the same pan, heat the oil. Add the onions and garlic and sauté, stirring often, until onion is tender and golden. Return the meat to the pan. Add the chili powder and sugar; stir; add the enchilada sauce, half the olives, and all the green chilies. Stir to combine well. Simmer over low heat for 15 minutes.

While the sauce cooks, cut the tortillas into quarters and fry them in hot oil, a few at a time, until crisp. Drain on paper towels.

In a small mixing bowl, stir together the cottage cheese and eggs and set aside.

To assemble the casserole: Pour ⅓ of the sauce in a shallow 6-quart casserole. Cover the sauce with a layer of tortillas, then top with ⅓ of the cottage cheese mixture and ⅓ of the jack cheese. Repeat the layering until all of the ingredients have been used. Top with the grated cheddar cheese.

Bake, uncovered, for 30 minutes, or until the cheese is melted and the casserole is heated through. Serve with sour cream, chopped green onions, and remaining olives.

	PER SERVING				
STANDARD RECIPE:	CALORIES 693	FAT 42G	PROTEIN 42G	CARBOHYDRATES 37G	CHOL 167MG
REDUCED FAT:	CALORIES 459	FAT 20G	PROTEIN 44G	CARBOHYDRATES 38G	CHOL 101MG

Mexican food, with all its bold flavors, can be just as tasty when made with low-fat ingredients. Using lean ground beef (7 percent fat) is a good place to start. Also, crisp the tortillas in the oven at 350°F for just a few minutes instead of frying them, to significantly help your heart! Low-fat cottage cheese, liquid egg substitute, reduced-fat cheeses, and light sour cream bring this dish back to reality and still create a delicious, flavorful casserole.

HELPFUL HINTS FROM THE WIZARD
- Don't substitute flour tortillas for the corn. Flour tortillas contain fat, while the ones made from corn do not!

Moussaka

MAKES 8 SERVINGS

Moussaka, known all over the world as the Greek national dish, is guaranteed to satisfy the biggest hunger on the coldest winter night. This eggplant and lamb casserole (moussaka can also be made with beef instead of lamb) is a taverna staple; it's perfect prepared a day before you're planning to serve it. (See Chef's Note for reheating tips.)

For the casserole:

2 tablespoons (1 ounce) unsalted butter
1 medium yellow onion, finely chopped
2 garlic cloves, minced
½ teaspoon cayenne pepper
2 pounds ground lamb
2 (28-ounce) cans Italian-style chopped tomatoes in juice, drained
½ cup dry red wine
3 tablespoons tomato paste
vegetable oil, for frying
2 large eggplants (about 2 pounds total) cut lengthwise into ¼-inch thick slices

all-purpose flour, for dredging
2 potatoes, peeled and sliced lengthwise

For the sauce:

2 sticks (8 ounces) unsalted butter
1 cup all-purpose flour
1 quart (4 cups) milk, warmed
2 large eggs, lightly beaten
1 cup freshly grated Parmesan cheese
pinch of nutmeg
salt & pepper, to taste

Preheat the oven to 350°F. Lightly grease a shallow 2-quart baking dish.

Melt the 2 tablespoons of butter in a large skillet. Add the onion and sauté over medium heat, stirring often, until tender, about 8 minutes. Add the garlic and cayenne pepper, and sauté for 1 minute longer. Remove the onion mixture and set aside.

Using the same pan, over high heat, sauté the lamb in batches, breaking the lamb up with the back of a spoon, until browned and cooked through. Return all of the browned meat to the pan and add the onion mixture. Stir in the tomatoes, wine, and tomato paste. Cook the sauce, uncovered, over medium heat for about 30 minutes, or until thickened. Season with salt and pepper.

PER SERVING

STANDARD RECIPE:	CALORIES 551	FAT 32G	PROTEIN 39G	CARBOHYDRATES 34G	CHOL 172MG
REDUCED FAT:	CALORIES 455	FAT 15G	PROTEIN 35G	CARBOHYDRATES 35G	CHOL 128MG

Meanwhile, heat about a ½-inch of oil in a large frying pan. Season the eggplant slices with salt and pepper, then dredge each slice in flour and shake off any excess. Sauté the eggplant slices on both sides in the hot oil until golden brown. After frying the eggplant, season the potato slices with salt and pepper and fry them in the same skillet until golden.

To make the sauce: Melt the butter in a medium saucepan. Add the flour and stir to create a paste. Gradually add the milk, whisking constantly over low heat, to form a smooth, thick sauce. Remove the sauce from the heat and add the eggs, stirring constantly. Place the sauce back on the heat and add the cheese. Stir over low heat until the cheese is melted and the sauce is smooth. Season with nutmeg, salt, and pepper.

To assemble the casserole: Arrange half the potatoes in the baking dish. Arrange half the eggplant slices on top of the potatoes. Pour half the sauce on top. Repeat to create one more layer. Pour the prepared cream sauce over the casserole. Place the baking dish on a cookie sheet with sides (to catch any drips) bake 1 hour or until golden and bubbly. Let stand 15 minutes before serving.

Chef's Note: To reheat the moussaka, bring the casserole to room temperature. Reheat in a 400°F oven for 30 minutes or until heated through.

CHEF JAMIE'S LOW-FAT TIP

This dish transforms incredibly into a hearty, low-fat meal. Prepare the low-fat Moussaka by first sautéing the onion mixture in only 1 tablespoon of butter along with a liberal spray of non-stick cooking spray. Substitute ground turkey for the lamb, and be sure to remove any fat from the pan after browning.

For the eggplant and potato, first, preheat the broiler. Line a baking sheet with aluminum foil and arrange the eggplant slices on top. Brush the eggplant slices on both sides with a minimal amount of olive oil, then broil until golden, about 4 minutes per side. Boil the potatoes whole, in a large pot of boiling salted water, until just tender, about 5 minutes. Then slice the potatoes ¼ inch thick.

To top it off, prepare the lightened version with yogurt rather than the customary sauce. Disregard preparing the sauce all together. Bake the moussaka as is, after assembling, for 45 minutes. Whisk together 3 cups of plain yogurt (not low-fat or non-fat, just regular!) and 3 egg yolks. Remove the moussaka from the oven and press the layers down using the back of a spoon. Pour the yogurt mixture over the top of the casserole to cover completely. Bake for 15 minutes more or until yogurt is just set. Let stand 15 minutes before serving.

Parmigiano Di Melanzane

MAKES 6 SERVINGS

You know this dish as "Eggplant Parmesan" but you may not realize that its use of mozzarella and tomato sauce marks it as a dish typical of the area surrounding Naples.

For the marinara sauce:
4 tablespoons extra-virgin olive oil
1 small yellow onion, minced
4 garlic cloves, finely chopped
2 anchovy fillets (optional)
2 tablespoons dried basil
2 teaspoons dried oregano
3 tablespoons tomato paste
1 teaspoon sugar
salt and pepper, to taste
2 (28-ounce) cans plum tomatoes, drained and coarsely chopped

For the casserole:
4 medium-sized eggplants, washed and cut into ½-inch slices
salt
1 cup bread crumbs
1 tablespoon dried oregano
¾ cup all-purpose flour
4 large eggs, well beaten
8 tablespoons olive oil
4 cups marinara sauce
16 ounces mozzarella cheese, thinly sliced
1 cup freshly grated Parmesan cheese

To make the marinara sauce: Heat the olive oil in a saucepan over moderate heat. Add the onion and garlic and cook for about 10 minutes, stirring frequently, until the onion is tender but not brown. Add the optional anchovies, if desired, and sauté to break up the fillets. Add the tomatoes, basil, oregano, tomato paste, sugar, salt, and pepper, and simmer over low heat for 30 minutes, stirring occasionally. Makes approximately 5 cups.

To make the casserole: Preheat the oven to 325°F.

Sprinkle the eggplant slices lightly with salt and place on paper towels for 30 minutes to drain. Place the eggs in a shallow bowl. Mix the bread crumbs and oregano in a shallow bowl. Dry the eggplant slices, dust each slice with flour, then dip in the beaten eggs and coat with the bread crumb mixture. Shake off any excess bread crumbs. Continue with remaining eggplant.

Heat half of the olive oil in a large skillet over medium heat and sauté the eggplant slices in batches until golden brown, about 5 minutes per side. Repeat, using the remaining oil and remaining eggplant slices. Place a thin coating of marinara sauce in the bottom of a baking pan large enough to hold half the eggplant in a single layer. Arrange the eggplant slices on the sauce.

		PER SERVING			
STANDARD RECIPE:	CALORIES 730	FAT 52G	PROTEIN 30G	CARBOHYDRATES 28G	CHOL 211MG
REDUCED FAT:	CALORIES 584	FAT 34G	PROTEIN 34G	CARBOHYDRATES 28G	CHOL 188MG

Place a slice of mozzarella on top of each eggplant slice and sprinkle with the Parmesan cheese. Repeat to create a second layer, ending with Parmesan cheese. Bake 20 to 25 minutes or until cheese is melted and the casserole is heated through.

CHEF JAMIE'S LOW-FAT TIP

Low-fat mozzarella cheese melts beautifully and works well in this cheesy dish. To lower your fat intake, use only 1 tablespoon of olive oil in each batch of sautéed eggplant, but supplement this by using non-stick cooking spray along with the oil. Also, decrease the amount of Parmesan cheese to ¼ cup and use it only for the top of the casserole. For the sauce, reduce the oil to 1 tablespoon for flavor, and use non-stick cooking spray here also.

HELPFUL HINTS FROM THE WIZARD

- Although eggplant is fat-free, it absorbs oil more easily than any other vegetable, and is sometimes called the "vegetable fat sponge."

Lasagna with Meat Sauce and Three Cheeses *MAKES 6 SERVINGS*

A marvelous one-dish meal, lasagna is a specialty in the Emilia-Romagna region of Italy, where the pasta is made with only flour and eggs. Today, of all the types of lasagna noodles you can buy (dried, pre-cooked, and fresh), I like the fresh noodles for their flavor and texture. For a vegetarian version, use grilled vegetables instead of the meat. To make the lasagna creamier, try adding goat cheese or a soft herbed cheese.

For the meat sauce:

3 tablespoons olive oil
½ cup yellow onion, diced
1 carrot, peeled and diced
2 garlic cloves, minced
½ pound ground beef
1 raw sweet or hot Italian sausage, squeezed from its casing
1 (28-ounce) can tomato puree
¼ cup dry red wine

For the lasagna:

1 (12-ounce) package lasagna noodles
1 cup (8 ounces) ricotta cheese
1 cup freshly grated Parmesan
½ cup Monterey Jack cheese, shredded

To make the sauce: Heat the oil in a large saucepan over medium heat. Add the onion, carrot, and garlic, and sauté until tender. Add the beef and raw sausage, and cook over high heat, stirring constantly and breaking up the meat with the back of the spoon. Add the red wine and tomato puree, and stir to combine. Simmer the sauce for 30 minutes, stirring occasionally.

To make the lasagna: Preheat the oven to 375°F.

Cook the noodles in boiling salted water and pat dry. Line the bottom of an 8-inch-square baking dish with a single layer of cooked noodles, cutting the noodles to fit. Top with a layer of sauce. Place half the ricotta in spoonfuls on top of the sauce to cover, then sprinkle with Parmesan cheese. Repeat the layers, using the remaining noodles, half of the remaining sauce, and the rest of the ricotta and Parmesan. Finish with a layer of the remaining sauce. Top with the shredded Jack cheese.

Cover loosely with aluminum foil and bake 1 hour or until heated all the way through.

CHEF JAMIE'S LOW-FAT TIP

Low-fat lasagna is easy to prepare using reduced-fat ingredients. First, use only 1 tablespoon of extra-virgin oil in the sauce, for great flavor. Using ground turkey and turkey sausage in place of beef and pork will reduce the fat in the sauce. Also, use non-fat ricotta cheese and a good quality non-fat Jack cheese in the filling.

		PER SERVING			
STANDARD RECIPE:	CALORIES 678	FAT 33G	PROTEIN 35G	CARBOHYDRATES 62G	CHOL 90MG
REDUCED FAT:	CALORIES 582	FAT 19G	PROTEIN 32G	CARBOHYDRATES 68G	CHOL 61MG

Baked Ziti

MAKES 8 SERVINGS

Ziti, literally translated from Italian, means "grooms," a name it earned from the tradition of serving it at weddings. I remember, as a child, loving baked ziti—so rich and creamy with the incredible sweetness of the tomato sauce, compounded in flavor from having baked in the oven! This is homey food at its finest. . .and still one of my favorites.

1 tablespoon unsalted butter
1 tablespoon olive oil
1 yellow onion, diced
1 garlic clove, minced
32 ounces (4 cups) tomato sauce, homemade or purchased
16 ounces (2 cups) ricotta cheese
1 cup cottage cheese

2 tablespoons fresh parsley, chopped
2 large eggs, beaten
salt & pepper, to taste
1 pound ziti or mostaccioli noodles, cooked and drained
16 ounces mozzarella cheese, shredded

Preheat the oven to 350°F. Grease a large, shallow baking dish.

Heat the butter and oil in a large sauté pan. Add the onion and garlic; sauté until the onion is tender, about 10 minutes. Stir in the tomato sauce and simmer 10 minutes.

In a large mixing bowl, combine the ricotta cheese, cottage cheese, parsley, and eggs, and mix well. Season with salt and pepper. Add the cooked ziti and mozzarella cheese. Add half of the tomato sauce mixture and mix to combine well. Spoon into the prepared baking dish. Spoon the remaining sauce on top.

Cover and bake the casserole for 20 minutes. Remove the lid and bake 10 minutes more.

CHEF JAMIE'S LOW-FAT TIP

For a great low-fat meal, omit the cottage cheese and substitute 4 cups of parboiled broccoli florets (boil the broccoli florets for about 3 minutes, then rinse with cold water and drain). Use only 8 ounces of the ricotta cheese (non-fat works well), and 8 ounces of the mozzarella cheese, part-skim please. Prepare the rest of the recipe according to the standard directions for a dish that is nutritionally balanced and low in fat.

HELPFUL HINTS FROM THE WIZARD

- If the cottage cheese has liquid on top, mix it back in. The liquid is whey, a good protein.

			PER SERVING		
STANDARD RECIPE:	CALORIES 293	FAT 23G	PROTEIN 25G	CARBOHYDRATES 34G	CHOL 137MG
REDUCED FAT:	CALORIES 246	FAT 1G	PROTEIN 18G	CARBOHYDRATES 33G	CHOL 115MG

Good Italian Spaghetti and Meatballs

MAKES 8 SERVINGS

This hearty dish illustrates why we love Italian food so much! Simmering the meatballs in the homemade sauce creates incredibly rich flavor.

For the meatballs:
1½ pounds ground beef
½ pound ground veal
2 raw sweet Italian sausages, squeezed from their casings
1 large egg
1 cup ketchup
¾ cup seasoned bread crumbs
½ cup Parmesan cheese
½ cup fresh parsley, chopped
½ cup beef broth
3 slices white bread
1 yellow onion, finely chopped
2 celery stalks, finely chopped

For the sauce:
¼ cup olive oil
3 garlic cloves, minced
½ cup dry red wine
1 (28-ounce) can tomato puree
1 (28-ounce) can tomato sauce
salt & pepper, to taste
1 pound spaghetti

To make the meatballs: In a large mixing bowl, combine the ground beef, ground veal, sausage, egg, ketchup, bread crumbs, Parmesan cheese, parsley, beef broth, and bread. Mix thoroughly. Then add half the onion, half the carrots, and half the celery, and stir to combine. Reserve the other half of the vegetables. Mix all of the ingredients thoroughly, then form meatballs about 1½ inches in diameter. Heat the oil in a large non-stick sauté pan and brown the meatballs in batches. Set the browned meatballs aside and discard the oil.

To make the sauce: In a saucepan, heat the oil and add the garlic. Sauté briefly over medium heat. Add the reserved onion, carrots, and celery, and sauté for 3 minutes, stirring often. Add the red wine and deglaze the pan by stirring to loosen browned bits from the bottom. Add the tomato puree and tomato sauce, and stir to combine. Add the meatballs to the sauce and simmer 30 minutes. Adjust seasoning with salt and pepper.

When ready to serve, cook the spaghetti in a pot of boiling salted water. Drain well, then toss with the sauce.

	PER SERVING				
STANDARD RECIPE:	CALORIES 729	FAT 37G	PROTEIN 45G	CARBOHYDRATES 28G	CHOL 147MG
REDUCED FAT:	CALORIES 647	FAT 27G	PROTEIN 45G	CARBOHYDRATES 28G	CHOL 135MG

Use ground turkey in place of the ground beef and veal, and substitute turkey sausage for the Italian pork-based kind. As for the olive oil, use only 1 tablespoon when sautéing the meatballs and prevent sticking by adding a few liberal sprays of non-stick cooking spray to the pan with the oil before browning each batch of meatballs. In the sauce, 2 tablespoons of olive oil will still give you great flavor but will cut down on your fat intake. Use non-stick cooking spray when sautéing the vegetables for the sauce, too!

HELPFUL HINTS FROM THE WIZARD

- If you rub a small amount of butter around the inside of the pot near the rim, the pot will not boil over.
- Be sure the colander is warm before draining pasta to prevent the pasta sticking together.

Linguine with White Clam Sauce

MAKES 4 SERVINGS

If fresh clams are not available, use canned whole baby clams.

4 dozen raw clams (littleneck or cherrystones), shucked and coarsely chopped

or 2 (10-ounce) cans whole baby clams, undrained

1 to 2 cups bottled clam juice

⅓ cup extra-virgin olive oil

4 tablespoons (2 ounces) unsalted butter

6 garlic cloves, peeled and minced

½ cup dry white wine

½ cup fresh parsley, finely chopped

1 teaspoon fresh thyme, chopped *or* ½ teaspoon dried thyme

salt & pepper, to taste

8 ounces dry linguine

16 fresh clams, in their shells for garnish, optional

If you are using fresh clams, shuck them, reserving any juices they leak, and chop them coarsely. If using canned clams, drain the clams in a fine strainer over a bowl, reserving the juice. Add enough bottled clam juice to the reserved clam liquid to make 2½ cups. Heat the butter and olive oil in a medium saucepan over low heat. Add the garlic, and sauté until golden, about 3 minutes. Stir in the reserved clam juice, wine, chopped parsley, chopped thyme, salt, and pepper, and cook for 10 minutes, stirring frequently. (The sauce can be prepared ahead of time up to this point.)

Meanwhile, if you are garnishing with fresh clams, scrub them well and place then in a large sauté pan with a lid. Add 1 inch of water to the pan, cover, and set over high heat. Shake often, cooking the clams for 3 to 5 minutes, or until the clams open. Reserve the clams in their shells.

Cook the linguine in salted boiling water; drain well and keep hot.

Just before serving, reheat the sauce if you have allowed it to cool. Add the chopped clams and heat for 1 to 2 minutes. Overcooked clams become tough and rubbery. Serve clam sauce over pasta. Garnish with the steamed clams in their shells.

CHEF JAMIE'S LOW-FAT TIP

I altered the fat and calories in this dish by reducing the olive oil to 3 tablespoons and by using only 2 tablespoons of reduced-fat (50 percent-less-fat) butter. Add a tablespoon of flour to the pan after you brown the garlic if you like a thicker sauce!

			PER SERVING		
STANDARD RECIPE:	CALORIES 717	FAT 36G	PROTEIN 52G	CARBOHYDRATES 44G	CHOL 219MG
REDUCED FAT:	CALORIES 546	FAT 21G	PROTEIN 52G	CARBOHYDRATES 44G	CHOL 203MG

Penne Puttanesca

MAKES 8 SERVINGS

This incredibly flavorful pasta sauce is not for the faint-hearted. Filled with potent garlic, anchovy, olives, and capers, it pairs beautifully with a glass of red wine and a simple green salad.

⅓ cup olive oil

2 garlic cloves, peeled and left whole

1 anchovy fillet

2 (28-ounce) cans whole peeled tomatoes

20 kalamata olives, pitted and halved

1 tablespoon capers

1 teaspoon dried basil

¼ teaspoon red pepper flakes

¼ teaspoon dried oregano

1 garlic clove, peeled and left whole

1 lb. penne pasta, cooked and well drained

Heat the oil in a large sauté pan. When the oil is hot, add the 2 garlic cloves and cook until the garlic is golden brown. Remove the garlic. Add the anchovy fillet to the hot oil and stir to dissolve. Add the tomatoes, olives, capers, red pepper flakes, oregano, basil, and the other garlic clove. Cover and simmer the sauce for half an hour. Remove the garlic clove and discard it.

When ready to serve, toss the cooked pasta with enough sauce to coat.

CHEF JAMIE'S LOW-FAT TIP

Big, bold flavors mask the loss of fat, and this recipe is certainly a perfect example of this phenomenon! Reduce the amount of olive oil in the recipe to 3 tablespoons, but keep the heat low so as not to burn the precious garlic.

HELPFUL HINTS FROM THE WIZARD

- Make sure the red pepper flakes are fresh for the spiciest flavor. Wash the flakes to reduce the heat, if you wish.

			PER SERVING		
STANDARD RECIPE:	CALORIES 234	FAT 12G	PROTEIN 3G	CARBOHYDRATES 27G	CHOL 35MG
REDUCED FAT:	CALORIES 194	FAT 7G	PROTEIN 3G	CARBOHYDRATES 27G	CHOL 35MG

Chapter 6

Delectable Meat Dishes

*O*ur *"center of the plate" mentality means that a tender, succulent meat dish takes pride of place at important meals, and whether we choose to make the centerpiece beef, lamb, or pork, it always seems to satisfy. Here you'll find recipes for casual favorites like juicy meatloaf and country maple spareribs as well as dressier entrees like osso bucco and braised lamb shanks with rosemary.*

A Really Great Cheeseburger

MAKES 4 SERVINGS

A big, fat, juicy burger is about as traditional as you can get! The hamburger is said to have made its first appearance at the 1904 Louisiana Purchase Exposition in St. Louis, and continues to be one of America's favorite foods. When you buy ground beef, make sure the meat is bright red and the fat white, not yellow, as that is a sign of age. The best tasting burger meat is a combination of chuck and sirloin, as you see in this recipe, giving you the perfect combination of flavor and fat. Your doctor won't approve, but your taste buds will!

½ pound ground chuck
½ pound ground sirloin
salt & pepper, to taste
2 tablespoons soy sauce

4 slices cheddar or American cheese
unsalted butter, melted, as needed
4 hamburger buns
lettuce, tomato & condiments

In a large mixing bowl combine the chuck and sirloin. Season with salt and pepper and mix thoroughly. Shape into 4 patties.

Heat a cast-iron skillet until hot. Add the patties to the pan and press down, using the back of a metal spatula. Add the soy sauce to the pan and cover the pan immediately with a lid or heatproof plate. Cook about 4 to 5 minutes or until golden brown on the bottom. Remove the lid and turn the burgers over. Cover and cook 2 minutes more.

Remove the lid and place the cheese slices on top of the burgers. Cover the pan again and cook for 1 minute longer or until the cheese has melted.

Meanwhile, lightly butter and toast the buns. Top the toasted buns with the cheeseburgers. Garnish with condiments.

CHEF JAMIE'S LOW-FAT TIP

Using all sirloin would significantly reduce the fat in this burger, however, low-fat ground turkey is necessary to really reduce the fat content. Again, low-fat or fat-free cheese helps save your arteries! The buns can also be sprayed with olive oil rather than buttered, to further reduce the calories.

HELPFUL HINTS FROM THE WIZARD

- Use reduced-salt soy sauce for a healthier alternative.
- Butter should always be allowed to soften at room temperature to retain its flavor.

			PER SERVING		
STANDARD RECIPE:	CALORIES 512	FAT 34G	PROTEIN 35G	CARBOHYDRATES 46G	CHOL 120MG
REDUCED FAT:	CALORIES 414	FAT 19G	PROTEIN 33G	CARBOHYDRATES 46G	CHOL 91MG

Just-Like-Mom-Used-to-Make Meat Loaf

MAKES 6 SERVINGS

My mother remembers her mother making meat loaf just this way. The onion-soup mix provides all of the seasoning, making this soft, moist, and flavorful meat loaf comfort food at its finest! Serve the meat loaf with Jamie's Garlicky Mashed Potatoes (see page 172) for an incrediblly homey meal!

2 pounds ground beef
2 large eggs beaten
1½ cups cracker or bread crumbs
¼ cup yellow onion, grated
1 package onion soup mix

1¼ cups ketchup
¼ cup warm water
salt & pepper, to taste

Preheat the oven to 350° F. In a large mixing bowl, combine the ground beef, eggs, cracker crumbs, onion, onion soup mix, ¾ cup of the ketchup, and the water. Mix thoroughly. Season with salt and pepper.

Pack the meat loaf into a loaf pan and place on a cookie sheet with sides, to catch any drippings during cooking. Spread the remaining ½ cup of ketchup over the top of the meat loaf. Bake 1 hour.

CHEF JAMIE'S LOW-FAT TIP

Make a turkey meat loaf using ground white meat turkey. If you choose to use beef, use super-lean ground beef or ground sirloin to lower your fat intake. Also, during the cooking process, remove the meat loaf from the oven every 15 minutes and drain the fat from around the loaf to eliminate the absorption of the oil into the meat. Half a cup of egg substitute in place of the whole eggs will bind the meat loaf.

HELPFUL HINTS FROM THE WIZARD

- Be sure to buy low-fat ground turkey; since some ground turkey has as much fat as ground beef. You may have to ask your butcher to grind turkey breast for you!

		PER SERVING		
STANDARD RECIPE:	CALORIES 372	FAT 19G	PROTEIN 27G	CARBOHYDRATES 25G	CHOL 83MG
REDUCED FAT:	CALORIES 295	FAT 13G	PROTEIN 22G	CARBOHYDRATES 24G	CHOL 50MG

Kick-Butt Chili

MAKES 8 SERVINGS

This hot and spicy chili should really be called by another name (if you know what I mean!), but since this recipe was created when I was on Home & Family, we had to name it something "television appropriate"! In this dish, good-quality sirloin is mixed with my favorite chili ingredients. Be sure to have lots of cool condiments such as sour cream, cheese, chips, and beer to put out the fire!

¼ cup olive oil
2 yellow onions, chopped
3 garlic cloves, minced
1 jalapeño pepper, seeded and minced
2 pounds sirloin steak, cut into 1-inch cubes
½ cup dry red wine
2 (28-ounce) cans diced tomatoes, with the juice
1 (15-ounce) can red kidney beans, drained

½ cup fresh parsley, chopped
2 tablespoons chili powder
1 tablespoon cumin
1 tablespoon dried basil
1 tablespoon dried oregano
1 tablespoon sugar
½ tablespoon ground cayenne pepper
salt & pepper, to taste
sour cream, grated cheddar and/or Jack cheese, tortilla chips and/or cornbread etc., for garnish

Heat the oil in a large pan over medium heat. Add the onions, garlic, and jalapeño, and sauté for 5 minutes, stirring often. Increase the heat to high and add the steak. Season with salt and pepper, and brown the meat on all sides. Add the red wine and deglaze the pan by stirring to loosen browned bits from the bottom of the pan. Add the chili powder, cumin, cayenne, basil, oregano, sugar, parsley, tomatoes, and kidney beans, and stir to combine well.

Simmer over low heat for 1½ hours, stirring occasionally. Serve the chili with the "cool" garnishes.

CHEF JAMIE'S LOW-FAT TIP

Using ground turkey or chicken instead of sirloin and only 2 tablespoons of olive oil makes this chili extremely low in fat. Add the ground meat just when you would add the sirloin, but be sure to break it up using the back of a spoon to achieve the proper crumbled effect.

HELPFUL HINTS FROM THE WIZARD

- To reduce the heat of the jalapeño peppers, remove the ribs and wash well under cold water.

PER SERVING

STANDARD RECIPE:	CALORIES 434	FAT 22G	PROTEIN 37G	CARBOHYDRATES 27G	CHOL 100MG
REDUCED FAT:	CALORIES 298	FAT 13G	PROTEIN 38G	CARBOHYDRATES 27G	CHOL 52MG

Beef Stroganoff

MAKES 4 SERVINGS

4 tablespoons all-purpose flour
salt & pepper, to taste
1 pound beef sirloin, cut into ¼-inch
   strips
2 tablespoons (1 ounce) unsalted
   butter
1 tablespoon olive oil

1 yellow onion, chopped
½ pound mushrooms, sliced
1 (10-ounce) can beef broth
1 cup sour cream
¼ cup dry sherry
1 (8-ounce) package egg noodles,
   cooked and drained

Place the flour in a small mixing bowl and season with salt and pepper. Dredge the beef strips in the flour and shake off any excess.

In a large skillet, heat the butter and oil until hot. Add the floured beef and brown the meat on all sides. Remove the meat from the skillet and set aside. Add the onion to the same pan and sauté over medium heat until tender. Add the remaining tablespoon of butter and the mushrooms; sauté over high heat until the mushrooms are softened, about 3 minutes, then add to the meat.

Over medium heat, add the beef broth to the pan, scraping the brown bits from the bottom. Add the beef and onion/mushroom mixture to the sauce and simmer, stirring often, for 15 minutes or until slightly thickened.

Remove from the heat and stir in the sour cream and sherry. Season to taste with salt and pepper. Serve over hot egg noodles.

CHEF JAMIE'S LOW-FAT TIP

Use strips of turkey breast in place of the beef for a delicious low-fat alternative. Non-stick cooking spray in place of the butter will suffice here. Light sour cream is another great substitute creating a truly "light" Stroganoff.

	PER SERVING				
STANDARD RECIPE:	CALORIES 653	FAT 45G	PROTEIN 36G	CARBOHYDRATES 41G	CHOL 99MG
REDUCED FAT:	CALORIES 333	FAT 12G	PROTEIN 41G	CARBOHYDRATES 42G	CHOL 11MG

Veal Parmesan

MAKES 4 SERVINGS

This is the Veal Parmesan I had growing up, prepared with a simple marinara sauce. This is a tasty traditional recipe, great for kids and adults alike.

5 tablespoons olive oil
1 yellow onion, diced
1 garlic clove, minced
2 cups crushed tomatoes in juice
1 teaspoon dried basil
1 teaspoon sugar
salt & pepper, to taste

2 large eggs, beaten
1 cup seasoned bread crumbs
¼ cup grated Parmesan cheese
4 (4-ounce) veal cutlets, cut ¼ inch thick
8 slices mozzarella cheese

Preheat oven to 350° F.

In a small saucepan, heat 2 tablespoons of the oil. Add the onions and garlic, and sauté until tender, stirring often. Next, add the crushed tomatoes, basil, sugar, and salt and pepper. Bring to a boil, then reduce the heat and simmer 30 minutes.

Place the beaten eggs in a shallow mixing bowl. In another shallow mixing bowl, stir together the bread crumbs and Parmesan cheese. Dip the veal cutlets into the beaten eggs, then into the bread crumbs. Coat both sides, shaking off excess crumbs.

In a large skillet, heat the remaining 3 tablespoons oil until very hot. Fry the breaded cutlets until golden on both sides, about 2 minutes on each side. Drain on paper towels.

Place cutlets in a baking dish and spread the marinara sauce over the top. Place two slices of mozzarella cheese on top of each cutlet. Bake 15 minutes or until the cheese is melted and bubbly.

CHEF JAMIE'S LOW-FAT TIP

Use part-skim mozzarella cheese and reduce the oil in the sauce to 1 tablespoon. Also, panfry the veal cutlets using a generous amount of non-stick cooking spray instead of oil.

HELPFUL HINTS FROM THE WIZARD

- Freshly grated Parmesan cheese is more flavorful than the packaged kind.
- If the veal is too thick, just pound it with a meat pounder until it is ¼ inch thick.

		PER SERVING		
STANDARD RECIPE:	CALORIES 753	FAT 46G	PROTEIN 56G	CARBOHYDRATES 28G	CHOL 328MG
REDUCED FAT:	CALORIES 546	FAT 24G	PROTEIN 56G	CARBOHYDRATES 28G	CHOL 327MG

You-Won't-Believe-It's-This-Easy
Roasted Pork Chops *MAKES 4 SERVINGS*

This recipe is so simple and delicious, you won't believe it!

all-purpose flour, as needed
salt & pepper, to taste
4 (1-inch-thick) pork chops
1 tablespoon unsalted butter

3 tablespoons olive oil
1 cup smooth applesauce
1½ cups sour cream

Preheat the oven to 350° F.

Season the flour with salt and pepper. Dredge each pork chop in the flour to coat and shake off any excess.

Heat the oil and butter in a large sauté pan over high heat. Add the pork chops and brown on both sides. Place in a baking dish.

Meanwhile, in a saucepan, heat the applesauce and sour cream until warm and pour over the chops. Cover and bake 45 minutes or until chops are tender.

CHEF JAMIE'S LOW-FAT TIP

Brown the pork chops using non-stick cooking spray instead of oil. Non-fat sour cream works terrifically in this dish, and you won't sacrifice flavor or texture.

		PER SERVING			
STANDARD RECIPE:	CALORIES 665	FAT 50G	PROTEIN 32G	CARBOHYDRATES 32G	CHOL 126MG
REDUCED FAT:	CALORIES 521	FAT 31G	PROTEIN 28G	CARBOHYDRATES 35G	CHOL 122MG

Country Maple Spareribs

MAKES 8 SERVINGS

I find pork spareribs particularly succulent. This recipe yields ribs that are sweet with a bit of spice. Beware. . .these finger-licking ribs are the kind that require lots of napkins!

4 pounds pork spareribs
salt & pepper, to taste
½ cup maple syrup
¼ cup light brown sugar
¼ cup mild chili sauce
¼ cup ketchup

¼ cup yellow onion, chopped
2 teaspoons dry mustard
1 teaspoon apple cider vinegar
1 teaspoon lemon juice
1 teaspoon Worcestershire sauce
1 garlic clove, minced

Preheat the oven to 350°F.

Cut the spareribs into serving-size portions and season with salt and pepper. Place the spareribs in a baking dish, cover, and bake for 1 hour. Remove the ribs and drain off any liquid. Place the ribs back in the pan and set aside.

Meanwhile, in a saucepan, combine the maple syrup, brown sugar, chili sauce, ketchup, onion, dry mustard, vinegar, lemon juice, Worcestershire suace, and garlic. Bring to a boil, then reduce the heat to simmer and allow the sauce to cook for 15 minutes, stirring occasionally. Remove from heat and set aside.

Pour half the sauce over the ribs to coat them well. Return to the oven and bake, uncovered, for 45 minutes longer, basting every 10 minutes with the remaining sauce. Serve the ribs with extra sauce for dipping.

Chef's Note: After baking the ribs, you can grill them on your barbecue for great smoky flavor. Grill the ribs until golden and bubbly, about 2 minutes on each side.

	PER SERVING				
STANDARD RECIPE:	CALORIES 982	FAT 68G	PROTEIN 66G	CARBOHYDRATES 23G	CHOL 272MG
REDUCED FAT:	CALORIES 824	FAT 42G	PROTEIN 66G	CARBOHYDRATES 23G	CHOL 245MG

Country Maple Spareribs *(continued)*

CHEF JAMIE'S LOW-FAT TIP

Country-style pork ribs are from the blade end of the loin (very meaty, more like chops) and slightly less fatty than spareribs. But all ribs are fatty! Try boiling the ribs first to remove any extra fat, then marinate them. As a rib lover myself, I say, "Splurge!"

HELPFUL HINTS FROM THE WIZARD

- Boiling ribs before cooking and seasoning them further is a chef's favorite way to tenderize sometimes-tough ribs.

Corned Beef & Cabbage

MAKES 6 SERVINGS

Every year, I look forward to St. Patrick's Day just so I can savor this old Irish dish. This recipe is beautifully flavorful, and has a few non-traditional ingredients to liven it up. I like to eat my corned beef and cabbage with spicy mustard for dipping!

4 pounds corned beef
½ pound salt pork, cut into chunks
12 cups water
¼ cup sugar
3 bay leaves
2 garlic cloves
12 baby red potatoes

6 small turnips, peeled
6 carrots, peeled and cut into
    ½-inch pieces
12 small boiling onions, peeled
6 parsnips, peeled and cut into
    3-inch pieces
1 head green cabbage

Soak the corned beef in cold water for 30 minutes, then drain. In a large Dutch oven, combine the corned beef, salt pork, and water. Place over medium heat and bring to a boil. Add the sugar, bay leaves, and garlic. Reduce the heat to low, cover partially with a lid, allowing steam to escape, and simmer 3 hours.

Remove the bay leaves and add the potatoes, turnips, carrots, onions, and parsnips. Continue cooking for 20 minutes, or until the vegetables are just tender.

Cut the head of cabbage into 6 wedges. Place cabbage on top of the meat, cover completely, and cook for 15 minutes, allowing the cabbage to steam and the vegetables to continue cooking.

Remove the cabbage and vegetables and set them aside, keeping them warm. Remove the corned beef and slice into long thin slices. Serve the corned beef over the cabbage wedges with the vegetables.

CHEF JAMIE'S LOW-FAT TIP

Corned beef and salt pork do not have low-fat alternatives! And, since it is only one day a year. . .just enjoy! The salt pork can be left out, if you desire.

PER SERVING

STANDARD RECIPE: CALORIES 1860 FAT 123G PROTEIN 24G CARBOHYDRATES 23G CHOL 1431MG

French Beef Stew

MAKES 6 SERVINGS

During the 1960s, a potful of wine-soaked beef, whose recipe originated in France, made a great impact on America as the first ethnic beef stew. This wonderful stew, rich with flavor, is prepared in the style of Provence. It tastes best when prepared the day before, as the flavors meld together and only get richer.

3 tablespoons olive oil
2 pounds bottom round, cut into 2-inch cubes
salt & pepper, to taste
1 yellow onion, peeled and quartered
1 pound white mushrooms, caps and stems separated
2 celery stalks, cut into 1-inch pieces
3 carrots, cut into 1-inch pieces
3 garlic cloves, minced

¼ cup all-purpose flour
¼ cup port
2 cups dry red wine
4 sprigs fresh thyme
1 bay leaf
1 strip fresh orange peel, 2 to 3 inches long
18 pearl onions
24 green pitted olives
4 plum or roma tomatoes, diced
¼ cup fresh parsley, chopped

In a large, heavy saucepan, heat the oil until just smoking. Season the meat with salt and pepper. Add the meat in a single layer and brown thoroughly on all sides. Brown the meat in batches if necessary. Remove the browned meat and set aside.

Add the onion, mushroom stems (not the caps), celery, carrots, and garlic to the pan and sauté for 1 minute. Pour off the excess fat from the pan and return the meat to the pan with the vegetables. Sprinkle in the flour and stir to dissolve. Add the port and deglaze, scraping any brown bits from the bottom of the pan into the sauce. Add the wine, thyme, bay leaf, and orange peel; stir to combine.

Bring to a boil, reduce the heat to simmer. Simmer, covered, for 1 hour, stirring occasionally. Check occasionally to make sure the liquid is still covering the ingredients. If it isn't, add water or broth and return to a simmer.

After the stew has cooked for 1 hour, add the pearl onions and the mushroom caps. Simmer for ½ hour longer.

Remove and discard the bay leaf, thyme sprigs, and orange peel. Just before serving, stir in the olives, tomatoes, and parsley.

		PER SERVING		
STANDARD RECIPE:	CALORIES 643	FAT 30G	PROTEIN 77G	CARBOHYDRATES 15G	CHOL 224MG
REDUCED FAT:	CALORIES 423	FAT 14G	PROTEIN 79G	CARBOHYDRATES 15G	CHOL 152MG

Choose the leanest beef available and eliminate the oil entirely, using non-stick cooking spray when sautéing.

HELPFUL HINTS FROM THE WIZARD

- If celery gets limp, just place it in a bowl of ice water and refrigerate for 1 hour.

Braised Lamb Shanks with Rosemary

MAKES 6 SERVINGS

These lamb shanks, stewed in a sauce of red wine, herbs, and garlic, couldn't be simpler or more welcome on a cold winter night. Lamb shanks are the last leg of the joint, and when cooked long and slow, emerge from the pot tender and moist and filled with a deep lamb flavor. Serve them on a bed of Jamie's Garlicky Mashed Potatoes (see page 172) or couscous.

6 lamb shanks, whole (not cracked)
salt & pepper, to taste
⅓ cup all-purpose flour
3 tablespoons olive oil
2 medium onions, chopped
10 garlic cloves, peeled and cut in half lengthwise
4 medium carrots, peeled and cut into 1-inch pieces
2 tablespoons fresh rosemary, minced
1 tablespoon tomato paste
2½ cups dry red wine
1½ cups water

Preheat the broiler to high.

Place the lamb shanks, in a single layer, in a large, shallow roasting pan, and season them with salt and pepper. Broil the shanks about 4 inches away from the heat, turning occasionally, until well browned all over, about 15 minutes.

Remove the browned shanks and generously dust them with flour, shaking off any excess.

In a large stockpot, heat the oil. Add the onions and garlic, and sauté, stirring often for 5 minutes. Add the carrots, rosemary, tomato paste, floured lamb shanks, red wine, and water. Bring to a boil over medium heat. Reduce heat to low, cover, and simmer, turning the meat occasionally, until the shanks are tender when pierced with a knife, about 1½ hours.

Uncover and increase the heat. Boil until the liquid is thickened and reduced slightly, about 15 minutes. Season with additional salt and pepper and serve.

CHEF JAMIE'S LOW-FAT TIP

Eliminating the oil completely from this recipe makes it a no-added-fat recipe (use non-stick cooking spray instead). Be sure to remove any excess fat from the shanks before cooking and again before eating. Roasting the lamb shanks in the oven until golden, as opposed to browning them in oil, is a great trick for creating a low-fat meat dish with lots of flavor!

	PER SERVING				
STANDARD RECIPE:	CALORIES 353	FAT 20G	PROTEIN 51G	CARBOHYDRATES 15G	CHOL 90MG
REDUCED FAT:	CALORIES 293	FAT 13G	PROTEIN 51G	CARBOHYDRATES 15G	CHOL 90MG

Pork Roast with Apricots

MAKES 8 SERVINGS

This handsome roast is perfect for a special dinner. . .and it makes incredible leftovers too! Serve the pork loin with dilled potatoes, green beans, and a crisp salad of endive and grapes.

1 pound dried apricots
dry white wine
4 tablespoons butter
2 tablespoons olive oil
1 pork loin, about 5 pounds
salt & pepper, to taste
1 medium yellow onion, chopped
3 garlic cloves, thinly sliced

2 teaspoons freshly grated ginger or ¼ teaspoon powdered ginger
bouquet garni (a few sprigs each of fresh parsley and thyme, 2 bay leaves, and 3 whole cloves, tied in cheesecloth)
1 cup chicken broth
1 tablespoon arrowroot

Place the dried apricots in a small saucepan and add white wine to cover. Bring to a boil over medium heat, then remove from the heat and allow to stand until the apricots plump, several hours or overnight. (You can use water for part or all of the wine, if you like.)

Preheat the oven to 325°F. Heat the butter and oil in a large sauté pan. Season the roast with salt and pepper, and place in the hot pan. Brown the roast on all sides. Remove the roast and set aside.

Add the onion to the same pan and sauté over medium heat, stirring often, until tender but not brown. Add the garlic and sauté briefly. Place the sautéed onion mixture in a large glass baking dish, along with the ginger and the bouquet garni. Pour the chicken broth and 1 cup of the poaching liquid from the apricots into the pan. Place the browned roast in the baking dish and cover the dish tightly. Roast the loin for about 1½ hours, basting often.

After 1½ hours of cooking, remove the lid, scatter the apricots around the roast, and return the pan to the oven. Continue roasting the meat, uncovered, basting often, until a meat thermometer placed in the center of the roast reaches 160°.

PER SERVING

STANDARD RECIPE:	CALORIES 861	FAT 60G	PROTEIN 72G	CARBOHYDRATES 7G	CHOL 230MG
REDUCED FAT:	CALORIES 664	FAT 35G	PROTEIN 72G	CARBOHYDRATES 7G	CHOL 233MG

Remove the pork roast and the apricots and place them on a serving platter. Degrease the sauce in the baking dish by skimming the fat from the surface, and transfer the sauce to a small saucepan. Bring the sauce to a simmer. In a small bowl, stir together the arrowroot with one tablespoon of the warm sauce. Add the arrowroot slurry to the saucepan and stir to combine. Bring the sauce back to a simmer, stirring constantly, and cook the sauce until thickened slightly, about 1 minute. Serve the pork with the sauce and the apricots.

CHEF JAMIE'S LOW-FAT TIP

The reduced fat analysis shown is based on using very lean pork that has 100 percent of all visible fat removed. Remove the butter from the recipe and sauté the roast in just 1 tablespoon of olive oil along with non-stick cooking spray. Spray the baking dish liberally with non-stick cooking spray to prevent the onions from burning.

Osso Bucco

MAKES 6 SERVINGS

This famous specialty of Milan, which literally mean "bone with a hole," creates the most wonderful braised veal shanks you have ever eaten. I think Osso Bucco is especially loved, not only for the incredible flavor and tenderness of the meat, but for the challenge of getting all of the meat off the bone and digging for the marrow!

6 veal shanks
salt & pepper, to taste
½ cup all-purpose flour
4 tablespoons butter
2 tablespoons olive oil
1 large carrot, chopped
1 yellow onion, chopped
6 garlic cloves, minced
2 anchovy fillets
3 cups fresh or canned tomatoes, chopped

2 cups beef broth
¾ cup cream sherry
2 tablespoons tomato paste
2 tablespoons fresh parsley, chopped
2 (1-inch) pieces fresh lemon peel
2 (1-inch) pieces fresh orange peel
1 bay leaf
1 tablespoon arrowroot
chopped parsley, for garnish

Preheat the oven to 350°F.

Season the veal shanks with salt and pepper. Dredge each shank in flour and shake off any excess. Heat 2 tablespoons of the butter and the oil in a large skillet. Add the floured shanks and brown well on all sides. Remove the shanks from the skillet and place them in a large baking dish.

Add the remaining 2 tablespoons of butter to the pan, along with the carrot, onion, and garlic. Sauté over medium heat, stirring often, until the onions are tender and light golden. Add the anchovy fillet and stir to dissolve. Stir in the tomatoes, beef broth, sherry, tomato paste, parsley, lemon peel, orange peel, and bay leaf. Pour the sauce over the veal shanks and cover the baking dish.

Bake for 1½ hours or until meat is very tender. Remove the veal shanks and keep warm. Discard the bay leaf, lemon peel and orange peel.

Transfer the sauce to a saucepan and bring it to a simmer. Place the arrowroot in a small mixing bowl and stir in 1 tablespoon of the warm sauce. Stir to dissolve any lumps. Whisking constantly, add the arrowroot mixture back to the saucepan and cook over low heat for 1 to 2 minutes or until the sauce thickens to the consistency of heavy cream. Pour half the sauce over the warm veal shanks and serve the remaining sauce on the side. Garnish with chopped parsley before serving.

	PER SERVING				
STANDARD RECIPE:	CALORIES 449	FAT 18G	PROTEIN 58G	CARBOHYDRATES 31G	CHOL 167MG
REDUCED FAT:	CALORIES 421	FAT 11G	PROTEIN 58G	CARBOHYDRATES 31G	CHOL 167MG

Osso Bucco *(continued)*

Orange-Glazed Veal Scallopini

MAKES 4 SERVINGS

These wonderfully thin veal cutlets are luxuriously bathed in a sweet and tangy orange sauce. This recipe makes a great throw-together meal too, since most of the dry ingredients are most likely to be staple items in your pantry and the veal can be kept frozen, as a standby, for those last-minute dinners. A good grinding of black pepper on top makes the dish perfect!

¾ cup orange juice concentrate, thawed but not diluted
⅓ cup light molasses
¼ cup ketchup
3 tablespoon Dijon mustard
2 tablespoon soy sauce
½ teaspoon garlic powder

¼ teaspoon cayenne pepper
⅛ teaspoon cumin
1 pound veal cutlets, pounded thin (scallopini)
2 tablespoons olive oil
1 tablespoon unsalted butter

In a small bowl, whisk together the juice concentrate, molasses, ketchup, mustard, soy sauce, garlic powder, cayenne, and cumin for the marinade. Remove ½ cup of marinade to use as a sauce for dipping; set aside.

Place the veal slices in the remaining marinade, cover bowl tightly with plastic wrap, and allow to marinate for one hour or overnight in the refrigerator.

When ready to serve, drain the cutlets from the marinade. Heat ½ tablespoon of butter with 1 tablespoon of olive oil in a large sauté pan over medium heat. Add some of the cutlets, without crowding the pan, and cook 2 to 3 minutes on each side, or until golden and cooked through. Remove and keep warm. Repeat the sautéing process using the remaining butter, oil and cutlets.

Before serving, in a small saucepan, bring the reserved sauce to a boil. Cook 2 minutes. Serve the scallopini with the warm sauce, garnished with parsley.

CHEF JAMIE'S LOW-FAT TIP

These flavorful cutlets can be made very low in fat by sautéing them with non-stick cooking spray only. Use turkey cutlets or turkey-breast slices pounded thin, for a leaner meat alternative. The turkey tastes just as good!

		PER SERVING		
STANDARD RECIPE:	CALORIES 452	FAT 20G	PROTEIN 43G	CARBOHYDRATES 40G	CHOL 188MG
REDUCED FAT:	CALORIES 271	FAT 5G	PROTEIN 49G	CARBOHYDRATES 25G	CHOL 126MG

Chapter 7

Classic Seafood

*F*resh, flavorful seafood, perfectly prepared, makes a wonderful meal. When purchasing fish, remember that fresh fish looks fresh: the flesh should appear bright, moist, firm, and almost translucent. When buying live shellfish, check for a fresh briny aroma and make sure that the shells are tightly closed (if you tap an open shell, a live shellfish will close; discard any that are not alive). The following classic recipes feature sweet and delicate seafood dishes that almost melt in your mouth!

Bouillabaisse

MAKES 6 SERVINGS

This fish stew was created in Marseilles, and eventually found its way all over the Mediterranean. The earliest records of the fish stew date back as far as 600 B.C., when it was called "kakavia" and seasoned with saffron, fennel seeds, and orange zest. Bouillabaisse often sends cooks running because it seems complicated and time-consuming. To make life simpler, this version uses only seafood that is readily available—and while the stew has a lot of ingredients, it is not difficult to prepare. You can even prepare the base and freeze it for a great meal at a later time: just add the fish before serving. When serving the bouillabaisse, place toasted slices of French bread on the table for dunking.

¼ cup olive oil
1 onion, sliced
1 leek, washed and diced
4 garlic cloves, minced
½ cup white wine
1 (14-ounce) can chopped plum
    tomatoes with juice
¼ cup fresh parsley, chopped
1 teaspoon fennel seed or
    1 tablespoon Pernod
1 teaspoon dried thyme
1 bay leaf

1 pinch saffron, optional
salt & pepper, to taste
8 cups (1 quart) water
18 mussels, scrubbed and debearded
18 clams, well scrubbed
2 dozen jumbo shrimp, shelled and
    deveined
2 pounds very fresh fish fillets, cut
    into chunks
2 (2 × 1-inch) pieces fresh orange
    peel

Heat the olive oil in a large stockpot. Add the onion, leek, and garlic, and sauté over medium heat, stirring often, for about 10 minutes or until the vegetables are tender. Add the white wine and deglaze the pot, scraping any browned bits from the bottom. Stir in the tomatoes, parsley, fennel, thyme, bay leaf, saffron, and salt and pepper. Add the water and bring to a boil. Reduce the heat to low and allow to simmer 45 minutes. (At this stage you can cool the broth and freeze for later use.)

When ready to serve, bring the broth to a slow simmer and add the mussels, clams, shrimp, and chunks of fish. Cover and cook over low heat until the mussels and clams open and the fish is cooked through.

Ladle the soup into bowls and serve immediately.

CHEF JAMIE'S LOW-FAT TIP

This fisherman's stew is actually a very healthy soup. Use only 1 tablespoon of olive oil in the lower-fat preparation, and eat to your heart's content.

		PER SERVING			
STANDARD RECIPE:	CALORIES 259	FAT 13G	PROTEIN 21G	CARBOHYDRATES 8G	CHOL 48MG
REDUCED FAT:	CALORIES 200	FAT 6G	PROTEIN 21G	CARBOHYDRATES 8G	CHOL 48MG

Fish & Chips
MAKES 4 SERVINGS

This English specialty began the revolution for crispy, tender fish that even kids would eat. Batter seals the fish superbly and keeps it incredibly moist. This recipe was borrowed from a good-old-diner in Pennsylvania. Using pancake mix for the batter makes it easy and scrumptious...if you don't believe me, try it for yourself! I guarantee you'll like it!

4 large russet potatoes
canola oil for frying
salt & pepper, to taste
2 pounds cod fillets

1¼ cups milk
1¼ cups pancake mix, such
   as Bisquick

Peel the potatoes and cut them into long wedges, about 8 wedges per potato. Place the wedges in ice water and let them stand for 30 minutes. Drain the potatoes well and dry them with paper towels.

In a deep skillet or an electric fryer, heat the oil to 375°F. Fry the potato wedges, a few at a time, until golden brown, about 3 to 5 minutes. Drain on paper towels and season with salt and pepper while still hot.

Meanwhile, cut the cod fillets into strips and season the fish with salt and pepper. In a mixing bowl, whisk together the milk and pancake mix until well combined. Add the cod strips and let soak for 1 minute. In the same skillet used to fry the potatoes, fry the battered fish fillets for 3 to 5 minutes or until golden brown.

CHEF JAMIE'S LOW-FAT TIP
You can achieve a lighter version by baking the fish instead of frying it. A low-fat version of pancake mix is available and is a perfect substitute in this recipe. If you are baking the fish and chips, be sure to spray the fish and potatoes directly, along with the baking sheet, with non-stick cooking spray before placing in a 375°F oven.

HELPFUL HINTS FROM THE WIZARD
- To make sure the fillets are fresh, put a small amount of pressure on the side of the package, then remove your fingers—if the pressure of your fingers leaves an indentation, the fish is old.

		PER SERVING			
STANDARD RECIPE:	CALORIES 235	FAT 13G	PROTEIN 5G	CARBOHYDRATES 25G	CHOL 10G
REDUCED FAT:	CALORIES 135	FAT 3G	PROTEIN 5G	CARBOHYDRATES 25G	CHOL 10G

Oven-Fried Fish

MAKES 6 SERVINGS

This is one of those simple yet fabulous dishes that never goes out of style! You can use almost any kind of firm whitefish, from bass to fluke. You can even bread the fillets in advance and refrigerate them for up to an hour before frying. (The refrigeration process actually helps the breading adhere better!) The fish is delicious when served with lots of fresh lemon wedges, with a sweet and spicy tartar sauce, or even with ketchup (that's the way I grew up eating it. . . so good!).

1 cup all-purpose flour, for dredging
salt & pepper, to taste
1 large egg, beaten
3 tablespoons milk
2 cups dry bread crumbs, plain or
   Italian style (with herbs)

6 whitefish fillets
1 stick (4 ounces) unsalted
   butter, melted
¼ cup capers, for garnish, optional
lemon wedges, for garnish

Preheat the oven to 500°F.

Season the flour with salt and pepper, and mix to combine well. Lay out a large piece of waxed paper and put the seasoned flour on it. In a shallow bowl, whisk together the egg and milk and set next to the flour. Lay out another sheet of waxed paper and put the bread crumbs on it. Season the fillets with salt and pepper on both sides.

Working in batches, dredge fish fillets in the flour and shake off excess. Next, dip each fillet into the egg mixture and let any excess drain off. Coat each fillet with bread crumbs, pressing gently to adhere the coating. Refrigerate, uncovered, for half an hour before cooking to allow the coating to adhere to the fish.

Line a large glass casserole dish (or baking pan with sides) with foil. Place half of the butter in the pan and place the pan in the oven. Heat 4 to 5 minutes, being sure the butter does not burn (it should brown just slightly). Remove from the oven and immediately place the fillets in it. Pour the remaining butter over the fillets.

Bake the fish for about 10 minutes, or until the fish flakes easily and is golden brown.

Garnish with lemon wedges and capers.

	PER SERVING				
STANDARD RECIPE:	CALORIES 389	FAT 13G	PROTEIN 24G	CARBOHYDRATES 42G	CHOL 102MG
REDUCED FAT:	CALORIES 341	FAT 6G	PROTEIN 24G	CARBOHYDRATES 42G	CHOL 88MG

CHEF JAMIE'S LOW-FAT TIP

Oven-fried fish translates beautifully to a low-fat dish. Use low-fat milk when breading and be sure to refrigerate the fillets before cooking. Instead of using all that butter, panfry the fillets on top of the stove using a liberal amount of cooking spray and a bit of olive oil for added flavor. Heat a large sauté pan over medium heat. Add 1 teaspoon olive oil to the pan and a few sprays of non-stick cooking spray. Cook the fillets in batches until golden in color and cooked through, adding more spray before turning over to cook on the underside.

Fillet of Sole Piccata

MAKES 4 SERVINGS

This classic needs no introduction. . . it is the simplest preparation for the sweetest fish.

1 cup all-purpose flour
salt & pepper, to taste
3 large eggs, lightly beaten
1 cup bread crumbs
8 sole fillets
¼ cup olive oil

¼ cup dry white wine
juice of 2 lemons
4 tablespoons capers
1 tablespoon unsalted butter
4 tablespoons fresh parsley, chopped

Season the flour with salt and pepper; mix to combine. Lay out a large piece of waxed paper and put the seasoned flour on it. In a shallow bowl, whisk the eggs and set next to the flour. Lay out another sheet of waxed paper and put the bread crumbs on it. Season the fillets with salt and pepper on both sides.

Working in batches, dredge the fish fillets in the flour and shake off excess. Next, dip each fillet into the egg mixture and let excess drain off. Finally, coat each fillet with bread crumbs, pressing gently so the coating adheres. Refrigerate the fish, uncovered, for half an hour before cooking, to allow the coating to adhere to the fish.

Heat the olive oil in a large sauté pan until hot but not smoking. Sauté the fillets, working in batches, until golden on both sides. Place the fish on a serving platter and keep warm. Add the wine and lemon juice to the same sauté pan and scrape up any bits that are stuck to the bottom of the pan. Add the capers to the sauce and cook 2 minutes. Remove the sauce from the heat and gently stir in the butter. Adjust the seasonings and pour the sauce over the fish. Garnish with chopped parsley and serve.

CHEF JAMIE'S LOW-FAT TIP

The sweet, wonderful flavor of fresh sole will hide the low-fat substitutions in this dish. Use ¾ cup of liquid egg substitute in place of the whole eggs and use only 1 tablespoon of olive oil and a liberal amount of non-stick cooking spray when sautéing the fillets.

			PER SERVING		
STANDARD RECIPE:	CALORIES 622	FAT 26G	PROTEIN 35G	CARBOHYDRATES 53G	CHOL 246MG
REDUCED FAT:	CALORIES 412	FAT 8G	PROTEIN 32G	CARBOHYDRATES 59G	CHOL 78MG

Mussels Meuniére

MAKES 6 SERVINGS

4 tablespoons (2 ounces) unsalted butter
3 tablespoons shallots, minced
6 dozen fresh mussels, cleaned and scrubbed
2 cups white wine
½ cup crème fraiche (see *Chef's Note* on page 160) *or* heavy cream
½ cup tomato, diced, for garnish
chopped fresh parsley, for garnish
lots of warm French bread, for dipping

Melt the butter in a medium-large sauté pan over medium heat. Add the shallots and sauté 1 minute. Add the mussels and the white wine and bring to a simmer. Cover the pan and allow to cook 3 to 4 minutes or until mussels open.

Remove the mussels and place them in a large serving bowl. Add the crème fraiche to the sauté pan and stir to combine. Allow the sauce to cook 30 seconds, then pour the sauce over the mussels in the bowl.

If you are using heavy cream, add the cream and simmer the sauce for about 5 minutes or until slightly thickened.

Sprinkle the mussels with the chopped diced tomato and chopped parsley and serve immediately.

CHEF JAMIE'S LOW-FAT TIP

We all know that French food certainly isn't light, but you could prepare this dish with just a tablespoon or two of cream, in homage to the richness of great French food. After removing the mussels, reduce the cooking liquid to strengthen the flavor of the sauce, then stir in the cream. Pour the sauce over the mussels and serve.

HELPFUL HINTS FROM THE WIZARD

- Before cooking, make sure the mussels' shells are closed tight, which means they're alive.

		PER SERVING		
STANDARD RECIPE:	CALORIES 728	FAT 29G	PROTEIN 82G	CARBOHYDRATES 30G	CHOL 218MG
REDUCED FAT:	CALORIES 633	FAT 19G	PROTEIN 75G	CARBOHYDRATES 30G	CHOL 218MG

Scampi à la Jamie

MAKES 4 SERVINGS

What could be better than large broiled shrimp in garlic butter? This is one of my all-time favorite indulgences!

1 stick (4 ounces) unsalted butter
¼ cup shallots, minced
¼ cup olive oil
2 tablespoons freshly squeezed lemon juice
1½ tablespoons garlic, minced

salt & pepper, to taste
2 pounds large fresh shrimp, shelled with tails left on, and deveined
lemon wedges, for garnish
¼ cup fresh parsley, chopped

Preheat the broiler to high. In a shallow, ovenproof sauté or baking pan, just large enough to hold the shrimp in a single layer, melt the butter over low heat, being careful not to let it brown. Add the olive oil and shallots; cook 1 minute. Add the lemon juice, garlic, salt, and pepper, and stir to combine. Add the shrimp and toss them in the butter to coat.

Place the pan under the broiler about 3 to 4 inches from the heat and broil for 2 minutes. Turn the shrimp over and broil 2 minutes longer or until the shrimp are golden in color and are just cooked through. (They will continue to cook after you remove them from the oven.)

Transfer the shrimp to a serving platter and pour the sauce from the pan over them. Garnish with chopped parsley and lemons wedges and serve immediately.

CHEF JAMIE'S LOW-FAT TIP

Lower-fat shrimp scampi can be done! To begin, place one stick of reduced-fat (50 percent-less-fat) butter in a small saucepan. Melt the butter over low heat, then continue simmering the butter for 10 minutes more to evaporate some of the water content and compound the flavor. Prepare the scampi using only 2 tablespoons olive oil and the reduced-fat butter.

HELPFUL HINTS FROM THE WIZARD

- Shrimp is easily overcooked and, when it is, becomes very tough, so be careful!

		PER SERVING			
STANDARD RECIPE:	CALORIES 588	FAT 42G	PROTEIN 48G	CARBOHYDRATES 4G	CHOL 424MG
REDUCED FAT:	CALORIES 361	FAT 16G	PROTEIN 48G	CARBOHYDRATES 4G	CHOL 391MG

Chapter 8

Poultry Favorites

*P*oultry, a most versatile meat, can be roasted,
grilled, sautéed, poached, or braised, and can be
served hot, warm, or cold. Some chicken and turkey
dishes are meant to be eaten with the most elegant of
silver, while others are best when picked up and eaten
with your fingers. The recipes in this chapter represent
my all-time poultry favorites.

The Very Best Southern-Fried Chicken

MAKES 4 SERVINGS

One of the great American classics, crispy fried chicken has been enjoyed in this country for more than a hundred years. But Americans weren't the first to fry their chickens—cooks in almost every country, from Italy to Vietnam, have a version of fried chicken. It is thought that Scottish immigrants who settled in the South introduced the method to the United States. It wasn't until the early 1900s that recipes for fried chicken began appearing in popular cookbooks.

The brining and the cornmeal crust are the tricks to this lusciously moist and crispy chicken! Plan to brine the chicken the night before, or be sure to allow 3 hours for quick brining. Also, don't let the amount of cayenne scare you, it really just adds flavor!

6 cups water
½ cup kosher salt (use ¼ cup if soaking overnight)
1 (3-to-4 pound) chicken, cut into pieces
2 cups buttermilk
a few dashes of Tabasco

1½ cups yellow cornmeal
1½ cups all-purpose flour
2 teaspoons cayenne pepper
2 teaspoons dried thyme
salt & pepper, to taste
canola oil, for frying

To brine the chicken: In a large mixing bowl or stockpot, combine the water and salt. Stir to dissolve. Add the chicken pieces and submerge them completely in the brine. Refrigerate, allowing the chicken to soak for 3 hours. (Use ¼ cup salt and soak overnight, if desired.)

To prepare the chicken: Drain the chicken pieces and pat them dry. In a separate bowl, stir together the buttermilk and Tabasco. Place the chicken pieces in the buttermilk and toss to coat. Allow the chicken to soak for at least ½ hour in the buttermilk.

When ready to fry, heat ¾ inch oil in a large cast-iron skillet to 350°. Combine the cornmeal, flour, cayenne, and thyme in a large zip-lock bag. Season liberally with salt and pepper. Seal the bag and shake to combine. Drain the chicken from the buttermilk but do not pat dry. Place a few pieces of chicken at a time in the cornmeal mixture, seal the bag, and shake to coat. Carefully place the coated chicken pieces, skin side down, in the hot oil, being sure not to crowd the pan. Cover and cook for 5 minutes. Remove the lid and cook, uncovered, until the underside of the chicken is golden brown. Turn and continue to cook until golden all over, about 20 to 25 minutes total cooking time. Repeat with remaining chicken pieces.

		PER SERVING			
STANDARD RECIPE:	CALORIES 1,304	FAT 38G	PROTEIN 138G	CARBOHYDRATES 28G	CHOL 452MG
REDUCED FAT:	CALORIES 914	FAT 20G	PROTEIN 138G	CARBOHYDRATES 28G	CHOL 391MG

CHEF JAMIE'S LOW-FAT TIP

Baked "fried chicken" is delicious. Spray the cornmeal-and-flour coated chicken pieces liberally with non-stick cooking spray and bake at 350°F for 30 minutes. Turn the chicken over and bake an additional 15 to 20 minutes or until golden brown all over and cooked through.

HELPFUL HINTS FROM THE WIZARD

- Never reuse frying oil; it develops trans-fatty acids, which are bad for the body.

Chicken and Dumplings

MAKES 4 SERVINGS

Who doesn't have fond memories of their grandmother's chicken and dumplings? The nice thing about this version of the popular classic is that the flour from the dumplings thickens the chicken broth to a tasty gravy. Be sure to let the dough rest before rolling it out and cutting it. This allows the gluten to develop and produces light, flaky dumplings!

For the chicken:
1 (3- to- 4-pound) chicken, cut into pieces
salt & pepper, to taste
2 tablespoons olive oil
4 cups chicken broth
2 stalks celery, cut into 2-inch pieces
2 carrots, peeled and cut into 2-inch pieces
1 small yellow onion, quartered
1 garlic clove, peeled and quartered
1 bay leaf
4 sprigs fresh parsley
1 tablespoon lemon juice

For the dumplings:
1 cup all-purpose flour
1½ teaspoons baking powder
salt & pepper, to taste
2 tablespoons fresh parsley, chopped
2 tablespoons solid vegetable shortening
⅓ cup whole milk

To make the chicken: Rinse the chicken pieces well and pat them dry. Season the chicken liberally with salt and pepper. Heat the oil in a large pot or Dutch oven over medium heat. Add the chicken pieces and brown them on all sides. Pour off the fat from the pan before continuing.

Add the celery, carrots, onion, garlic, bay leaf, parsley, lemon juice, and chicken broth to the chicken in the pot and bring to a boil. Lower the heat, cover, and simmer 45 minutes.

With a slotted spoon, transfer the chicken and vegetables to a platter and keep warm.

To make the dumplings: Combine the flour, baking powder, salt, pepper, and parsley in a mixing bowl. With a pastry blender or your fingertips, cut in the shortening until the mixture resembles coarse crumbs. Add the milk and stir just until moistened. Gather the dough into a ball and let it rest 5 to 10 minutes. Knead once or twice, then roll out on a floured surface to about a ½-inch thickness. Cut into 12 squares.

PER SERVING					
STANDARD RECIPE:	CALORIES 878	FAT 36G	PROTEIN 32G	CARBOHYDRATES 14G	CHOL 90MG
REDUCED FAT:	CALORIES 365	FAT 11G	PROTEIN 32G	CARBOHYDRATES 14G	CHOL 81MG

Bring the broth back to a simmer, then drop in the dumplings. Cover and simmer the dumplings until they have puffed up and are cooked through, about 20 minutes.

To serve, arrange the chicken, vegetables, and dumplings in four bowls. Remove the bay leaf from the gravy. Ladle some of the gravy into each bowl and serve immediately.

CHEF JAMIE'S LOW-FAT TIP

This recipe actually translates quite well to a low-fat version. Be sure to remove the skin from the chicken and use only 1 tablespoon of oil when browning the pieces. For the dumplings, make the dough lower in fat by eliminating the vegetable shortening altogether and using ½ cup of low-fat milk in place of the whole milk in the original recipe.

Myles' Favorite Chicken Pot Pie

MAKES 6 SERVINGS

A childhood favorite, chicken pot pie is homey, warm, and comforting. It is believed that English settlers brought the tradition of the pot pie with them when they came to America. But while the dish may have originated in England, we made it our specialty, so much so that in 1951 Swanson began mass-producing this classic and selling it on freezer shelves everywhere! The frozen pot pie was an immediate hit, and remains the third-best-selling frozen food item today. But homemade always tastes best, and this lovingly made American tradition is still the ultimate recipe for using leftovers. Leftover chicken or turkey and any vegetables you happen to have around always taste great in a creamy sauce topped with a flaky crust!

For the crust:
1¼ cups all-purpose flour
¼ teaspoon salt
4 tablespoons unsalted butter, cut into small pieces and chilled
3 to 4 tablespoons water

For the filling:
2 tablespoons unsalted butter, chilled
4 carrots, cut into ½-inch slices, parboiled until just tender
1 cup mushrooms, sliced
2 cups fresh or frozen peas
2 cups cooked chicken, diced
1 teaspoon fresh thyme, chopped
salt & pepper, to taste
3 tablespoons unsalted butter
1 cup chicken broth
1 cup half & half

To make the crust: In a mixing bowl, combine the flour and salt. Add the chilled butter and, using a pastry blender or a fork, blend until it resembles coarse meal. Add the water one tablespoon at a time, stirring just until the dough holds together. Form into a ball and wrap in plastic wrap. Refrigerate at least 1 hour.

To make the filling: In a large sauté pan, melt the 2 tablespoons butter over medium heat. Add the cooked carrots and mushrooms, and sauté 5 minutes. Add the peas, chicken, and thyme and season to taste with salt and pepper. Sauté 5 minutes longer.

In a separate small pan, melt the 3 tablespoons butter. Add the flour and stir constantly over low heat until golden brown to make a roux. Slowly whisk in the chicken broth to create a smooth sauce. Cook, stirring constantly, for 2 minutes or until thick.

Add the sauce to the vegetable/chicken mixture and stir to combine well. Stir in the half & half. Pour into a 6-cup casserole dish.

	PER SERVING				
STANDARD RECIPE:	CALORIES 556	FAT 31G	PROTEIN 30G	CARBOHYDRATES 38G	CHOL 225MG
REDUCED FAT:	CALORIES 281	FAT 16G	PROTEIN 29G	CARBOHYDRATES 41G	CHOL 145 MG

Roll out the chilled dough into a circle large enough to fit over the top of the casserole dish with an extra inch of dough for overhang. Place the dough over the casserole dish and press to the sides of the dish to create a seal. Cut a few slits in the top to allow steam to escape. Bake at 425°F for 30 to 35 minutes or until the crust is golden brown.

CHEF JAMIE'S LOW-FAT TIP
Using 50 percent-less-fat butter and 1 percent milk in place of the half & half will significantly lessen the fat in this dish. The chicken pot pie should still taste as creamy and delicious as you remember from your childhood.

HELPFUL HINTS FROM THE WIZARD
• Make sure that you remove all of the skin from the chicken before cooking.

Chicken Divan

This is my favorite chicken dish of all time! The chicken, with its creamy topping, combined with fresh broccoli and sweet peaches, is delectable! Growing up, I remember asking my mom to make this recipe for every special event. . .every birthday, celebration dinner, and so on. I still love it!

1 (3-pound) chicken, cut into pieces
salt & pepper, to taste
1 tablespoon olive oil
3 tablespoons unsalted butter
3 garlic cloves, minced
1 cup sour cream

1½ cup mayonnaise
¼ cup Parmesan cheese
1 (16-ounce) can sliced peaches, drained
1 bunch broccoli with stems left on, cut into large pieces

Preheat the oven to 350°F.

Season the chicken pieces with salt and pepper. Heat the oil and butter in a large skillet over medium heat. Add the garlic and sauté 30 seconds. Remove the pan from the heat and add the chicken pieces. Coat each piece well with the butter mixture.

Remove the chicken pieces and place them in a large, shallow baking dish. Cover the pan loosely with foil and bake for 20 minutes. Baste the chicken with the pan juices once during baking.

Meanwhile, in a small mixing bowl, combine the sour cream and mayonnaise. Steam the broccoli until tender but still crisp.

When the chicken is done, remove the pan from the oven and discard the foil. Using only half of the sour cream mixture, place a dollop of sauce on top of each piece of chicken. Bake for 20 minutes more.

When the chicken is cooked through, remove the pan from the oven and set the oven to broil. Place the broccoli pieces and peach slices around the chicken and top them with the remaining sauce. Sprinkle the entire dish with Parmesan cheese.

Broil, about 6 inches from the heat, for 5 minutes or until golden and bubbly.

	PER SERVING				
STANDARD RECIPE:	CALORIES 947	FAT 51G	PROTEIN 102G	CARBOHYDRATES 15G	CHOL 323MG
REDUCED FAT:	CALORIES 780	FAT 29G	PROTEIN 102G	CARBOHYDRATES 15G	CHOL 299MG

CHEF JAMIE'S LOW-FAT TIP

Low-fat Chicken Divan is very close to the original and incredibly delicious! To begin, sauté the garlic in just 1 tablespoon of olive oil, then rub on the *skinless* chicken pieces for flavor. For the topping, light sour cream and low-fat mayonnaise (even the non-fat counterparts taste good here) taste incredibly good in this dish. Eliminate the Parmesan cheese for an even lower-fat version.

HELPFUL HINTS FROM THE WIZARD

- When choosing broccoli, make sure that the florets are closed and that there is no yellow on them.

Chicken Cacciatore

MAKES 6 SERVINGS

This dish got its name in honor of hunters (cacciatore *is Italian for* "hunter"), who often gathered mushrooms while hunting in the forest. Tomatos and onions were readily available in summer and easily preserved or stored for winter. Serve the chicken, with plenty of sauce, over spaghetti or linguine.

½ cup all-purpose flour
salt & pepper, to taste
1 (3-pound) chicken, cut into pieces
6 tablespoons olive oil
2 yellow onions, sliced
½ pound mushrooms, sliced
2 garlic cloves, minced

½ cup dry red wine
2 (8-ounce) cans tomato sauce
1 (14-ounce) can diced tomatoes, in their juice
2 tablespoons fresh basil, chopped
1 teaspoon fresh oregano, chopped
½ cup fresh parsley, chopped

Fill a large resealable plastic bag with the flour, salt, and pepper. Shake the bag well to mix. Place one piece of chicken at a time in the bag, seal, and shake to coat. Shake off excess coating and repeat with the remaining chicken pieces.

In a large, deep pan, over medium-high heat, heat 4 tablespoons of the oil. Add the floured chicken pieces without crowding, and brown on all sides. Remove and set aside.

Add the remaining oil and the onions to the pan. Sauté until tender, about 5 to 8 minutes. Add the garlic and mushrooms, and sauté 2 minutes. Add the red wine, scraping any browned bits from the bottom of the pan. Stir in the tomatoes, tomato sauce, basil, and oregano. Return the chicken to the pan and cook, covered, 1 hour.

Season to taste with salt and pepper before serving. Garnish with chopped parsley.

Chef's Note: You can prepare this dish with just chicken breasts or thighs, if you prefer, and dried herbs can substitute if you have difficulty finding fresh. Use half the amount of dried herbs that you would fresh.

PER SERVING

STANDARD RECIPE:	CALORIES 675	FAT 27G	PROTEIN 79G	CARBOHYDRATES 25G	CHOL 210MG
REDUCED FAT:	CALORIES 487	FAT 16G	PROTEIN 75G	CARBOHYDRATES 24G	CHOL 160MG

Chicken Cacciatore (continued)

CHEF JAMIE'S LOW-FAT TIP
Reduce the olive oil by half, using 2 tablespoons to brown the chicken and only 1 tablespoon to brown the onions. Also, removing the skin from the chicken pieces before flouring will greatly reduce your fat intake.

HELPFUL HINTS FROM THE WIZARD
- Fresh herbs make a big difference in this recipe. Though you can use dried instead, it's worth the trip to the green market or gourmet grocery to buy the fresh ones.

Chicken Tetrazzini

MAKES 4 SERVINGS

This chicken and spaghetti dish was invented for the opera star Luisa Tetrazzini, who sang in the days when calories really didn't count. The low-fat version of this recipe fits better with today's times, but the original is still so incredibly good!

For the velouté sauce:
2 tablespoons unsalted butter
3 tablespoons all-purpose flour
1 cup chicken broth, warmed
¼ cup heavy cream
salt & pepper, to taste

For the chicken:
2 tablespoons unsalted butter
¼ cup yellow onion, minced
1 cup white mushrooms, sliced

¼ cup dry sherry
1 cup velouté sauce (recipe below)
½ cup heavy cream, warmed
¼ cup Parmesan cheese, grated
3 cups cooked chicken, cubed
salt & pepper, to taste
2 tablespoons fresh parsley, chopped
3 cups cooked spaghetti, well drained

To make the velouté sauce: Melt the butter in a small saucepan. Stir in the flour. Cook over low heat for 2 minutes, stirring often, until pale golden in color. Whisk in the broth and the cream, and bring to a slow simmer. Do not boil. Season with salt and pepper. Simmer gently, stirring often, for 10 minutes, or until thickened.

To make the chicken: Melt the butter in a large saucepan over medium heat. Add the onion and mushrooms and sauté, stirring often, until the onion is tender. Stir in the sherry.

Stir in the velouté sauce, cream, and Parmesan cheese. Simmer 3 minutes, stirring often, to melt the cheese. Add the chicken to the sauce and mix well. Season with salt and pepper.

When ready to serve, stir the chopped parsley into the sauce. Serve the chicken mixture on a bed of hot spaghetti.

CHEF JAMIE'S LOW-FAT TIP

A quick and low-fat version can be prepared using reduced-fat condensed cream of chicken soup in place of the velouté sauce, and water in place of the heavy cream. You will still achieve rich and flavorful Tetrazzini!

			PER SERVING		
STANDARD RECIPE:	CALORIES 725	FAT 45G	PROTEIN 54G	CARBOHYDRATES 41G	CHOL 1,107MG
REDUCED FAT:	CALORIES 603	FAT 23G	PROTEIN 53G	CARBOHYDRATES 32G	CHOL 188MG

Chicken Dijonnaise

MAKES 4 SERVINGS

This mustard-flavored chicken is both easy and versatile. While the recipe calls for a combination of Dijon-style mustard and whole-grain mustard, you can substitute any mustard that appeals to you. The chicken is delicious served hot, and just as good when chilled and shredded into a salad.

¼ cup whole-grain mustard
¼ cup Dijon mustard
1 (3- to 3½-pound) chicken, quartered
salt & pepper, to taste
⅓ cup dry white wine
½ cup crème fraiche (see *Chef's Note*) or heavy cream

In a small mixing bowl, combine the two mustards. Remove 3 tablespoons of the mustard mixture and set aside.

Place the chicken in a large baking dish and coat with the mustard mixture. Allow the chicken to marinate in the refrigerator for at least 2 hours or overnight.

Preheat the oven to 350°F.

'Season the chicken with salt and pepper, and pour the white wine around the chicken pieces.

Bake the chicken, uncovered, for 35 to 40 minutes or until the chicken is cooked through. You may have to bake the dark meat pieces an additional 5 to 10 minutes.

Remove the chicken from the oven and place the chicken pieces on a serving platter. Keep warm.

Pour any remaining juices from the baking dish into a saucepan. Bring to a boil, then stir in the reserve mustard and the crème fraiche or heavy cream. Lower the heat to medium low and cook 5 minutes to blend flavors. Season with salt and pepper to taste.

Spoon the sauce over the chicken and serve.

Chef's Note: Crème fraiche (tangy, thickened cream) is what I call "the ultimate sour cream"! Its rich body and tart flavor make it an ideal addition to sauces (since it can be boiled without separating) and a delicious topping for desserts! You can make crème fraiche by whisking together 1 cup heavy cream and 1 cup sour cream. Place in a clean jar and close the lid tightly. Let sit at room temperature overnight, or until thickened. Shake the jar a few times during the thickening process. (In cold weather, it might take up to 24 hours to thicken.) When thick, refrigerate for at least 4 hours, after which the crème fraiche will be quite thick. Keep in the refrigerator for up to 2 weeks.

PER SERVING

STANDARD RECIPE:	CALORIES 799	FAT 34G	PROTEIN 110G	CARBOHYDRATES 1G	CHOL 358MG
REDUCED FAT:	CALORIES 522	FAT 12G	PROTEIN 111G	CARBOHYDRATES 1G	CHOL 233MG

The potent mustard flavor masks the loss of fat in this recipe quite well. Use light sour cream in the sauce, but, to keep the sour cream from breaking, be sure not to bring the sauce to a boil. Also, be sure to remove the skin from the chicken before coating it with the mustard. (Note: The reduced-fat recipe statistics have been calculated for skinless white meat.)

Chicken with White Wine Mushroom Sauce *MAKES 4 SERVINGS*

This is one of the best of the basics! Create a very simple dish by using white button mushrooms or make an elegant main course by using shiitakes, criminis, and lobster mushrooms. These luscious wild mushrooms dress up the dish and add an incredible woodsy flavor.

For the chicken:
4 boneless, skinless chicken breast
    halves
½ cup all-purpose flour
1 teaspoon dried thyme
1 teaspoon dried basil
salt & pepper, to taste
2 tablespoons unsalted butter
1 tablespoon olive oil
cooked spaghetti (optional)

For the sauce:
1 tablespoon unsalted butter
2 cups mushrooms, sliced
¼ cup dry white wine
¼ cup chicken broth
¼ cup heavy cream
¼ cup chopped fresh parsley,
    for garnish

To make the chicken: Pound the chicken breasts between two layers of plastic wrap or wax paper until they are thin cutlets.

Stir the flour, thyme, basil, salt, and pepper in a shallow mixing bowl. Dredge each chicken breast in the flour mixture and shake off excess.

Heat the butter and olive oil in a large sauté pan over medium heat. Add the floured chicken breasts to the pan and brown on both sides. Remove the chicken and set aside.

To make the sauce: To the same pan, melt the butter over high heat. Add the mushrooms and sauté 2 minutes, or until golden. Return the chicken to the pan and add the white wine and chicken broth. Lower the heat and simmer 1 minute more. Add the heavy cream and simmer 1 minute or until the sauce thickens slightly. Be careful not to cook the dish too long or the chicken will become tough.

Serve the chicken with the sauce over pasta, garnished with the parsley.

CHEF JAMIE'S LOW-FAT TIP
Try using just 1 tablespoon of heavy cream in the sauce and use 1 tablespoon of reduced-fat (50 percent-less-fat) butter and 1 teaspoon of olive oil when sautéing the *skinless* chicken breasts.

		PER SERVING		
STANDARD RECIPE:	CALORIES 652	FAT 34G	PROTEIN 66G	CARBOHYDRATES 17G	CHOL 247MG
REDUCED FAT:	CALORIES 527	FAT 19G	PROTEIN 65G	CARBOHYDRATES 18G	CHOL 202MG

Lemon Chicken

MAKES 4 SERVINGS

Terrific hot or cold, this chicken is especially delicious on a picnic. I love the crisp golden crust and the zing from the fresh lemon.

1 (3- to 3½-pound) chicken, quartered
1 cup fresh lemon juice
1 cup all-purpose flour
1 teaspoon salt
½ teaspoon pepper

½ cup vegetable oil
1 tablespoon lemon zest
2 tablespoons brown sugar
¼ cup chicken broth
½ teaspoon lemon extract
2 lemons, sliced paper-thin

Combine the chicken pieces and lemon juice in a nonreactive mixing bowl just large enough to hold the pieces comfortably. Cover the bowl and allow the chicken to marinate in the refrigerator overnight, turning occasionally.

Drain the chicken and pat dry. Discard the lemon juice.

Fill a large resealable plastic bag with the flour, salt, and pepper. Shake the bag well to mix. Place one piece of chicken at a time in the bag, seal, and shake to coat. Shake off excess coating from the chicken and repeat with the remaining chicken pieces.

Preheat the oven to 350°F.

Heat the oil in a large frying pan or cast-iron skillet until hot. Fry the chicken pieces in batches, until brown and crisp on all sides.

Arrange the browned chicken pieces in a single layer in a large baking dish. Sprinkle the chicken pieces with the brown sugar and lemon zest. In a small mixing bowl, combine the chicken broth and lemon extract. Pour around the chicken pieces and place a slice of lemon on top of each piece of chicken.

Bake, uncovered, for 25 to 30 minutes.

CHEF JAMIE'S LOW-FAT TIP

Create pungent, flavorful chicken without all the fat by reducing the oil you fry in to 1 tablespoon per batch of frying and supplementing with non-stick cooking spray. Be sure to brown the chicken over medium heat to reduce the risk of burning. Use skinless chicken breasts or skinless chicken pieces to cut the fat even more.

Chef's Note: For a more intense lemon flavor, use Meyer lemons and omit the lemon extract.

		PER SERVING		
STANDARD RECIPE:	CALORIES 1,115	FAT 54G	PROTEIN 114G	CARBOHYDRATES 15G	CHOL 332MG
REDUCED FAT:	CALORIES 841	FAT 24G	PROTEIN 114G	CARBOHYDRATES 15G	CHOL 297MG

Chicken Enchiladas

MAKES 6 SERVINGS

Enchiladas are one of those filling comfort foods, like lasagna, that supposedly got heavier and cheesier after being adapted for American palates. This dish is a great way to use up leftover meats.

2 tablespoons unsalted butter
1 tablespoon olive oil
1 yellow onion, chopped
1 garlic clove, minced
1 (16-ounce) can diced tomatoes in juice, drained
1 (8-ounce) can tomato puree
1 (4-ounce) can diced green chiles
1 teaspoon sugar

1 teaspoon ground cumin
½ teaspoon salt
½ teaspoon dried oregano
½ teaspoon dried basil
12 burrito-size flour tortillas
2 cups Monterey Jack cheese, shredded
2 cups shredded cooked chicken
½ cup sour cream

Preheat the oven to 350°F. Lightly grease a 9 × 13-inch baking dish.

Melt the butter with the oil in a large sauté pan over medium heat. Add the onion and garlic, and sauté until tender. Add the tomatoes, chiles, tomato puree, sugar, cumin, salt, oregano, and basil. Bring the sauce to a boil, then reduce the heat and simmer, covered, for 20 minutes.

To assemble the enchiladas, dip each tortilla in the sauce. Place 2 tablespoons of chicken and 2 tablespoons of grated cheese on each tortilla. Roll the tortilla and place seam-side down in the prepared baking dish. Repeat, using remaining tortillas and filling. Blend the sour cream into the remaining sauce and pour over tortillas. Sprinkle with the remaining cheese. Cover and bake 40 minutes.

CHEF JAMIE'S LOW-FAT TIP

This recipe adjusts well by eliminating the butter and sautéing in just olive oil, stirring often so the onions don't burn, and by using low-fat cheese and low-fat or even fat-free sour cream in the assembly.

HELPFUL HINTS FROM THE WIZARD

- Corn tortillas are fat-free; flour tortillas have a very small amount of unsaturated fat.

			PER SERVING		
STANDARD RECIPE:	CALORIES 261	FAT 36G	PROTEIN 39G	CARBOHYDRATES 12G	CHOL 139MG
REDUCED FAT:	CALORIES 225	FAT 19G	PROTEIN 38G	CARBOHYDRATES 12G	CHOL 94MG

Spicy Piquant Chicken

MAKES 6 SERVINGS

This sumptuously spicy one-pot meal is always well received. Serve the chicken over rice or pasta for a hearty meal.

½ cup olive oil
2 (3-pound) chickens, cut into pieces
salt & pepper, to taste
2 yellow onions, diced
2 cups celery, diced
1 red bell pepper, cut into thin strips
1 green bell pepper, cut into thin strips
salt & pepper, to taste
¼ cup all-purpose flour
2 (28-ounce) cans crushed tomatoes

1 cup chicken broth
1 (6-ounce) can tomato paste
3 tablespoon fresh lemon juice
1 teaspoon crushed red pepper flakes
½ teaspoon Tabasco
4 garlic cloves, chopped
1 bay leaf
16 green olives
4 scallions, chopped
2 tablespoons fresh parsley, chopped

In a large stockpot, heat half the olive oil. Season the chicken pieces with salt and pepper. Brown the chicken in batches, using more oil as needed, until the chicken is golden on all sides. Remove and set aside.

In the same pan, sauté the onions, celery, and peppers over medium heat until tender. Season to taste with salt and pepper. Remove the vegetables and set aside.

Drain all but 1 tablespoon of the oil from the pan. Stir in the flour and cook for 1 minute. Add the crushed tomatoes, chicken broth, tomato paste, lemon juice, red pepper flakes, pepper, Tabasco, garlic, bay leaf, and sautéed vegetables to the pot. Bring to a boil, then reduce the heat to a simmer. Add the chicken pieces to the pot and cook, partially covered, until the sauce is thickened, about 1 hour.

Remove the bay leaf and skim excess fat before serving. Stir in the olives, scallions, and parsley before serving.

		PER SERVING			
STANDARD RECIPE:	CALORIES 798	FAT 34G	PROTEIN 83G	CARBOHYDRATES 38G	CHOL 210MG
REDUCED FAT:	CALORIES 639	FAT 15G	PROTEIN 83G	CARBOHYDRATES 38G	CHOL 210MG

Spicy Piquant Chicken (continued)

CHEF JAMIE'S LOW-FAT TIP

Instead of browning the chicken in oil, broil (set the broiler to high and set the chicken quite close to the heat source) until golden on all sides. Use only 1 tablespoon of olive oil along with liberal amounts of non-stick cooking spray to sauté the vegetables and avoid any scorching.

HELPFUL HINTS FROM THE WIZARD

- Tabasco is now made in two types, the traditional red pepper sauce and a milder green jalapeño version.

Spicy Stir-Fry Orange Chicken with Vegetables
MAKES 4 SERVINGS

I especially like this recipe because it reminds me of the sweet and crispy orange chicken at my favorite Chinese restaurant. I eliminated the deep-frying method and added the crunch of a few vegetables to modernize the dish. Serve with steamed white or brown rice.

½ cup chicken broth
⅓ cup orange juice
3 tablespoons soy sauce
1 tablespoon cornstarch
2 teaspoons sugar
2 teaspoons rice vinegar
1 teaspoon sesame oil
½ cup all-purpose flour
salt & pepper, to taste

4 chicken breasts, sliced crosswise
2 tablespoons olive oil
1 red bell pepper, cut into thin strips
1 cup snow peas, cleaned
1 green onion, thinly sliced
¼ cup orange zest
1 garlic clove, minced
¼ teaspoon crushed red pepper flakes

In a small mixing bowl, whisk together the chicken broth, orange juice, soy sauce, corn starch, sugar, rice vinegar, and sesame oil.

Fill a large resealable plastic bag with the flour, and salt and pepper. Shake the bag well to mix. Place the chicken pieces in the bag, seal, and shake to coat. Remove the chicken from the bag and shake off excess coating.

Heat the oil in a large skillet or wok until very hot. Add the floured chicken. Cook for about 1 minute, stirring constantly. Add the bell pepper, snow peas, green onion, orange zest, garlic, and red-pepper flakes. Sauté for 2 minutes, stirring often, until the vegetables are tender but still crisp. Stir in the sauce and simmer 2 to 3 minutes, or until the chicken is cooked through and the sauce thickens slightly.

CHEF JAMIE'S LOW-FAT TIP
The beauty of Chinese cooking is the truly amazing heat distribution a good wok gives you. This dish becomes quite healthy when you eliminate flouring the chicken and sauté using only ½ teaspoon of olive oil and non-stick cooking spray to coat the wok. Use ¼ teaspoon of sesame oil in the marinade for flavor!

		PER SERVING		
STANDARD RECIPE:	CALORIES 611	FAT 27G	PROTEIN 66G	CARBOHYDRATES 27G	CHOL 176MG
REDUCED FAT:	CALORIES 497	FAT 12G	PROTEIN 66G	CARBOHYDRATES 27G	CHOL 176MG

Spicy Stir-Fry Orange Chicken with Vegetables
(continued)

HELPFUL HINTS FROM THE WIZARD
- Vegetables cooked quickly in a wok retain more nutrients than in virtually any other method of cooking. Make sure to cook them only until they deepen a bit in color, but still retain their firmness and fresh flavor.

Chapter 9

The Greatest Side Dishes

*S*ide dishes make a meal special. Their complementary and contrasting flavors and textures turn the ordinary into the extraordinary! Whether you decide to experiment with new combinations or rely on your time-honored favorites, serve these sides with your signature main course to make your meals come alive with flavor.

German Potato Salad

MAKES 6 SERVINGS

This mayonnaise-free potato salad was originally associated with German immigrants and therefore is referred to as "German Potato Salad." I have updated this picnic classic by requesting that you coddle the egg to lessen the risk of bacterial contamination.

4 pounds baby red potatoes, scrubbed
6 slices bacon, cut into ¼-inch dice
2 yellow onions, finely minced
½ cup white wine vinegar
2 teaspoons sugar

4 tablespoons vegetable oil
salt & pepper, to taste
1 egg, coddled, then beaten (see page 42)
2 tablespoons fresh chives, chopped

Place the potatoes in a large saucepan, cover with cold water, and add a generous pinch of salt. Bring to a boil, then reduce the heat to medium and cook just until tender, 30 to 40 minutes. Drain and set aside.

Sauté the bacon and onions in a large pan over medium heat. Cook, stirring often, until the onion softens but does not brown, about 5 minutes. Add the vinegar and sugar, and bring to a boil over high heat. Cook 1 minute, then remove from the heat and slowly whisk in the oil.

When the potatoes are cool enough to handle, but still warm, cut into ¼-inch slices. Place in a large mixing bowl and season with salt and pepper. Pour the warm bacon mixture and the egg over the potatoes. Mix gently and thoroughly. Sprinkle with chives and serve warm.

CHEF JAMIE'S LOW-FAT TIP
Using turkey bacon will greatly reduce the fat in this scrumptious salad.

HELPFUL HINTS FROM THE WIZARD
- Egg substitutes will not work well with this recipe.

PER SERVING

STANDARD RECIPE:	CALORIES 466	FAT 32G	PROTEIN 9G	CARBOHYDRATES 36G	CHOL 57MG
REDUCED FAT:	CALORIES 360	FAT 18G	PROTEIN 10G	CARBOHYDRATES 37G	CHOL 37MG

Jamie's Garlicky Mashed Potatoes

MAKES 4 SERVINGS

Mashed potatoes are a basic of the American table. . . comfort food at its finest! As for which potato to use, I use russet because I like fluffy, light mashed potatoes. If you like a heavier mashed potato, choose a low-starch potato such as a round white. To modernize the recipe even more, try using a potato of the yellow variety, like Yukon Gold, for extra creaminess.

6 russet potatoes, peeled
8 cloves of garlic, peeled and
    left whole
½ cup half & half
½ cup crème fraiche (see *Chef's
    Note* on page 160) *or* sour cream
2 tablespoon fresh thyme,
    finely chopped

2 tablespoon fresh tarragon,
    finely chopped
2 tablespoon fresh oregano,
    finely chopped
salt & pepper, to taste
½ stick unsalted butter, cut
    into pieces

Place the potatoes, garlic cloves, and a generous pinch of salt in a large pan and cover with cold water. Bring to a boil over high heat, then reduce to low and simmer until the potatoes are tender, about 45 minutes. Drain (do not discard the garlic cloves—leave them with the potatoes) and place in a large mixing bowl.

Meanwhile, in a small saucepan, combine the half & half, crème fraiche, herbs, and salt and pepper. Bring to a simmer over low heat, whisking to combine.

Add the butter and allow to melt. Add the hot milk mixture to the potatoes. Using an electric mixer on low speed (or a potato masher and some serious elbow grease), blend until smooth. Adjust the seasoning and serve.

CHEF JAMIE'S LOW-FAT TIP

The potent flavor of the garlic masks the loss of fat in this recipe. Eliminate the butter completely and instead of using half & half and crème fraiche, use low-fat milk and light sour cream.

HELPFUL HINTS FROM THE WIZARD

- If you use milk, be sure that it is very warm before adding it to the potatoes. Cold dairy liquids may cause the potatoes to become lumpy.
- A pinch of baking powder will fluff them up. Don't use baking soda, or they will turn black.

	PER SERVING				
STANDARD RECIPE:	CALORIES 288	FAT 21G	PROTEIN 4G	CARBOHYDRATES 22G	CHOL 55MG
REDUCED FAT:	CALORIES 135	FAT 2G	PROTEIN 3G	CARBOHYDRATES 20G	CHOL 13MG

Chef Jamie's Sweet Potato Pie

MAKES 8 SERVINGS

This sweet potato pie is a signature dish of mine, and the low-fat version, which I created years ago, is requested almost as much as the original. Both are equally good! There are many varieties of this large edible root, but the most widely grown is the "pale sweet potato," which is a relative of the yam. Yams originated in Asia, are less sweet, and contain 10 to 20 percent fewer nutrients than sweet potatoes. Both yams and sweet potatoes tend to decay faster than other potatoes due to their high sugar content.

For the crust:
2 cups graham cracker crumbs
2 teaspoons ground cinnamon
3 tablespoons unsalted butter, melted

For the filling:
3 pounds sweet potatoes
8 ounces cream cheese, softened
3 large eggs
4 tablespoons unsalted butter, melted

5 tablespoons pure maple syrup
¼ cup orange juice
2 tablespoons vanilla extract
1 tablespoon honey
1 teaspoon freshly grated orange zest
¼ teaspoon ground nutmeg
¼ teaspoon ground cloves
¼ teaspoon ground ginger
¼ teaspoon ground allspice
¼ teaspoon salt

To make the crust: Grease a 10-inch springform pan. In a large mixing bowl, combine the graham cracker crumbs, cinnamon, and melted butter, and mix until moist. Transfer the crumb mixture to the prepared pan and press it down firmly to cover the bottom of the pan evenly. Set aside.

To make the filling: Preheat the oven to 350°F. Prick the sweet potatoes with a fork and place them on a cookie sheet. Bake 1 hour or until very tender. When cool enough to handle, peel and place in the bowl of a food processor. Add the cream cheese and process until completely smooth. Add the eggs, butter, maple syrup, orange juice, vanilla, honey, orange zest, nutmeg, cloves, ginger, allspice, and salt, and blend thoroughly. Pour the filling into the prepared crust.

Bake about 1 hour, or until the center of the pie is firm and not sticky to the touch. Allow to cool for at least 1 hour before serving.

	PER SERVING				
STANDARD RECIPE:	CALORIES 294	FAT 25G	PROTEIN 10G	CARBOHYDRATES 18G	CHOL 145MG
REDUCED FAT:	CALORIES 226	FAT .6G	PROTEIN 7G	CARBOHYDRATES 19G	CHOL 13MG

Chef Jamie's Sweet Potato Pie *(continued)*

CHEF JAMIE'S LOW-FAT TIP

As I mentioned above, this recipe is equally—and I mean equally—as good in its low-fat form. Use 2 egg whites in place of the butter for the graham cracker crust. In the filling, use 6 large egg whites or ¾ cup of liquid egg substitute for the 3 whole eggs, and light cream cheese in place of regular. Eliminate the butter altogether in the filling and voilà, you have the ultimate low-fat sweet potato pie!

HELPFUL HINTS FROM THE WIZARD

• Store sweet potatoes with a small piece of ginger root to prevent the potatoes from sprouting.

Sweet Potato Casserole with Praline Topping   *MAKES 12 SERVINGS*

The combination of sweet potatoes and brown sugar can't be beat. This sweet, rich casserole will thrill your taste buds and make you "thankful" for the recipe, especially at Thanksgiving time!

3 pounds sweet potatoes, peeled and cubed
1 cup all-purpose flour
¾ cup brown sugar
¼ cup chopped pecans, toasted
2 tablespoons unsalted butter, melted

1 teaspoon ground cinnamon
¼ cup heavy cream
2 teaspoons grated orange peel
¼ teaspoon ground ginger
2 large eggs, beaten
salt & pepper, to taste

Cook the sweet potatoes in a large pan of boiling salted water until tender, about 30 minutes. Drain well.

Preheat oven to 350°F. Grease a 2-quart casserole dish.

In a small mixing bowl, combine the flour, ¼ cup of the brown sugar, the pecans, butter, and ¼ teaspoon cinnamon. Set aside.

Place the cooked sweet potatoes in a large mixing bowl with 1 cup of the topping mixture, the cream, orange peel, ginger, eggs, and the remaining ¼ cup brown sugar. Mash together until smooth. Season to taste with salt and pepper.

Spoon the mixture into the prepared casserole dish. Top with the remaining topping mixture. Bake 45 minutes, or until set and heated through.

CHEF JAMIE'S LOW-FAT TIP

This sweet side dish makes a lovely low-fat treat if you use reduced-fat (50 percent-less-fat) butter in place of real butter, orange juice in place of heavy cream, and 1 whole egg plus ¼ cup liquid egg substitute in place of the 2 eggs.

			PER SERVING		
STANDARD RECIPE:	CALORIES 283	FAT 8G	PROTEIN 8G	CARBOHYDRATES 56G	CHOL 43MG
REDUCED FAT:	CALORIES 257	FAT 4G	PROTEIN 4G	CARBOHYDRATES 50G	CHOL 3MG

Caramelized Onion, Mushroom, and Sage Stuffing   *MAKES 8 SERVINGS*

Stuffing isn't just for turkey anymore! There are hundreds of ways to make stuffing, a.k.a. dressing or filling. Some like it moist, others prefer it dry. Serve this stuffing with hearty meat dishes as an alternative to potatoes or rice. You could even add your favorite mix of mushrooms (shitake, crimini, or portabella), then use the filling to stuff a turkey breast for a truly elegant meal.

1 (16-ounce) loaf egg bread, cut into 1-inch cubes
4 tablespoons (2 ounces) unsalted butter
2 tablespoons olive oil
2 yellow onions, diced
3 celery stalks, diced
1 pound white mushrooms, sliced
½ pound brown or shitake mushrooms, sliced

¼ cup dry white wine
juice of one lemon
1 cup chicken broth
½ cup fresh parsley, chopped
2 large eggs, lightly beaten
2 teaspoons fresh sage, minced, *or* 1 teaspoon dried sage
salt & pepper, to taste

Preheat the oven to 325°F. Grease a 9 × 13-inch glass baking dish.

Place the bread cubes on a cookie sheet. Toast the bread in the oven, tossing often, until golden brown. Transfer the toasted bread cubes to a large bowl.

Heat the butter and oil in a large sauté pan over medium heat. Add the onions and reduce the heat to low. Cook until golden and caramelized, stirring often, about 20 minutes. Add the celery and mushrooms, and sauté for 3 minutes. Add the wine and lemon juice and stir to combine. Remove from the heat and stir the mushroom mixture into the cubed bread. Stir in the chicken broth, parsley, eggs, and sage. Season to taste with salt and pepper.

Place the stuffing in the prepared pan and cover with foil. Bake for 30 minutes, then remove the foil and bake an additional 30 minutes, or until golden.

CHEF JAMIE'S LOW-FAT TIP

The trick to this sweet, flavorful stuffing is the caramelized onion! You can reduce the oil and butter you sauté the onions in by half and still maintain their rich flavor. As for the eggs, liquid egg substitute works great in stuffing, so use ½ cup of egg substitute in place of the 2 whole eggs.

HELPFUL HINTS FROM THE WIZARD

- To get more juice from a lemon, microwave it for a few seconds before squeezing.

		PER SERVING			
STANDARD RECIPE:	CALORIES 146	FAT 11G	PROTEIN 4G	CARBOHYDRATES 6G	CHOL 70MG
REDUCED FAT:	CALORIES 74	FAT 6G	PROTEIN 4G	CARBOHYDRATES 7G	CHOL 35MG

Warm Rice Salad

MAKES 8 SERVINGS

This rice salad is delicious served hot or at room temperature. It makes a nice addition to a buffet or a potluck party. Use brown or wild rice for an innovative twist.

For the vinaigrette:
1 tablespoon Dijon mustard
4 tablespoons red wine vinegar
1 teaspoon sugar
½ cup extra-virgin olive oil
salt & pepper, to taste

For the salad:
8 cups hot, cooked white rice
1 cup dried currants or raisins

1 (10-ounce) package frozen peas, thawed and drained
1 red bell pepper, stemmed, cored and cut into thin strips
1 green bell pepper, stemmed, cored and cut into thin strips
½ cup pitted black olives, chopped
¼ cup fresh parsley, chopped
1 small red onion, diced

To make the vinaigrette: In a small mixing bowl, whisk together the red wine vinegar, mustard, and sugar. Slowly drizzle in the oil, whisking constantly. Season with salt and pepper.

To make the salad: Place the hot rice in a large mixing bowl. Pour the vinaigrette into the rice and toss well. Cool to room temperature.

Add the remaining ingredients and toss thoroughly. Adjust the seasonings.

CHEF JAMIE'S LOW-FAT TIP

Create a low-fat rice salad by using the following dressing in place of the oil-based vinaigrette in the original recipe. Simply whisk all the ingredients together in a small mixing bowl. I was served a low-fat dressing similar to this during a wonderful spa vacation, and duplicated the flavor as soon as I got back to my own kitchen! The dressing below is delicious on salads, too!

For the low-fat dressing:
1 cup low-fat buttermilk
½ cup unsalted tomato juice
½ cup red wine vinegar

1 teaspoon fresh basil, minced
1 small garlic clove, minced
1 teaspoon fresh dill, minced

		PER SERVING			
STANDARD RECIPE:	CALORIES 417	FAT 15G	PROTEIN 7G	CARBOHYDRATES 64G	CHOL 0MG
REDUCED FAT:	CALORIES 298	FAT 2G	PROTEIN 7G	CARBOHYDRATES 64G	CHOL 0MG

Baked Cheese Grits

MAKES 4 SERVINGS

The word "grits" refers to any coarsely ground grain such as corn, oats, or rice. I like to serve grits instead of mashed potatoes for variety. . . they are wonderful with leg of lamb!

1½ cups water
1½ cups whole milk
¾ cup quick-cooking grits
   (not instant)
salt & pepper, to taste
1 large egg, beaten

½ cup cheddar cheese, shredded
2 tablespoons unsalted butter
dash of hot sauce or cayenne pepper

Preheat the oven to 350°F. Grease a 1½-quart casserole dish.

In a saucepan, combine the water and milk. Bring to a boil over medium heat. Stir in grits, salt, and pepper. Reduce heat to medium low and cook, stirring constantly, for 5 minutes. Remove from the heat.

Add a small amount of the hot grits to the beaten egg and stir to combine. Return the egg mixture to the pan. Add the cheese and butter and stir until the cheese is melted and well blended.

Pour into the prepared dish. Bake 40 to 45 minutes or until golden brown and puffed.

CHEF JAMIE'S LOW-FAT TIP

Low-fat milk, liquid egg substitute, and low-fat cheese (one that melts well!) substitute beautifully in this dish. An extra dash of hot sauce will mask any loss of creamy texture caused by using the low-fat ingredient alternatives! Also, you can use 50 percent-less-fat butter in place of the regular butter.

		PER SERVING			
STANDARD RECIPE:	CALORIES 299	FAT 15G	PROTEIN 9G	CARBOHYDRATES 25G	CHOL 97MG
REDUCED FAT:	CALORIES 198	FAT 3G	PROTEIN 9G	CARBOHYDRATES 29G	CHOL 22MG

Cheese Spoon Bread

MAKES 6 SERVINGS

Unlike corn bread, spoon bread incorporates egg whites that are beaten separately, so it is more like a soufflé than a bread. The soufflé will sink if not served immediately out of the oven, so be sure to have everything on the table at the same time!

2 cups whole milk
1 cup yellow cornmeal
2 tablespoons sugar
1 tablespoon unsalted butter
½ teaspoon salt

6 ounces sharp cheddar cheese, grated
2 teaspoons baking powder
4 large eggs, separated

Preheat the oven to 375°F. Grease a 1½-quart soufflé pan.

Scald the milk in a medium saucepan. Remove from the heat and stir in the cornmeal. Over a very low flame, whisk for 2 minutes. Stir in the salt, sugar, and butter. Add the grated cheese and mix thoroughly. Set aside to cool slightly.

Stir the baking powder into the cornmeal mixture. Beat in the egg yolks.

In a separate bowl, beat the egg whites until stiff. Gently fold the beaten egg whites into the cornmeal mixture. Pour the batter into the prepared soufflé pan and bake 30 minutes, or until puffy and golden.

CHEF JAMIE'S LOW-FAT TIP

This recipe is just perfect for slimming down! Low-fat milk, reduced-fat (50 percent-less-fat) butter, low-fat cheese, and ¼ cup of liquid egg substitute in place of the egg yolks produce a delicious low-fat bread.

			PER SERVING		
STANDARD RECIPE:	CALORIES 334	FAT 19G	PROTEIN 16G	CARBOHYDRATES 27G	CHOL 188MG
REDUCED FAT:	CALORIES 213	FAT 4G	PROTEIN 13G	CARBOHYDRATES 27G	CHOL 10MG

Fresh Corn Pudding

MAKES 6 SERVINGS

This wonderful pudding is a lovely side dish for meat or poultry. The sugar in corn begins to turn to starch as soon as it is picked, so be sure to use the freshest corn you can find.

3 large eggs
¼ cup flour
1 teaspoon salt
½ teaspoon pepper

2 cups fresh corn kernels, cut from the cob
2 cups half & half
2 tablespoons butter, melted

Preheat the oven to 375°F.

In a large mixing bowl, beat the eggs until foamy. In a separate bowl, sift together the flour, salt, and pepper; then sift it again. Stir the sifted mixture into the eggs. Add the corn kernels, half & half, and melted butter, and stir gently to combine.

Pour into a greased 1½-quart casserole dish or individual ramekins. Place the casserole dish or ramekins in another pan and fill the pan with hot water, enough to reach one-quarter up the casserole dish or ramekins.

Bake 1 hour for a large casserole or 30 to 40 minutes for the ramekins, or until a cake tester inserted in the center of the pudding comes out clean. Serve hot.

CHEF JAMIE'S LOW-FAT TIP

Aeration of the eggs is essential to this light and airy pudding, as is the half & half for its creamy texture. To lessen your guilt, try using 3 egg whites and 1 whole egg. Also, use 1 cup of half & half (for creaminess and thickness) and 1 cup of low-fat milk (to lighten the load) for a delicious "lighter" pudding.

HELPFUL HINTS FROM THE WIZARD

• Corn kernels are easily removed from a cob with a shoehorn.

			PER SERVING		
STANDARD RECIPE:	CALORIES 256	FAT 11G	PROTEIN 7G	CARBOHYDRATES 20G	CHOL 155MG
REDUCED FAT:	CALORIES 174	FAT 9G	PROTEIN 7G	CARBOHYDRATES 20G	CHOL 53MG

Chef Jamie's Noodle Kugel

MAKES 6 SERVINGS

This incredible noodle kugel recipe is one of my top ten favorite foods! The cornflake crumbs are the key to a crispy topping, and the pineapple in the creamy noodle mixture adds just the right amount of sweetness!

8 ounces broad egg noodles
1 tablespoon canola oil
½ stick unsalted butter
½ cup sugar
3 large eggs
1 (20-ounce) can crushed pineapple, drained
¾ cup whole milk

¼ cup sour cream
¼ cup golden raisins
1 teaspoon vanilla extract
½ teaspoon cinnamon
1 cup cornflake crumbs
2 tablespoons brown sugar
2 tablespoons unsalted butter, melted

Preheat the oven to 325°F. Grease an 8-inch-square glass baking dish.

Cook the noodles according to package directions. Drain well and toss with the oil to prevent sticking. Set aside.

In a large mixing bowl, cream together the butter and sugar until light and fluffy. Beat in the eggs, one at a time. Add the pineapple, milk, sour cream, raisins, vanilla, and cinnamon; mix well. Add the cooked noodles and mix thoroughly. Spread in the prepared baking dish.

In a separate bowl, mix together the cornflake crumbs, sugar, and butter. Sprinkle the topping over the noodle mixture. Cover the kugel with aluminum foil and bake for 45 minutes. Remove the foil and bake 15 minutes more, or until a knife inserted in the center comes out clean.

CHEF JAMIE'S LOW-FAT TIP

A lighter version of this all-time tasty treat can be prepared using reduced-fat (50 percent-less-fat) butter or non-diet stick margarine, ½ cup of liquid egg substitute and 1 whole egg in place of the 3 eggs, low-fat milk, and light sour cream. Also, for the topping, use 1 egg white in place of the butter for a crisp topping with less fat!

		PER SERVING			
STANDARD RECIPE:	CALORIES 620	FAT 37G	PROTEIN 9G	CARBOHYDRATES 66G	CHOL 223MG
REDUCED FAT:	CALORIES 440	FAT 21G	PROTEIN 8G	CARBOHYDRATES 67G	CHOL 116MG

Twice-Baked Beans

MAKES 16 SERVINGS

This recipe is my take on authentic Boston Baked Beans. You could start from scratch using dried beans, but I find that doctoring the canned baked beans (thereby making them baked twice) intensifies the flavor and makes them taste even better!

12 ounces bacon, sliced
1 yellow onion, diced
2 (24-ounce) cans baked beans
1 (14-ounce) can red kidney beans

1 cup brown sugar
1 cup Dijon mustard
1 cup ketchup
1 (6-ounce) jar chili sauce

Preheat the oven to 200°F.

In a large sauté pan, cook the bacon in batches, reserving the grease. Crumble the cooked bacon and set aside.

In the same sauté pan, using 4 tablespoons of the bacon grease, sauté the onion until tender. Place the sautéed onions in a large, heavy-bottomed, ovenproof pan along with the crumbled bacon, baked beans, kidney beans, brown sugar, mustard, chili sauce, and ketchup. Mix well to combine all of the ingredients.

Cover and bake 5 hours without removing the lid.

CHEF JAMIE'S LOW-FAT TIP

These low-fat baked beans aren't quite as rich as the full-of-fat version in the standard recipe, but they are much better for you. Eliminate the bacon and sauté the onion in 2 tablespoons of olive oil. Look for the low-fat canned baked beans in your local supermarket for an added low-fat bonus.

PER SERVING (½ CUP)

STANDARD RECIPE:	CALORIES 441	FAT 34G	PROTEIN 28G	CARBOHYDRATES 72G	CHOL 50MG
REDUCED FAT:	CALORIES 167	FAT 10G	PROTEIN 13G	CARBOHYDRATES 72G	CHOL 32MG

Sweet & Creamy Coleslaw

MAKES 8 SERVINGS

Coleslaw was created by the Dutch—who called it "koolsla," literally "cabbage salad"—by blending shredded cabbage with dressing. It has since evolved to sometimes include bacon, pickles, peppers, and more, creating probably as many variations as there are cooks!

1 small head of green cabbage, cored and shredded
1 cup red cabbage, shredded
2 large carrots, peeled and grated
1 cup mayonnaise
½ cup sour cream

2 tablespoons heavy cream
1 (10-ounce) can crushed pineapple in its own juice, drained
1 teaspoon caraway seeds
salt & pepper, to taste

Combine the green cabbage, red cabbage, and carrot in a large mixing bowl.

In a separate mixing bowl, whisk together the mayonnaise, sour cream, and heavy cream. Stir in the drained pineapple and the caraway seeds.

Pour the mayonnaise mixture over the cabbage mixture and stir to combine well. Season liberally with salt and pepper. Cover and chill for at least 2 hours before serving.

Toss well and adjust the seasonings before serving.

CHEF JAMIE'S LOW-FAT TIP

Low-fat coleslaw can fool even the greatest slaw lover! Reserve the juice from the can of pineapple if you are making the low-fat version and use 2 tablespoons of pineapple juice in place of the heavy cream. Low-fat mayonnaise and light sour cream will reduce your calorie intake even more!

			PER SERVING		
STANDARD RECIPE:	CALORIES 203	FAT 13G	PROTEIN 2G	CARBOHYDRATES 21G	CHOL 16MG
REDUCED FAT:	CALORIES 142	FAT 3G	PROTEIN 2G	CARBOHYDRATES 22G	CHOL 6MG

Creamed Onions

MAKES 8 SERVINGS

Tender, sweet, and creamy, these tasty onions are fragrant with sage. A variation on the traditional recipe, which uses only heavy cream, this recipe incorporates a pungent cheese. For some people, a Thanksgiving just wouldn't be the same without creamed onions!

2 pounds small white boiling onions or pearl onions
2 (14-ounce) cans chicken broth
1 stick unsalted butter
¾ cup all-purpose flour
⅓ cup heavy cream

2 teaspoons fresh sage, minced, *or* 1 teaspoon dried sage
¾ cup Gruyere or Swiss cheese, cut into cubes
salt & pepper, to taste
¼ cup Parmesan cheese

To peel the onions, score an "X" on the stem end of each onion, then drop in boiling water for 1 minute. Remove the onions from the water and peel.

Place the onions with the chicken broth in a medium-sized pan and gently simmer until just tender, about 30 minutes. Remove the onions from the broth and layer them in a shallow baking dish. Reserve 3 cups of the broth.

Melt the butter in a small saucepan. Add the flour and whisk until smooth. Cook 2 minutes, stirring constantly, until light golden in color. Whisk in the cream and mix to combine well. Remove the sauce from the heat and set aside.

Heat the reserved chicken broth in a large saucepan until boiling. Add the cheese cubes and stir until melted. Whisk in the cream mixture to form a thick, creamy sauce. Stir in the sage and season with salt and pepper.

Pour the sauce over the onions. Sprinkle the Parmesan cheese over the top. Broil until sauce is bubbly and lightly browned.

		PER SERVING		
STANDARD RECIPE:	CALORIES 335	FAT 23G	PROTEIN 12G	CARBOHYDRATES 21G	CHOL 67MG
REDUCED FAT:	CALORIES 235	FAT 12G	PROTEIN 12G	CARBOHYDRATES 21G	CHOL 41MG

CHEF JAMIE'S LOW-FAT TIP

Creamed onions can be made with much less fat and still be delicious! Fifty percent-less-fat butter works well but you may need to cook the butter and flour a bit longer to achieve a light golden color, since the low-fat butter has a higher percentage of water and will therefore take a longer time to evaporate. Use half & half or whole milk in place of the heavy cream to lower your fat intake while preserving creaminess in the dish. Also, low-fat Swiss cheese is delicious and could fool even the harshest critic, since the bold flavor of the cheese masks the loss of fat.

HELPFUL HINTS FROM THE WIZARD

- Mini white pearl onions are the best. Purchase them loose, rather than in sealed bags, to be sure they are fresh.

Creamed Spinach

MAKES 4 SERVINGS

This is serious comfort food! So rich and soooo good! You can steam fresh spinach if you like, but I have found, after many test runs, that frozen chopped spinach, when squeezed of all its juice, works just as well.

2 tablespoons unsalted butter
¼ cup yellow onion, diced
1 garlic clove, chopped
2 (10-ounce) packages frozen chopped spinach, thawed and squeezed dry

½ cup heavy cream
1 tablespoon unsalted butter
3 tablespoons grated Parmesan cheese
salt & pepper, to taste

In a large skillet, melt the butter. Add the onions and garlic, and sauté over medium heat, stirring constantly, until the onions are tender. Add the spinach and mix well. Add the cream and butter; simmer for 5 minutes, or until thick. Stir in the Parmesan cheese and season with salt and pepper.

Serve the creamed spinach as is, or spoon it into individual soufflé dishes. Top each dish with a sprinkle of Parmesan cheese and broil until golden and bubbly. Serve immediately. (You can prepare the creamed spinach in advance and place it in the soufflé cups, then refrigerate until ready to serve. Be sure to reheat the creamed spinach in a 350°F oven, until hot all the way through, before broiling with extra cheese.)

CHEF JAMIE'S LOW-FAT TIP

Low-fat creamed spinach is possible! Use non-stick cooking spray to sauté the onions and garlic, being careful not to burn them. (Add a tablespoon or two of water to the onions when you first start cooking them to help them become tender.) Use reduced-fat (50 percent-less-fat) butter when mixing the creamed spinach, and substitute ¼ cup half & half in place of the heavy cream.

PER SERVING

STANDARD RECIPE:	CALORIES 173	FAT 18G	PROTEIN 3G	CARBOHYDRATES 3G	CHOL 54MG
REDUCED FAT:	CALORIES 64	FAT 5G	PROTEIN 2G	CARBOHYDRATES 2G	CHOL 14MG

Seasoned Collard Greens

MAKES 8 SERVINGS

Collard greens, the ultimate Southern side dish, have been updated here to create the perfect balance of tart and sweet. Bacon is a traditional partner to the greens, but collards certainly can be prepared without it. I like the sweetness of the fruit vinegar in this recipe mixed with the tartness of the greens. The trick to the greens is to cook them until very tender, but not scorched!

4 pounds collard greens, washed thoroughly
½ pound bacon
4 tablespoons unsalted butter
2 tablespoons sugar

1 teaspoon dried red pepper flakes
salt & pepper, to taste
½ cup water
¼ cup fruit vinegar, such as raspberry vinegar

Cut the stems from the greens just below the leaf and discard the stems. Cut the greens into ½-inch strips, being sure to cut across the center vein. Set the greens aside.

In a large stockpot over medium heat, fry the bacon until crisp. Add the butter to the crisp bacon and its grease, then add the cut greens. Sauté over medium-high heat until just beginning to wilt, about 3 minutes. Add the sugar, red pepper flakes, and salt and pepper, along with the water. Stir to combine well. Partially cover and cook over medium heat, stirring occasionally, for 30 minutes, or until the greens are tender; drain. Remove and discard the bacon. Add the vinegar and cook over medium heat for 3 minutes, stirring often.

CHEF JAMIE'S LOW-FAT TIP

Collard greens can be delicious without all the fat. Preparing this recipe with imitation bacon bits makes a huge difference, to say the least! Start by melting 2 tablespoons of butter with 2 tablespoons of olive oil. Add the greens and sauté, stirring often, until they are just beginning to wilt. Add the remaining ingredients and continue the recipe as written above. Stir in ¼ cup of bacon bits just before serving.

HELPFUL HINTS FROM THE WIZARD

• Collard greens are one of nature's most nutritious greens.

		PER SERVING		
STANDARD RECIPE:	CALORIES 288	FAT 26G	PROTEIN 5G	CARBOHYDRATES 11G	CHOL 40MG
REDUCED FAT:	CALORIES 103	FAT 6G	PROTEIN 2G	CARBOHYDRATES 11G	CHOL 17MG

Ginger Candied Carrots

MAKES 4 SERVINGS

These sweet and spicy carrots are not only delicious around the holidays but throughout the year!

8 medium-sized carrots, peeled and
    cut into ¾-inch pieces
3 tablespoons unsalted butter
3 tablespoons brown sugar

1½ teaspoons ground ginger
1 teaspoon freshly grated orange zest
salt & pepper, to taste

Place the carrots in a saucepan with enough cold water to cover. Cook over medium heat until tender, about 20 minutes.

Meanwhile, melt the butter in a small saucepan. Add the brown sugar, ginger, and orange zest, and cook, stirring constantly, until the sugar dissolves completely.

When the carrots are cooked, drain them well and return them to the pan. Pour the butter mixture over the carrots and mix well. Cook over low heat for 5 minutes, stirring occasionally. Serve hot.

CHEF JAMIE'S LOW-FAT TIP

For low-fat candied carrots, use just 1 tablespoon of reduced-fat (50 percent-less-fat) butter in the mix and only 2 tablespoons of brown sugar for a nice balance. Add a tablespoon of orange juice for body. Be sure to toss the carrots with the sauce to coat well.

	PER SERVING				
STANDARD RECIPE:	CALORIES 169	FAT 10G	PROTEIN 2G	CARBOHYDRATES 21G	CHOL 25MG
REDUCED FAT:	CALORIES 128	FAT 5G	PROTEIN 2G	CARBOHYDRATES 21G	CHOL 12MG

Potato Latkes

Great potato pancake recipes are passed from generation to generation. Wonderful memories of celebrating the Jewish holidays at my house come with this recipe, from my family to yours. Some people like to make the pancakes so thin that all of the parts are crispy and crunchy. . .but however you choose to make them, they are so good that they rarely reach the table before being eaten! Latkes can be made small, to serve as an hors d'oeuvre, or large, to accompany a meal.

6 large russet (or Idaho) potatoes, scrubbed
2 tablespoons fresh lemon juice
⅓ cup yellow onion, finely grated
2 large eggs, lightly beaten
1 cup matzo meal or all-purpose flour
½ teaspoon baking powder
salt & pepper, to taste
corn oil, for frying
sour cream and applesauce, for dipping

Using a hand grater or a food processor, coarsely grate the unpeeled potatoes and place in a glass or ceramic bowl. Toss with the lemon juice and let the potatoes sit for 5 minutes to allow them to release their liquid.

Transfer the potatoes to a large colander and drain well. Squeeze out any remaining liquid and place them back into the bowl.

Using a fork, stir the grated onion, eggs, matzo meal, and baking powder into the drained potatoes and mix thoroughly. Season liberally with salt and pepper.

Heat ⅛ inch of oil in a large non-stick skillet over medium-high heat. Using a slotted spoon, drop level spoonfuls of the potato mixture into the hot oil. Flatten the pancakes slightly and sauté until golden on both sides, about 2 minutes per side. As the pancakes are cooked, drain on paper towels and keep warm.

Add more oil to the skillet as needed for additional batches. Serve the pancakes immediately with sour cream and applesauce.

PER SERVING (4 LATKES)

	CALORIES	FAT	PROTEIN	CARBOHYDRATES	CHOL
STANDARD RECIPE:	442	53G	10G	62G	107MG
REDUCED FAT:	311	2.5G	10G	62G	107MG

Potato Latkes *(continued)*

Potato Latkes (continued)

CHEF JAMIE'S LOW-FAT TIP

For lower-fat latkes, use an infinitely smaller amount of oil! Heat the pan until medium-hot (the latkes tend to burn easier without the oil), then coat it with 1 teaspoon of canola oil. Cook the latkes until golden brown on both sides, adding an additional teaspoon of oil to the pan before turning the pancakes over. An even slimmer version can be prepared using non-stick cooking spray to coat the pan, with no oil at all! (The reduced-fat analysis uses non-stick cooking spray.)

HELPFUL HINTS FROM THE WIZARD

- Matzo meal works better than flour in this recipe, giving the pancake a more solid texture and some extra flavor.

Eggplant Fritters

MAKES ABOUT 1 DOZEN

A noted cook in Louisiana passed this recipe on to my Mom and me. It is not only a delicious comfort food, but also a good way to get kids to eat their vegetables. The fritters taste best when eaten hot, and the batter keeps uncooked in the refrigerator for 1 to 2 days.

1 medium-size eggplant
1 large egg
¼ to ⅓ cup all-purpose flour
1 ½ teaspoons baking powder
1 teaspoon vanilla extract

whole milk, as needed
canola oil, for frying
½ cup sugar, plus additional sugar
    for dusting

Preheat the oven to 350°F. Prick the eggplant with a fork about 8 to 10 times to allow the air to release during baking. Place the eggplant on a cookie sheet and roast for 45 minutes or until very tender. Allow to cool slightly, then scoop out the inside and, in a mixing bowl, mash well. Discard the skin.

Add the egg, flour, baking powder, vanilla, and just enough milk to the eggplant to make a stiff batter. (Think stiff biscuit dough).

Drop the batter by spoonfuls into hot oil. Fry until golden brown on all sides. Remove the fritters with a slotted spoon to paper towels and sprinkle with sugar. Enjoy immediately.

CHEF JAMIE'S LOW-FAT TIP

Baking instead of frying makes for a healthier fritter. Spray a cookie sheet liberally with non-stick cooking spray and place the spoonfuls of batter on the prepared sheet. Spray the tops of the unbaked fritters with non-stick cooking spray to aid in crisping. Bake at 425°F for about 30 minutes, or until golden and cooked through, turning once to ensure all-over color. Also, you won't sacrifice any flavor using low-fat milk in this recipe!

			PER FRITTER		
STANDARD RECIPE:	CALORIES 199	FAT 16G	PROTEIN 2G	CARBOHYDRATES 18G	CHOL 19MG
REDUCED FAT:	CALORIES 74	FAT 1G	PROTEIN 2G	CARBOHYDRATES 18G	CHOL 19MG

Zucchini Pancakes

MAKES 4 LARGE PANCAKES OR 12 MINI PANCAKES

The vast summer crop of zucchini encourages all of us to expand our repertoire of recipes for this prolific vegetable. There is evidence of squash being eaten in Mexico as far back as 550 B.C., and zucchini, a member of the squash family, is still the most widely eaten squash today. These pancakes make an elegant side dish for meat, fish, or chicken, and are also delicious when topped with a dollop of dilled sour cream and served as an hors d'oeuvre.

2 cups coarsely grated zucchini
2 large eggs, beaten
¼ cup yellow onion, minced
½ cup all-purpose flour
½ teaspoon baking powder
salt & pepper, to taste
¼ teaspoon dried oregano
canola oil, for frying

Place the zucchini in a large strainer and press out as much moisture as possible. In a large mixing bowl, combine the drained zucchini, eggs, and onion, stirring to combine well.

In a separate bowl, combine the flour, baking powder, salt, pepper, and oregano. Stir the dry ingredients into the zucchini mixture. Mix well.

Using a large sauté pan, heat ¼ inch of oil over medium-high heat. Drop the dough by tablespoons into the hot oil and press lightly to form small pancakes. Cook, turning once, until golden brown on both sides. Remove the pancakes from the oil and drain briefly on paper towels. Serve immediately.

CHEF JAMIE'S LOW-FAT TIP

These tasty little pancakes are delicious minus the oil. After preparing the batter, heat a large non-stick skillet over medium heat. Spray the pan liberally with non-stick cooking spray and sauté the pancakes over medium heat until golden on both sides and cooked through. Be sure to spray the pan liberally with cooking spray again before turning the pancakes!

HELPFUL HINTS FROM THE WIZARD

• Mixing the batter frequently will aerate it, producing lighter pancakes.

		PER LARGE PANCAKE			
STANDARD RECIPE:	CALORIES 159	FAT 16G	PROTEIN 5G	CARBOHYDRATES 16G	CHOL 109MG
REDUCED FAT:	CALORIES 107	FAT 2G	PROTEIN 5G	CARBOHYDRATES 16G	CHOL 109MG

Quick Corn Relish

There is nothing more delicious than fresh, sweet corn, rushed from the garden to your kitchen. This wonderful corn relish keeps indefinitely in the refrigerator, and the flavor only improves with time!

1 cup white wine vinegar
⅓ cup sugar
2 teaspoons salt
1 teaspoon celery seed
½ teaspoon mustard seed
½ teaspoon Tabasco

3 cups cooked corn kernels or 2 (16-ounce) cans whole kernel corn, drained
¼ cup green bell pepper, minced
2 tablespoons green onion, minced
2 tablespoons chopped pimento
2 tablespoons olive oil

Combine the vinegar, sugar, salt, celery seed, mustard seed, and Tabasco in a large nonreactive saucepan. Bring to a boil over medium heat. Cook for 2 minutes, then remove from the heat and cool.

Place the remaining ingredients in a large mixing bowl. Add the cooled vinegar mixture and stir to combine.

Store in an airtight container in the refrigerator.

CHEF JAMIE'S LOW-FAT TIP

Relishes, by nature, are usually quite low in fat and full of flavor. Eliminating the olive oil in this recipe (it adds a bit of flavor and texture, but can be left out) sacrifices very little taste and creates a terrific low-fat side dish, accompaniment, or healthy snack!

HELPFUL HINTS FROM THE WIZARD

• The milder green Tabasco may be used, if desired.

			PER SERVING		
STANDARD RECIPE:	CALORIES 326	FAT 9G	PROTEIN 4G	CARBOHYDRATES 65G	CHOL 0MG
REDUCED FAT:	CALORIES 266	FAT 2G	PROTEIN 4G	CARBOHYDRATES 65G	CHOL 0MG

Cold Cucumber Sauce

MAKES 1 ½ CUPS

This traditional Greek sauce, known as tzatziki, is often served as a dip with pita bread, or as sauce for cold poached salmon or lamb. Popular versions of this cucumber and yogurt dish are served throughout the Middle East, each with its own slight variation. The Greek version contains the most garlic!

2 cups plain yogurt
1 cup cucumber, peeled, seeded, and shredded
1 teaspoon lemon juice

1 garlic clove, minced
¼ teaspoon sugar
salt & pepper, to taste

Line a fine sieve with a large piece of cheesecloth. Place the yogurt in the sieve and let it drain over a bowl for 2 hours in the refrigerator.

Discard the drained liquid and place the thickened yogurt in a mixing bowl. Stir in the cucumber, lemon juice, garlic, sugar, and salt and pepper.

Refrigerate 1 hour before serving.

CHEF JAMIE'S LOW-FAT TIP

Create a fat-free cucumber sauce by using non-fat plain yogurt.

HELPFUL HINTS FROM THE WIZARD

- To remove the bitterness from a cucumber, just slice off 1 inch from the end of the cucumber and rub the two exposed surfaces together in a circular motion, then pull them apart. Repeat with the other end. This will neutralize the chemical in the cucumber that causes bitterness.

PER SERVING (¼ CUP)

STANDARD RECIPE:	CALORIES 47	FAT 3G	PROTEIN 3G	CARBOHYDRATES 4G	CHOL 10MG
REDUCED FAT:	CALORIES 44	FAT 0G	PROTEIN 3G	CARBOHYDRATES 5G	CHOL 4MG

Homemade Tartar Sauce

MAKES 1 ½ CUPS

I love tartar sauce on fried fish, crab cakes, and catfish! It tastes best when made fresh.

1 cup mayonnaise
2 tablespoons fresh lemon juice
dash of Tabasco
¼ cup pickle relish

¼ cup fresh parsley, chopped
2 tablespoons shallots, minced
2 tablespoons capers, finely chopped
salt & pepper, to taste

Combine the mayonnaise, lemon juice, and Tabasco in a mixing bowl and whisk to combine. Stir in the relish, parsley, shallots, and capers. Season to taste with salt and pepper. Cover the sauce and refrigerate for 1 hour before serving.

CHEF JAMIE'S LOW-FAT TIP
To make non-fat tartar sauce, substitute fat-free mayonnaise for the full-of-fat kind.

PER SERVING (2 TABLESPOONS)					
STANDARD RECIPE:	CALORIES 42	FAT 4G	PROTEIN .1G	CARBOHYDRATES 3G	CHOL 3MG
REDUCED FAT:	CALORIES 36	FAT 0G	PROTEIN .1G	CARBOHYDRATES 3G	CHOL 1.6MG

Chapter 10

Bakers' Delights—
Savory & Sweet

There is no scent more welcoming than that of freshly baked bread. Hearty Russian black bread, sesame dinner rolls, and quickbreads like cranberry bread and zucchini bread add depth to any meal. Whether you decide on sweet or savory breads, you'll find that the satisfaction that comes from baking is immeasurable!

Sweet Cream Biscuits

MAKES 6 DOZEN

The word "biscuit" comes from the French "bis cuit," meaning twice cooked, and in France refers to a flat, thin cookie or cracker. This American version has come a long way! They are light, fluffy, and tender. Biscuits freeze beautifully. . . but don't be surprised if they disappear before you can wrap any up!

1¾ cups all-purpose flour
1 tablespoon sugar
1 tablespoon baking powder
½ teaspoon salt

6 tablespoons cold unsalted butter, cut into small pieces
¾ cup heavy cream

Preheat the oven to 450°F.

Sift the flour, sugar, baking powder, and salt together into a large mixing bowl. Using a pastry blender or your fingertips, cut the butter into the dry ingredients until the mixture resembles coarse crumbs. Add the cream and stir until just combined; do not over mix.

Turn the dough out onto a floured surface and knead just until the dough forms. Pat out the dough to ¼-inch thickness.

Cut out rounds using a small biscuit cutter (¾-inch or 1-inch in diameter). Gather the dough scraps and pat out the dough again. Cut out additional rounds and continue using gathered dough scraps until all is used.

Transfer the rounds to an ungreased cookie sheet. Bake 10 minutes, or until golden brown.

CHEF JAMIE'S LOW-FAT TIP

This recipe becomes lower in fat when you use buttermilk in place of cream and reduced-fat (50 percent-less-fat) butter in place of regular butter. Add 1 tablespoon of minced fresh herbs, rosemary, or thyme, for added flavor.

HELPFUL HINTS FROM THE WIZARD

- When kneading dough, keep in mind that a wooden board works better than plastic or glass. The dough tends to catch better on the wood and is easier to work with.

			PER BISCUIT		
STANDARD RECIPE:	CALORIES 27	FAT 2G	PROTEIN .4G	CARBOHYDRATES 3G	CHOL 5MG
REDUCED FAT:	CALORIES 19	FAT 1G	PROTEIN .4G	CARBOHYDRATES 3G	CHOL 4MG

Russian Black Bread

MAKES 2 LOAVES (28 SERVINGS)

This is one of the best homemade bread recipes, especially warm from the oven, when the hearty loaf is served buttered and topped with thin slices of sweet red onion.

2 ½ cups water
½ stick unsalted butter
¼ cup white vinegar
¼ cup dark molasses
1 ounce (1 square) unsweetened chocolate
4 cups rye flour
2 cups whole-bran cereal

2 packages (2 tablespoons) dry yeast
2 tablespoons caraway seeds, crushed
2 teaspoons instant coffee
2 teaspoons salt
1 teaspoon sugar
½ teaspoon fennel seeds, crushed
2 ½ to 3 cups all-purpose flour

Lightly grease a large bowl and 2 standard-size loaf pans.

In a 2-quart saucepan, combine the water, butter, vinegar, molasses, and chocolate. Place over medium heat and cook, stirring often, until the chocolate is just melted, but is still lukewarm. Transfer to the bowl of an electric mixer.

In a separate mixing bowl, combine the rye flour, bran cereal, yeast, caraway seeds, coffee, salt, sugar, and fennel seeds. Add to the wet mixture in the mixer.

On low speed, begin beating. Gradually add the all-purpose flour, about ½ cup at a time, to make a soft dough. After all of the flour has been added, beat 3 minutes.

Turn onto a lightly floured work surface. Cover with a bowl and allow to rest for 15 minutes. Knead the dough until smooth and elastic, about 10 minutes, adding additional all-purpose flour as needed. Place the kneaded dough in the greased bowl, turning to coat the entire surface. Cover with plastic wrap and set it in a warm place until the dough doubles in size. (Setting the bowl on top of the clothes dryer, on low heat, works especially well for this process, called proofing.)

Preheat the oven to 350°F.

Punch down the dough and turn it onto a lightly floured work surface. Cut in half and shape into 2 balls. Place the dough in the prepared pans. Cover with plastic wrap and leave in a warm place, once again, until the dough doubles in size.

		PER SLICE		
STANDARD RECIPE:	CALORIES 152	FAT 5G	PROTEIN 5G	CARBOHYDRATES 38G	CHOL 9MG
REDUCED FAT:	CALORIES136	FAT 3G	PROTEIN 5G	CARBOHYDRATES 38G	CHOL 5MG

Place the pans in the oven, on the center rack, and bake 45 minutes, or until the loaves sound hollow when tapped. Remove the breads from the pans and allow them to cool on racks.

CHEF JAMIE'S LOW-FAT TIP
This bread is so full of goodness that it needs little fat to make it delicious. Reduced-fat (50 percent-less-fat) butter or non-diet stick margarine can substitute for real butter, and non-stick cooking spray works well for greasing the bowl and the pans.

Homemade Hamburger Buns

MAKES 24

A really great hamburger or cheeseburger on a homemade bun is hard to resist.

8 cups all-purpose flour
2 packages (2 tablespoons) active dry yeast
2 cups warm (not hot) water

¾ cup vegetable oil
⅓ cup sugar
1 tablespoon salt
3 large eggs

In a large mixing bowl, combine 4 cups of the flour with the yeast.

In a separate bowl, combine the water, oil, sugar, and salt. Mix well. Add the liquid mixture to the flour mixture and stir just until combined. Let stand 5 minutes.

Meanwhile, beat the eggs with an electric mixer on low speed for 30 seconds. Turn the speed to high and beat the eggs for 3 minutes longer.

Add the beaten eggs to the flour/water mixture, along with the remaining 4 cups of flour. Mix well to form a ball of dough. Turn out onto a well-floured surface and knead the dough until smooth. Place in a large greased bowl, turning once to coat the surface. Cover with plastic wrap and let rise in a warm place until the dough has doubled in size.

Preheat the oven to 375°F.

Punch down the dough and divide it into 3 sections. Cover and let rise for 5 minutes.

Divide each portion into 8 equal balls and turn each ball in your hands to fold the edges under and make even circles. Press the balls flat. Place the disks of dough on a greased baking sheet and let rise until doubled in size.

Bake the buns for 10 minutes or until golden.

CHEF JAMIE'S LOW-FAT TIP

You can make this recipe lighter by reducing the vegetable oil to ½ cup and using 2 eggs and ¼ cup of liquid egg substitute in place of the 3 whole eggs. Be prepared for a slightly stiffer dough and a bit more kneading. For a healthier version, use 100 percent whole-wheat flour and canola oil.

PER BUN

STANDARD RECIPE:	CALORIES 232	FAT 8G	PROTEIN 5G	CARBOHYDRATES 34G	CHOL 27MG
REDUCED FAT:	CALORIES 198	FAT 4G	PROTEIN 5G	CARBOHYDRATES 34G	CHOL 18MG

Sesame Dinner Rolls

MAKES 3 DOZEN

These crusty rolls are made from a treasured old-fashioned recipe.

4 cups warm water (120°F to 130°F)
1 tablespoon salt
1 tablespoon sugar

8 to 9 cups all-purpose flour
3 packages (3 tablespoons) dry yeast
1 cup sesame seeds

Grease a large bowl and 3 (12-compartment) muffin tins.

In a mixing bowl, combine the water, salt, and sugar; stir to dissolve.

In the bowl of an electric mixer, combine 4 cups of the flour with the yeast. Add the water and beat until well combined, about 3 minutes. Leave in the bowl and cover with plastic wrap. Set in a warm place and allow the dough to rise until doubled in size.

Add the remaining flour to the dough and knead until smooth and elastic (the dough will be quite sticky). Place the dough in the greased bowl, turning to coat the entire surface. Cover with plastic wrap and set in a warm place until the dough doubles in size. (Setting the bowl on top of the clothes dryer, turned on low, works especially well for this process, called proofing.)

Preheat the oven to 400°F.

Punch the dough down and knead briefly. Cut into 6 even pieces and cut each piece into 6 even pieces again (in the end, you will have 36 pieces). Shape the dough into balls (lightly oiling your hands makes shaping easier). Roll each ball in sesame seeds and place in the prepared muffin tins. Cover the tins lightly with plastic wrap and let rise in a warm place until doubled in size.

Bake 20 to 30 minutes, or until golden brown.

CHEF JAMIE'S LOW-FAT TIP

Eliminating the sesame seeds to make plain dinner rolls makes these piping-hot goodies almost fat-free.

		PER ROLL		
STANDARD RECIPE:	CALORIES 115	FAT 2.2G	PROTEIN 3G	CARBOHYDRATES 24G	CHOL 0MG
REDUCED FAT:	CALORIES 115	FAT .3G	PROTEIN 3G	CARBOHYDRATES 24G	CHOL 0MG

Skillet Corn Bread

MAKES 8 SERVINGS

Crisp on the outside and crumbly on the inside, this flavorful bread is hard to resist.

2 teaspoons canola oil
½ cup yellow cornmeal
½ cup white cornmeal
½ cup all-purpose flour
¼ cup sugar
1 teaspoon baking powder
pinch of salt

2 large eggs
½ cup milk
⅓ cup vegetable oil
1 (15-ounce) can cream-style corn
1 (4-ounce) can diced mild green
   chiles, drained

Preheat the oven to 400°F. Oil a 10-inch cast-iron skillet using the canola oil, covering the bottom and sides of the pan well. Place the skillet in the oven while the oven is heating.

Combine the yellow and white cornmeal, flour, sugar, baking powder, and salt in a large mixing bowl.

In a separate bowl, combine the eggs, milk, and vegetable oil. Add the liquid mixture to the cornmeal mixture and stir just until combined. Stir in the corn and chiles.

Remove the hot skillet from the oven and pour the batter into the skillet. Bake for 20 to 25 minutes, or until a cake tester inserted in the center comes out clean. Invert the corn bread onto a plate, then, using another plate, turn the corn bread right side up. Cut into wedges and serve.

Chef's Note: If you don't have a cast-iron skillet, don't fret! Use a greased 8-inch-square baking pan instead.

CHEF JAMIE'S LOW-FAT TIP

Robustly flavored corn bread, like this one, can easily be made low in fat. Use 1 egg plus ¼ cup of liquid egg substitute, reduced-fat (50 percent-less-fat) butter, and non-fat milk. You can cut the oil down to ¼ cup without losing much, but don't eliminate it completely or the soft texture of the bread will be lost entirely. Spray the pan with non-stick cooking spray instead of greasing it with oil for an added cutback or, to lower the fat even more, heat the pan in the oven without the coating of oil. Spray the hot pan with non-stick cooking spray before adding the batter.

PER SERVING

STANDARD RECIPE:	CALORIES 355	FAT 19G	PROTEIN 6G	CARBOHYDRATES 41G	CHOL 68MG
REDUCED FAT:	CALORIES 312	FAT 11G	PROTEIN 6G	CARBOHYDRATES 43G	CHOL 27MG

Zucchini Bread

MAKES 2 LOAVES OR 1 BUNDT CAKE (16 SERVINGS)

For the best flavor, wrap the bread once it's cool and let it stand overnight before serving. This cake-like tea bread freezes well, too!

4 large eggs
2 cups sugar
1 cup vegetable oil
3 cups shredded zucchini, blotted dry
3 cups all-purpose flour

1½ teaspoon baking soda
1½ teaspoon baking powder
1 teaspoon salt
1 teaspoon cinnamon
¼ teaspoon ground cloves
1 cup chopped walnuts, optional

Preheat the oven to 350°F. Grease and flour 2 loaf pans or 1 bundt pan.

In a large mixing bowl, whisk together the eggs, sugar, and oil until well combined. Stir in the zucchini to coat.

In a separate bowl, sift together the flour, baking soda, baking powder, salt, cinnamon, and cloves. Add the sifted mixture to the zucchini mixture, and mix well. Stir in the walnuts.

Pour the batter into the prepared pans. Bake 1 hour, or until a cake tester inserted into the center of the cake comes out clean.

CHEF JAMIE'S LOW-FAT TIP

Using applesauce in place of half of the oil produces great results in this quick bread. The applesauce adds incredible moisture, and its smooth texture fools your mouth into thinking "This can't be low fat!" Use 2 whole eggs and ½ cup of liquid egg substitute and eliminate the walnuts for a truly light and delicious bread. (Note: Reduced-fat recipe analysis was calculated without walnuts.)

PER SERVING

STANDARD RECIPE:	CALORIES 292	FAT 11G	PROTEIN 6G	CARBOHYDRATES 42G	CHOL 53MG
REDUCED FAT:	CALORIES 186	FAT 4G	PROTEIN 3G	CARBOHYDRATES 44G	CHOL 26MG

Peach–Pecan Muffins

MAKES 10

The secret to these sweet and flavorful muffins is the preserves. . . they keep the muffins moist and tender! These easy goodies make a perfect breakfast treat, but they also make a great accompaniment at a summer barbecue or picnic.

1 ¾ cups all-purpose flour
½ cup sugar
1 teaspoon baking powder
½ teaspoon baking soda
½ teaspoon salt

½ cup sour cream
½ cup peach preserves
1 large egg
1 teaspoon vanilla extract
1 cup chopped pecans, toasted

Preheat the oven to 400°F. Line 10 muffin cups with cupcake papers.

Sift together the flour, sugar, baking powder, baking soda, and salt into a large mixing bowl.

In a separate bowl, whisk together the sour cream, preserves, egg, and vanilla. Mix well. Add the sour cream mixture and the pecans to the dry ingredients, and stir just until combined; do not over mix.

Divide the batter among the muffin cups. Bake 20 minutes, or until a cake tester inserted in the center of the muffins comes out clean. Cool 15 minutes before serving.

CHEF JAMIE'S LOW-FAT TIP

This recipe actually tastes incredible in its low-fat form (fat from the pecans remains, but there is no added fat). Use fat-free sour cream, ¼ cup liquid egg substitute in place of the egg, and only ¼ cup of the pecans for an incredible low-fat treat.

HELPFUL HINTS FROM THE WIZARD

* For the best results, make sure the baking soda and baking powder are fresh.

	PER MUFFIN				
STANDARD RECIPE:	CALORIES 335	FAT 18G	PROTEIN 5G	CARBOHYDRATES 60G	CHOL 21MG
REDUCED FAT:	CALORIES 219	FAT 4G	PROTEIN 2G	CARBOHYDRATES 39G	CHOL 4MG

Lana's Pumpkin Bread

MAKES 1 LOAF (12 SERVINGS)

Everyone seems to love my mom's pumpkin bread, with its sweet, spicy aroma. It is so easy to prepare and it freezes beautifully, too.

1 cup sugar
⅓ cup dark molasses
½ cup vegetable oil
2 large eggs
1 cup pumpkin puree (canned or fresh)
1 tablespoon freshly grated orange zest

1⅓ cups all-purpose flour
½ teaspoon nutmeg
½ teaspoon cinnamon
½ teaspoon ground cloves
½ teaspoon salt
¼ teaspoon baking powder
1 cup chopped walnuts

Preheat the oven to 350°F. Lightly oil a 9-inch loaf pan.

Using an electric mixer, beat together the sugar, molasses, and oil. Add the eggs, one at a time, beating well after each addition. Add the pumpkin and orange zest; blend thoroughly. Sift the flour, nutmeg, cinnamon, cloves, salt, and baking powder into the pumpkin mixture; blend well. Stir in the walnuts.

Pour the batter into the prepared pan and bake for 1½ hours, or until a toothpick inserted in the center of the loaf comes out clean.

Allow the bread to cool for ½ hour before removing from the pan.

CHEF JAMIE'S LOW-FAT TIP

Create a low-fat bread by replacing half of the oil with smooth applesauce. The 2 whole eggs can be replaced with 1 whole egg and ¼ cup liquid egg substitute. Reduce the nuts to ¼ cup for just a hint of texture.

	PER SERVING				
STANDARD RECIPE:	CALORIES 424	FAT 22G	PROTEIN 6G	CARBOHYDRATES 52G	CHOL 36MG
REDUCED FAT:	CALORIES 311	FAT 13G	PROTEIN 5G	CARBOHYDRATES 52G	CHOL 18MG

Cranberry Bread

MAKES 1 LOAF (10 SERVINGS)

This sweet-tart loaf is perfect for breakfast, at teatime, or as a simple dessert. When baked in miniature loaf pans, cranberry bread is also a lovely homemade holiday gift! The trick to bringing this bread to its full potential is allowing the flavors to mellow for a full day before you serve it!

2 cups all-purpose flour
½ cup sugar
1 tablespoon baking powder
½ teaspoon salt
⅓ cup apple juice
2 large eggs, lightly beaten

3 tablespoons (1½ ounces) unsalted butter melted
1 teaspoon vanilla extract
1¼ cups cranberries, coarsely chopped
½ cup chopped walnuts

Preheat the oven to 350°F. Grease a 9-inch loaf pan.

Sift the flour, sugar, baking powder, and salt into a large mixing bowl.

Make a well in the center of the flour mixture and pour in the apple juice, eggs, melted butter, and vanilla. Mix the ingredients just to combine. Do not over mix. Fold in the walnuts and cranberries.

Pour the batter into the prepared pan and bake for 45 to 50 minutes, or until a cake tester inserted in the center comes out clean.

Allow to cool in the pan for 10 minutes. Remove from the pan and cool completely on a rack.

Wrap the bread well with plastic wrap and leave it on the counter for one day before serving.

CHEF JAMIE'S LOW-FAT TIP

My friends and family hail my low-fat cranberry bread as a great success! Use 1 whole egg instead of 2 eggs, and use 2 tablespoons of canola oil or reduced-fat (50 percent-less-fat) butter in place of the butter in the original recipe. I also found a way to make this delectable bread with no added sugar by using 6 ounces of frozen apple juice concentrate, thawed but not diluted, in place of the sugar *and* the regular apple juice in the recipe! The low-fat, no-sugar-added bread turned out to be quite delicious!

HELPFUL HINTS FROM THE WIZARD

- To check cranberries to see if they are fresh, just bounce them. If they are firm and bounce back, you have fresh berries!

			PER SLICE		
STANDARD RECIPE:	CALORIES 247	FAT 13G	PROTEIN 8G	CARBOHYDRATES 35G	CHOL 35MG
REDUCED FAT:	CALORIES 188	FAT 8G	PROTEIN 8G	CARBOHYDRATES 28G	CHOL 23MG

Chapter 11

Desserts—
Ending the Meal
with a Flair

*W*ho doesn't love a happy ending? Dark, rich
devil's food cake, dreamy coconut cake, classic
apple pie, summer berry trifle. . .one of the scrumptious
traditional desserts in this chapter is sure to spark
childhood memories and satisfy your sweet tooth.

Devil's Food Cake

MAKES 12 SERVINGS

Devil's Food Cake was allegedly named for the belief that consuming the rich, dark, incredibly chocolaty treat could cause one to faint. While traditionally all chocolate, this version of the cake has a fluffy white frosting that you could eat with a spoon, without even missing the cake! The cake batter is wonderfully moist from the addition of sour cream, and is perfectly light and airy because of the careful sifting.

For the cake:
4 cups cake flour
3 cups sugar
½ cup cocoa powder
2 teaspoons baking soda
pinch of salt
4 large eggs
2 teaspoons vanilla extract
2 cups sour cream
2 cups buttermilk

For the frosting:
1 cup sugar
3 egg whites
¼ cup light corn syrup
3 tablespoons water
¼ teaspoon cream of tartar
1 teaspoon vanilla extract

Preheat the oven to 350°F. Grease two 9-inch round cake pans.

To make the cake: Sift cake flour, sugar, cocoa powder, baking soda, and salt together three times. In a separate bowl, beat the eggs with the vanilla until light and foamy. Add the sour cream and buttermilk and blend well. Fold in the dry ingredients, just until combined. Do not over mix.

Pour the batter into the prepared cake pans and bake 30 minutes, or until a cake tester inserted in the center of the cake comes out clean. Allow to cool for 10 minutes, then remove the cakes from the pans. Cool completely before frosting.

To make the frosting: Combine all of the ingredients in the top of a double boiler. Over simmering water, beat with an electric mixer until peaks form when beaters are raised. Remove from the heat and beat in the vanilla. Cool the frosting before spreading on the cakes.

To assemble the cake, place one layer on a cake plate. Spread the top with a ½-inch layer of frosting. Top with the remaining cake layer. Frost the top and sides to cover completely.

CHEF JAMIE'S LOW-FAT TIP

The low-fat version of this recipe is just as flavorful as the original. Substitute 2 eggs and ½ cup of liquid egg substitute for the 4 whole eggs and use light sour cream and low-fat buttermilk in the batter. As for the frosting, it's delectably fat-free already!

		PER SERVING		
STANDARD RECIPE:	CALORIES 578	FAT 10G	PROTEIN 11G	CARBOHYDRATES 115G	CHOL 86MG
REDUCED FAT:	CALORIES 543	FAT 4G	PROTEIN 11G	CARBOHYDRATES 115G	CHOL 44MG

Chocolate Cocoa Cake

MAKES 12 SERVINGS

Before the 1900s, around the time Hershey's Cocoa was first marketed, chocolate was considered an unconventional flavoring for cakes. It wasn't until after World War I that cocoa powder was used for much more than just making hot cocoa.

For the cake:
unsalted butter, for greasing the pans
cocoa, for dusting the pans
2 cups sugar
1¾ cups all-purpose flour
¾ cup unsweetened cocoa
1½ teaspoons baking powder
1½ teaspoons baking soda
1 teaspoon salt
1 cup milk, room temperature

½ cup vegetable oil
2 large eggs, lightly beaten
2 teaspoons pure vanilla extract
1 cup boiling water

For the frosting:
2 sticks (8 ounces) unsalted butter
1⅓ cups unsweetened cocoa
6 cups powdered sugar, sifted
⅓ cup milk (more if needed)
2 teaspoons vanilla extract

Preheat the oven to 350°. Lightly butter two 9-inch round cake pans. Line the bottom of the pans with parchment paper and dust the sides with cocoa; tap out excess. Set aside.

To make the cake: In a large bowl, combine the sugar, flour, cocoa powder, baking powder, baking soda, and salt. Add the oil, milk, eggs, and vanilla. Using an electric mixer on medium speed, beat for 2 minutes. Add the boiling water and beat to combine (batter will be thin). Divide evenly between the prepared pans.

Bake 30 to 35 minutes, or until a tester inserted in the center comes out clean. Cool the cakes in the pans for 10 minutes. Run a small knife around the edges to loosen the cakes from the pans. Invert onto wire racks to cool completely.

To make the frosting: In a medium saucepan, melt the butter. Add the cocoa, and beat with an electric mixer to blend well.

Alternately add the powdered sugar and milk, beating on medium speed until frosting reaches a spreading consistency. Add vanilla and beat to combine. Add more milk as needed to achieve a good consistency for frosting.

	PER SERVING				
STANDARD RECIPE:	CALORIES 901	FAT 30G	PROTEIN 5G	CARBOHYDRATES 144G	CHOL 84MG
REDUCED FAT:	CALORIES 793	FAT 19G	PROTEIN 5G	CARBOHYDRATES 139G	CHOL 79MG

To assemble the cake: Place one layer on a serving plate and frost with 1 cup frosting. Top with the remaining cake layer, bottom side up, and frost the entire cake with remaining frosting.

CHEF JAMIE'S LOW-FAT TIP

For the cake, substitute 50 percent-less-fat butter for the oil, but be sure to have the eggs and milk at room temperature so the butter does not coagulate. You can also substitute ¼ cup of liquid egg substitute for 1 of the whole eggs, to lower your cholesterol. For the frosting, use my recipe below. Use non-fat cream cheese in place of the light cream cheese to lower the fat content even more.

REDUCED-FAT CHOCOLATE FROSTING

8 ounces light cream cheese

4 tablespoons diet margarine, softened

6 tablespoons non-fat milk

6 cups powdered sugar

1 ½ cups unsweetened cocoa

pinch of salt

2 teaspoons vanilla extract

In a large mixing bowl, beat together the cream cheese, margarine, and milk until smooth. In a separate bowl, combine the sugar, cocoa, and salt. Gradually add the sugar mixture to the cream cheese mixture, beating at low speed until well blended. Add vanilla and beat to combine. Makes about 4 cups, enough to frost a 2-layer cake.

Dreamy Coconut Cake

MAKES 12 SERVINGS

This incredible coconut cake was originally served at the famous Brown Derby Restaurant in Hollywood. This decadent creation is made especially delicious with the addition of grapefruit juice to the batter. I have topped the cake with my favorite white frosting to create the ultimate dessert!

For the cake:
1½ cups cake flour
¾ cup sugar
1½ teaspoons baking powder
¼ teaspoon salt
½ cup vegetable oil
¼ cup water
3 large eggs, separated
3 tablespoons grapefruit juice
1 teaspoon freshly grated lemon zest
¼ teaspoon cream of tartar

For the frosting:
¾ cup sugar
¼ cup light corn syrup
¼ cup water
3 egg whites, at room temperature
1 teaspoon vanilla extract
½ teaspoon almond extract

To assemble:
1½ cups shredded coconut

Preheat the oven to 350°F. Grease a 9-inch springform pan.

To make the cake: Sift the flour, sugar, baking powder, and salt in a large mixing bowl. Make a well in the center of the dry ingredients and add the water, oil, egg yolks, grapefruit juice, and lemon zest. Using an electric mixer, beat until very smooth.

In a separate bowl, beat the egg whites with the cream of tartar until stiff peaks form. Gently fold the beaten egg whites into the batter until just combined. Do not over mix. Pour the batter into the prepared pan and bake about 25 minutes, or until the top of the cake springs back lightly when touched. Cool the cake in the pan for 15 minutes, then loosen the edges of the cake with a knife and remove it from the pan. Allow to cool completely before frosting.

To make the frosting: Combine the sugar, corn syrup, and water in a saucepan. Insert a candy thermometer and partly cover the pan. Bring to a boil over medium heat. Remove the lid and boil without stirring until the thermometer registers 240°F.

	PER SERVING				
STANDARD RECIPE:	CALORIES 260	FAT 12G	PROTEIN 4G	CARBOHYDRATES 51G	CHOL 53MG
REDUCED FAT:	CALORIES 190	FAT 2G	PROTEIN 4G	CARBOHYDRATES 52G	CHOL 30MG

Meanwhile (before the syrup reaches 240°F), beat the egg whites, using an electric mixer, until soft peaks form. When the syrup reaches the proper temperature, set the mixer containing the egg whites on high speed. Carefully pour the syrup into the egg whites in a slow, thin stream. Beat the frosting until glossy and firm enough to hold shape. Beat in the vanilla and almond extracts.

To assemble the cake: Cut the cake in half horizontally, using a serrated knife, to make 2 even layers. Place one layer on a serving platter and top with ⅓ of the frosting. Spread the frosting to cover, then top with remaining cake half. Frost the top and sides with the remaining frosting. Carefully pat the coconut onto the top and sides of the cake.

CHEF JAMIE'S LOW-FAT TIP

Don't tell the Brown Derby, but this coconut cake, with a few changes made, tastes delicious without all of the fat. Reduce the oil in the cake batter to ¼ cup and supplement the remaining ¼ cup with smooth applesauce, for texture. As for the eggs, use 1 egg yolk and 2 tablespoons of liquid egg substitute instead of all yolks. For the assembly, use only ¼ cup of shredded coconut on the top of the cake only, for decoration and far fewer fat grams!

HELPFUL HINTS FROM THE WIZARD

- Cake flour is all soft flour and makes for a lighter, moister cake, so don't try to substitute all-purpose flour.

Cream Cheese Pound Cake

MAKES 16 SERVINGS

Originally, pound cake was made with one pound each of flour, butter, and eggs. While the measurements have changed and variations have developed, this wonderful, moist cake is still full of flavor. It's absolutely scrumptious when served with fresh berries and a dollop of whipped cream.

3 sticks (12 ounces) unsalted butter, softened
8 ounces cream cheese, softened
3 cups sugar

1½ teaspoons almond extract
3 cups cake flour (or use all-purpose flour, sifted 4 times)
6 large eggs

Grease and flour 2 loaf pans.

In a large mixing bowl, cream together the butter and cream cheese. Gradually add the sugar and mix well. Add the almond extract.

On low speed, alternately add the flour and the eggs in three additions, beating thoroughly after each addition.

Pour the batter into the prepared pans. Place the pans in a *cold* oven. Set the oven to 300°F and bake 1½ to 1¾ hours, or until a cake tester inserted in the center of the cake comes out clean.

Cool the cakes in the pans for 30 minutes before turning out. Continue cooling on a wire rack.

CHEF JAMIE'S LOW-FAT TIP

I know what you're thinking. . . how is she going to make this incredibly rich and delicious pound cake lower in fat? Well, it took some time and plenty of testing, but I think that you will truly enjoy the lighter version! Fifty percent-less-fat butter bakes beautifully, as long as you beat the batter very well, until extremely fluffy, before adding the sugar. I found that using non-fat cream cheese works great, too, and there was very little difference in flavor between the light and the fat-free versions. Also, using 4 whole eggs and ½ cup of liquid egg substitute allows the cake to rise properly and lowers your cholesterol intake!

PER SERVING					
STANDARD RECIPE:	CALORIES 471	FAT 26G	PROTEIN 6G	CARBOHYDRATES 56G	CHOL 145MG
REDUCED FAT:	CALORIES 365	FAT 11G	PROTEIN 5G	CARBOHYDRATES 57G	CHOL 53MG

Y. M.'s Banana Cake

MAKES 12 SERVINGS

I learned from my mom, Lana, that the best thing to do with aging bananas is to freeze them for later use in banana cake!

For the cake:
5 cups all-purpose flour
2⅓ cups sugar
2 sticks plus 2 tablespoons (9 ounces) unsalted butter, softened
2½ teaspoons baking powder
2½ teaspoons baking soda
½ teaspoon cinnamon
½ teaspoon salt
¼ teaspoon nutmeg
1⅓ cups buttermilk
2½ cups mashed bananas

5 large eggs
1 teaspoon vanilla extract
1⅛ cups walnuts, chopped

For the frosting:
12 ounces cream cheese, at room temperature
1 stick unsalted butter, at room temperature
4½ cups powdered sugar
1 tablespoon vanilla

Preheat the oven to 350°F. Grease and flour two 9-inch round cake pans.

To make the cake: In a large mixing bowl, beat together the flour, sugar, baking powder, baking soda, cinnamon, nutmeg, salt, butter, and half of the buttermilk for 3 minutes. Add the bananas, eggs, and remaining buttermilk, and continue to beat for 2 minutes longer. Gently fold the walnuts into the batter.

Pour into the prepared pans and bake 45 minutes. Let the cakes cool in the pans for 10 minutes, then turn onto racks and cool completely before frosting.

To make the frosting: Blend together the cream cheese and butter using an electric mixer. Slowly add the sugar and blend until fluffy. Stir in the vanilla.

To assemble the cake: Spread ½-inch of frosting on top of the first cake layer. Top with the other cake layer. Frost the sides and top of the cake with the remaining frosting.

	PER SERVING				
STANDARD RECIPE:	CALORIES 996	FAT 41G	PROTEIN 16G	CARBOHYDRATES 150G	CHOL 179MG
REDUCED FAT:	CALORIES 748	FAT 25G	PROTEIN 15G	CARBOHYDRATES 134G	CHOL 44MG

Y. M's Banana Cake *(continued)*

CHEF JAMIE'S LOW-FAT TIP

To lighten the cake layers, use 50 percent-less-fat butter and 2 whole eggs plus ¾ cup liquid egg substitute. For the frosting, beat together 6 tablespoons of light cream cheese with 3 cups of powdered sugar. Add 1 teaspoon of vanilla and enough low-fat milk (about 2 tablespoons) to reach a spreading consistency. This delectable cake is just as good in its low-fat form!

Apple Spice Cake

MAKES 9 SERVINGS

Moist, sweet, and spicy are three words that describe this perfect cake. The chunks of apple give it wonderful texture and the pureed cottage cheese adds incredible creaminess to the cake.

1 stick unsalted butter, at room temperature
¾ cup sugar
½ cup cottage cheese, pureed until smooth
3 tablespoons light corn syrup
1 teaspoon grated lemon zest
1 teaspoon vanilla extract
1½ cups all-purpose flour

1½ teaspoons baking powder
½ teaspoon cinnamon
⅛ teaspoon nutmeg
¼ cup whole milk
2 large eggs
2 green apples, cored, peeled, and diced
whipped cream, for serving

Preheat the oven to 350°F. Grease an 8-inch-square cake pan.

With an electric mixer, beat together the butter and sugar until light and fluffy. Add the cottage cheese and corn syrup; beat 3 minutes. Add the lemon zest and vanilla and mix to combine well.

In a separate mixing bowl, sift the flour with the baking powder, nutmeg, and cinnamon.

In a separate bowl, lightly whisk together the milk and eggs.

Add the flour mixture and the milk mixture, alternately, to the cottage cheese mixture in three additions, mixing well after each addition. Gently fold the apples into the batter, mixing until just combined.

Pour the batter into the prepared baking pan and bake 35 minutes, or until a cake tester inserted in the center of the cake comes out clean.

Allow the cake to rest for 10 minutes before serving. Cut the cake into squares and serve warm with whipped cream.

CHEF JAMIE'S LOW-FAT TIP

This cake can be made with remarkably less fat and still taste wonderful. Using 50 percent-less-fat butter, low-fat cottage cheese, low-fat milk, and 4 egg whites instead of 2 whole eggs will give you excellent low-fat results. Low-fat frozen yogurt is the perfect substitute for whipped cream, creating a scrumptiously light dessert!

PER SERVING

STANDARD RECIPE:	CALORIES 321	FAT 14G	PROTEIN 4G	CARBOHYDRATES 44G	CHOL 81MG
REDUCED FAT:	CALORIES 253	FAT 7G	PROTEIN 4G	CARBOHYDRATES 44G	CHOL 21MG

Apple Spice Cake (continued)

HELPFUL HINTS FROM THE WIZARD
- Make sure the lemon is very clean before zesting. It's best to scrub it with a soft brush.

Layered Apple Cake

MAKES 10 SERVINGS

This simple-to-prepare cake works best with Granny Smith apples, which stand up to baking without falling apart or getting mushy.

5 large green apples, cored, peeled and thinly sliced
2 tablespoons cinnamon
3 cups all-purpose flour
1½ cups sugar plus 3 tablespoons
1 tablespoon baking powder

pinch of salt
4 large eggs
2 teaspoons vanilla extract
1 cup vegetable oil
¼ cup unsweetened pineapple juice

Preheat the oven to 350°F. Grease a standard-size bundt pan.

In a bowl, toss the apples with the cinnamon and 3 tablespoons sugar; set aside.

In a large mixing bowl, combine the flour, sugar, baking powder, and salt. In a separate bowl whisk together the eggs, vanilla, oil, and pineapple juice. Stir the liquid mixture into the dry mixture until smooth.

Alternately layer the batter and apples in the prepared pan, ending with batter on top.

Bake the cake for 1 to 1¼ hours, or until a tester inserted in the center of the cake comes out clean. Cool the cake completely in the pan before inverting.

CHEF JAMIE'S LOW-FAT TIP

Applesauce is the savior here. To create a low-fat apple cinnamon cake, use ¼ cup vegetable oil and ¾ cup smooth applesauce. The moisture in the applesauce tends to lengthen the baking time slightly, so be sure to check the cake with a tester to ensure that it is baked through.

	PER SERVING				
STANDARD RECIPE:	CALORIES 467	FAT 25G	PROTEIN 7G	CARBOHYDRATES 54G	CHOL 85MG
REDUCED FAT:	CALORIES 320	FAT 8G	PROTEIN 7G	CARBOHYDRATES 55G	CHOL 85MG

14-Carat Carrot Cake

MAKES 16 SERVINGS

A family favorite, my mom's carrot cake is not to be beat. . .and now you finally have the recipe! The cake is prepared in loaf form, but you can easily make it a layer cake by using two 9-inch cake pans instead. The low-fat version tastes scrumptiously close to the original!

For the cake:
3 large eggs
¾ cup vegetable oil
¾ cup sugar
1 cup dark brown sugar
½ cup buttermilk
1 (4-ounce) jar carrot puree baby food
1 (6-ounce) can crushed pineapple, drained
3 cups all-purpose flour
2 teaspoons baking soda
2 teaspoons baking powder

2 teaspoons ground cinnamon
½ teaspoon allspice
¼ teaspoon salt
3 cups shredded carrots
1 cup chopped walnuts

For the frosting:
6 ounces cream cheese
½ stick (2 ounces) unsalted butter, at room temperature
2 cups powdered sugar
2 teaspoons vanilla extract

Preheat the oven to 350°F. Grease two 9 × 5-inch loaf pans.

To make the cake: In a large mixing bowl, beat together the eggs, oil, sugar, brown sugar, buttermilk, carrot puree, and pineapple. When combined, stir in the flour, baking soda, baking powder, cinnamon, allspice, and salt by hand. Fold in the shredded carrots and walnuts.

Divide the batter evenly between the two pans. Bake 40 minutes, or until a cake tester inserted in the center of each loaf comes out clean. Let cool in the pans 15 minutes, then let cool completely on wire racks.

To make the frosting: In a large mixing bowl, beat the cream cheese and butter until fluffy. Add the powdered sugar and vanilla; blend until well combined.

Frost the top and sides of the cooled cakes with the frosting.

CHEF JAMIE'S LOW-FAT TIP

This delicious cake can be prepared with 1 whole egg and 4 egg whites, and only ¼ of a cup of vegetable oil (or use canola, a healthier oil) and still be moist. Be sure to use low-fat buttermilk, too. Reduce the flour to 2½ cups for the low-fat version. For the frosting, eliminate the butter and use a total of 8 ounces of fat-free cream cheese.

		PER SERVING			
STANDARD RECIPE:	CALORIES 547	FAT 36G	PROTEIN 11G	CARBOHYDRATES 66G	CHOL 40MG
REDUCED FAT:	CALORIES 396	FAT 23G	PROTEIN 10G	CARBOHYDRATES 63G	CHOL 14MG

Good Luck Cake

MAKES 12 SERVINGS

A well-loved New Year's tradition, this cake has a coin baked into the batter (make sure to warn your guests of the possible surprise). The person who finds the coin in their slice is supposed to have good luck for the entire year!

2 sticks unsalted butter, softened
1¾ cups sugar, plus 1 tablespoon
3 large eggs, separated
2 large eggs
2 tablespoons water
2 teaspoons vanilla extract
3 cups all-purpose flour

1 teaspoon baking powder
pinch of salt
a quarter, washed and wrapped
   in foil
½ cup slivered almonds
2 tablespoons sesame seeds

Preheat the oven to 325°F. Grease and flour a 10-inch tube pan.

In a large mixing bowl, cream the butter with 1¾ cups sugar until light and fluffy. Gradually beat in 3 egg yolks, 2 whole eggs, water, and vanilla. In a separate bowl, stir the flour, baking powder, and salt in a separate bowl. Gradually beat the dry mixture into the butter mixture (the batter will be very thick).

Using clean, dry beaters in a clean bowl, beat the egg whites with the salt until soft peaks form. Add the remaining 1 tablespoon of sugar and beat until stiff but not dry. Gently fold the egg whites into the batter.

Pour into the prepared pan. Press the coin into the cake. Sprinkle the top of the batter with nuts and sesame seeds. Bake 1 hour and 10 minutes, or until a tester inserted in the center of the cake comes out clean. Cool completely in the pan. Run a knife around the edges of the cake to loosen it from the pan. Turn the cake out onto a plate. Wrap the cake tightly and store at room temperature until ready to serve.

CHEF JAMIE'S LOW-FAT TIP

This "lucky" cake is even luckier when prepared in its low-fat form. Use ¼ cup of liquid egg substitute in place of the 3 egg yolks (but keep the 2 whole eggs). Use only 1½ sticks of 50 percent-less-fat butter instead of the 2 sticks of whole butter, for less fat with just as much flavor. Do away with the almonds and sesame seeds and garnish the cake, before serving, with edible flowers for decoration.

		PER SERVING			
STANDARD RECIPE:	CALORIES 347	FAT 24G	PROTEIN 8G	CARBOHYDRATES 26G	CHOL 133MG
REDUCED FAT:	CALORIES 251	FAT 13G	PROTEIN 8G	CARBOHYDRATES 26G	CHOL 52MG

Angel Food Cake

MAKES 10 SERVINGS

I have always loved Angel Food Cake for its light, airy texture...and because it's fat-free! This cake keeps beautifully when tightly wrapped and left on the counter.

1 cup cake flour, sifted
1½ cups sugar
1½ cups egg whites
¼ teaspoon salt

1½ teaspoons cream of tartar
1 teaspoon vanilla extract
½ teaspoon almond extract

Preheat the oven to 350°F.

In a large mixing bowl, sift together the flour and ½ cup of the sugar four times.

In a separate mixing bowl, beat the egg whites with the salt until foamy. Add the cream of tartar, almond extract, and vanilla. Continue beating on medium-high speed until the egg whites hold soft peaks. Slowly add the remaining sugar, continuing to beat at medium-high speed until stiff, glossy peaks form.

By hand, stir one quarter of the sifted flour mixture into the beaten egg whites. Continue adding the flour mixture in three more additions, folding gently, until well combined.

Pour the batter into an ungreased 10-inch tube pan and "cut" the batter with a knife to remove any air pockets. Bake 35 minutes, or until the top is golden brown and the cake springs back when touched.

Invert the cake (in the pan) immediately after removing it from the oven and let cool. With a long knife, loosen the sides of the cake from the pan and remove to a serving plate.

CHEF JAMIE'S LOW-FAT TIP

Lucky me! This recipe needs no trimming, as it is already FAT-FREE! Angel Food Cake makes a delicious dessert when served with fresh berries, and it's also a special breakfast treat or a scrumptious snack. Try toasting or grilling the cake for an innovative dessert! The edges of the cake will caramelize and crisp slightly, bringing out its sweetness!

	PER SERVING				
STANDARD RECIPE:	CALORIES 172	FAT 0G	PROTEIN 3G	CARBOHYDRATES 406G	CHOL 0MG

Summertime Strawberry Shortcakes

MAKES 9 SERVINGS

If America were to choose a national dessert, this combination of warm biscuits, thick, sweet cream, and juicy red fruit would definitely be in the running!

For the filling:
6 cups strawberries, thinly sliced (about 5 [1-pint] baskets)
½ cup sugar, plus 2 teaspoons
1 cup heavy *or* whipping cream

For the biscuits:
2¼ cups all-purpose flour
¾ cup yellow cornmeal
⅓ cup sugar
3 teaspoons baking powder
pinch of salt
6 tablespoons chilled unsalted butter, cut into pieces
1 cup buttermilk

Combine the berries, ½ cup sugar, and lemon juice in a mixing bowl and stir to combine. Let stand for 30 minutes at room temperature or cover and chill for up to 3 hours before using.

To make the whipped cream: Combine the cream with the vanilla and the 2 teaspoons of sugar. Whip until thick. Refrigerate until ready to use.

To make the biscuits: Preheat the oven to 425°F. Lightly grease a large cookie sheet.

Place the flour, cornmeal, sugar, baking powder, and salt in the bowl of a food processor. Pulse to combine. Add the chilled butter and pulse just until the mixture resembles coarse crumbs. With the processor running, add the buttermilk and process just until moist clumps form.

Turn the dough out onto a lightly floured work surface and knead until smooth. Roll out the dough to a 9-inch square. Cut it into 9 (3-inch) squares. Transfer the squares of dough to the prepared baking sheet, spaced evenly. Bake until golden brown, about 20 minutes.

To assemble the shortcakes: Cut the warm biscuits in half horizontally. Place the bottom halves in individual serving bowls. Spoon the strawberries with their juice over the biscuit bottoms and add a dollop of whipped cream to each. Cover with the biscuit tops and serve.

	PER SERVING				
STANDARD RECIPE:	CALORIES 630	FAT 25G	PROTEIN 12G	CARBOHYDRATES 49G	CHOL 38MG
REDUCED FAT:	CALORIES 421	FAT 10G	PROTEIN 11G	CARBOHYDRATES 46G	CHOL 30MG

Summertime Strawberry Shortcakes (continued)

CHEF JAMIE'S LOW-FAT TIP

A fine recipe for low-fat strawberry shortcakes: Use the low-fat variation for the Sweet Cream Biscuits recipe on page 199. If you double the recipe and add ⅓ cup of sugar, you will have terrific low-fat biscuits for the shortcakes. Low-fat ice cream or frozen yogurt will finish off the desserts beautifully.

HELPFUL HINTS FROM THE WIZARD

- Do not remove the strawberry caps until after you wash them—without their caps, the berries will fill with water.

Pineapple Upside-Down Cake

MAKES 10 SERVINGS

This is one my favorite homemade desserts. I have found, from numerous tests, that this cake tastes best when prepared in a cast-iron skillet. If you don't have one, don't fret...it tastes pretty good no matter what you do to it!

6 tablespoons (3 ounces) unsalted butter
1½ cups brown sugar
6 large eggs
1½ cups sugar
¼ cup pineapple juice, reserved from the can

2 teaspoons vanilla extract
2 cups all-purpose flour
2 teaspoons baking powder
¼ teaspoon salt
1 (10-ounce) can pineapple slices, drained and juice reserved
maraschino cherries

Preheat the oven to 350°F.

Melt the butter in a cast-iron skillet or heavy sauté pan with high sides. Add the brown sugar and cook over low heat just until the sugar dissolves. Remove from the heat and allow to cool.

In a large mixing bowl, beat the eggs until frothy. Gradually beat in the sugar. Add the reserved pineapple juice and vanilla, and mix well.

In a separate bowl, sift together the flour, baking powder, and salt. Add the flour mixture to the egg mixture and blend thoroughly, but do not over mix.

Arrange the pineapple slices in the bottom of the cooled pan of butter/sugar mixture. Place maraschino cherries in the center of each pineapple ring.

Pour the batter over the pineapple rings. Bake 45 minutes, or until a cake tester inserted in the center comes out clean. To serve, loosen the cake from the pan and carefully invert onto a serving plate. Slice and serve.

CHEF JAMIE'S LOW-FAT TIP

This traditional favorite can easily be transformed into a low-fat tropical treat. Cut the amount of butter in half, using only 3 tablespoons (you can use 50 percent-less-fat butter also, for a truly lean treat). Prepare the cake batter using 2 whole eggs and 1 cup of liquid egg substitute. This will allow the cake to rise properly yet still keep your fat and cholesterol intake down!

HELPFUL HINTS FROM THE WIZARD

- Good-quality vanilla *extract* is more expensive, but worth the investment! Avoid lower-quality vanilla *flavoring*.

PER SERVING

STANDARD RECIPE:	CALORIES 517	FAT 11G	PROTEIN 7G	CARBOHYDRATES 100G	CHOL 148MG
REDUCED FAT:	CALORIES 459	FAT 5G	PROTEIN 5G	CARBOHYDRATES 101G	CHOL 52MG

Incredible Lemon Bundt Cake

MAKES 12 SERVINGS

This lemony cake is very easy to prepare, since the base is a store-bought cake mix. It happens to taste especially good in its guilt-free low-fat form!

For the cake:
1 (18-ounce) box white cake mix
1 cup sour cream
1 (6-ounce) can frozen lemonade, thawed
3 large eggs
4 ounces cream cheese, at room temperature

For the icing:
⅓ cup buttermilk
4 tablespoons unsalted butter, softened
2 tablespoons light corn syrup
1 tablespoon lemon zest
1 teaspoon lemon extract
pinch of salt
2 cups powdered sugar

Preheat the oven to 350°F. Grease a 12-cup bundt pan.

To make the cake: In a large mixing bowl, beat together the cake mix, sour cream, and lemonade. Add the cream cheese and mix thoroughly. Add the eggs, one at a time, blending well after each addition. Beat 4 minutes on medium speed. (If you beat this batter for less time it tends to separate...so do it just to be safe!)

Pour the batter into the prepared pan and spread evenly. Bake 1 hour, or until a cake tester inserted in the center comes out clean. Cool in the pan 15 minutes, then remove from the pan and place on a serving plate.

To make the icing: Place all the ingredients in a food processor or blender in the order listed, and blend until smooth.

Drizzle the icing over the warm cake. Refrigerate 2 to 3 hours before slicing. Bring the cake to room temperature before serving. Store any leftover cake in the refrigerator.

CHEF JAMIE'S LOW-FAT TIP

You can make this cake lighter by substituting light sour cream, low-fat cream cheese, and 1 whole egg plus 3 egg whites. For the icing, substitute reduced-fat (50 percent-less-fat) butter and be sure to use low-fat buttermilk.

		PER SERVING		
STANDARD RECIPE:	CALORIES 398	FAT 15G	PROTEIN 5G	CARBOHYDRATES 43G	CHOL 81MG
REDUCED FAT:	CALORIES 358	FAT 10G	PROTEIN 4G	CARBOHYDRATES 44G	CHOL 37MG

Really Easy Sour Cream Cheesecake

MAKES 10 SERVINGS

This simple recipe turns out creamy, perfect cheesecake every time. For a REALLY easy version, use a prepared graham cracker crust and cut the batter recipe in half, since purchased pie crusts hold less filling than a traditional pan. Notice that, in this recipe, the cheesecake bakes in a water bath at a low temperature. This ensures even baking and less cracking! For a smooth filling, be sure to allow the cream cheese to come to room temperature before creaming!

For the crust:
1 cup graham cracker crumbs
¼ cup coarsely chopped walnuts
2 tablespoons brown sugar
⅓ cup unsalted butter, melted

For the filling:
3 large eggs
1 cup sugar
2 tablespoons all-purpose flour
1½ cups sour cream
2 teaspoons fresh lemon juice
2 teaspoons lemon zest
16 ounces cream cheese, at room temperature

Preheat the oven to 325°F. Grease a 9-inch springform pan. Wrap the bottom of the pan in foil, extending the foil up the sides of the pan at least 2 inches all the way around.

To make the crust: Combine the crumbs, walnuts, brown sugar, and butter. Mix well. Press evenly into the bottom of the prepared pan. (If you are feeling adventurous, you can press the crust into the bottom and 2 inches up the sides of the pan!)

To make the filling: In a large mixing bowl, beat the eggs until pale yellow. Slowly add the sugar and flour; beat until well combined. Add the sour cream and the cream cheese; blend well. Stir in the lemon juice and lemon zest.

Pour the batter into the prepared crust. Place the springform pan in a baking dish large enough to hold it. Place the pan in the oven on the center rack. Pour enough hot tap water into the baking dish to come one inch up the sides of the pan. Bake 1 hour or until set. Let cool completely. Cover and refrigerate until thoroughly chilled (at least 8 hours).

PER SERVING

STANDARD RECIPE:	CALORIES 424	FAT 34G	PROTEIN 7G	CARBOHYDRATES 18G	CHOL 145MG
REDUCED FAT:	CALORIES 324	FAT 15G	PROTEIN 9G	CARBOHYDRATES 19G	CHOL 94MG

Really Easy Sour Cream Cheesecake (continued)

CHEF JAMIE'S LOW-FAT TIP

This creamy, dreamy cheesecake tastes delicious when created using low-fat ingredients. The trick is to use a combination of light and fat-free cream cheese in the filling (use 8 ounces of each) and low-fat sour cream, to maintain the creamy quality of the cheesecake. An almost fat-free crust can be prepared using 3 egg whites in place of the melted butter. Note that most graham crackers look and taste the same, but their fat content varies, so check labels and choose the leanest crackers.

HELPFUL HINTS FROM THE WIZARD

• Regular cream cheese is about 90 percent fat.

Apple Cobbler

MAKES 6 SERVINGS

The earliest written
reference to "cobbler,"
a deep-dish fruit dessert
with a crust on top,
is from a German
cookbook published in
1839. This wonderfully
homey dessert is delicious
served with vanilla bean
ice cream!

For the filling:
6 large Granny Smith apples, peeled
    & sliced
⅓ cup sugar
2 tablespoons tapioca flour
1 teaspoon cinnamon
1 teaspoon vanilla extract
1 teaspoon freshly grated lemon zest
1 teaspoon lemon juice
½ teaspoon nutmeg
pinch of salt

For the streusel topping:
1 cup all-purpose flour
¼ cup sugar
¼ cup brown sugar
½ cup sliced almonds
2 teaspoons cinnamon
1½ sticks cold unsalted butter,
    cut into small pieces

Preheat the oven to 350°F. Grease an 8-inch-square cake pan.

To make the filling: Lightly toss all of the filling ingredients in a large bowl. Pour into the prepared cake pan.

To make the streusel: In a food processor, pulse the white and brown sugar, flour, almonds, and cinnamon to combine. Add the cold butter pieces and pulse just until crumbly.

Top the filling with the streusel. Bake 45 minutes or until golden and bubbly. Serve warm.

CHEF JAMIE'S LOW-FAT TIP

Create a lower-fat cobbler by using only 1 stick of reduced-fat (50 percent-less-fat) butter in the streusel topping. Or, make the cobbler virtually fat free by crushing graham cracker crumbs and using them in place of the streusel topping. Prepare the cobbler by topping the fruit with the graham cracker crumbs and baking until the fruit is tender and the crumbs are golden. If you find the crumbs are getting too brown before the apples are tender, gently drape the top of the cobbler with a piece of aluminum foil to prevent burning.

		PER SERVING			
STANDARD RECIPE:	CALORIES 457	FAT 35G	PROTEIN 8G	CARBOHYDRATES 66G	CHOL 66MG
REDUCED FAT:	CALORIES 319	FAT 20G	PROTEIN 8G	CARBOHYDRATES 66G	CHOL 39MG

Fresh Fruit Crisp

MAKES 8 SERVINGS

A crisp is a wonderful showcase for fresh, seasonal fruit. Nothing more than fruit baked with a crumbly topping, a crisp is as easy to make as it is scrumptious. The following recipe is for a basic apple crisp, but almost any fruit or combination of fruits will taste delicious. My favorites include apple, apple-blackberry, peach, and blueberry-lemon. (See the Chef's Note below for these variations!)

For the topping:
1¼ cups old-fashioned oats
1 cup plus 2 tablespoons brown sugar
¾ cup walnuts
¾ cup all-purpose flour
½ teaspoon cinnamon
¼ teaspoon salt
1½ sticks cold unsalted butter, cut into small pieces

For the filling:
4 pounds Granny Smith or pippin apples, peeled, cored, and sliced
½ cup sugar
1 tablespoon fresh lemon juice
2 tablespoons all-purpose flour
¾ teaspoon cinnamon
¼ teaspoon ground ginger
vanilla ice cream, for serving

Preheat the oven to 375°F. Butter a 9 × 13-inch baking dish.

To make the topping: In a large mixing bowl, stir together the oats, brown sugar, walnuts, flour, cinnamon, and salt. Add the cold butter and, using a pastry blender or your fingers, mix until coarse crumbs form. Refrigerate until ready to use.

To make the filling: In a large mixing bowl, toss the sliced apples, sugar, lemon juice, flour, cinnamon, and ginger.

Transfer the apple filling to the prepared dish. Spread the topping over the filling. Bake 50 minutes or until golden brown. Serve warm with vanilla ice cream.

Chef's Note: Apple-blackberry crisp is easily prepared with 3 pounds of sliced apples and 1¼ cups fresh blackberries in the filling. For peach crisp, use 4 pounds of firm, ripe, sliced peaches. Blueberry-lemon crisp is made with 4 cups blueberries and 2 teaspoons freshly grated lemon zest.

CHEF JAMIE'S LOW-FAT TIP

Once again, 50 percent-less-fat butter saves the day! For an even lighter version, use only 1 stick of reduced-fat (50 percent-less-fat) butter and about 12 liberal sprays of refrigerated butter spray (I Can't Believe It's Not Butter is a good one) in the topping. Reduce your fat intake from the nuts by using only ¼ cup of the walnuts for flavor. Frozen yogurt or light ice cream tops this lower-fat dessert beautifully!

		PER SERVING			
STANDARD RECIPE:	CALORIES 828	FAT 46G	PROTEIN 15G	CARBOHYDRATES 102G	CHOL 9MG
REDUCED FAT:	CALORIES 575	FAT 21G	PROTEIN 8G	CARBOHYDRATES 99G	CHOL 9MG

- For a fancy treat, scoop out the ice cream in well-rounded balls and place them on a small cookie sheet in the freezer 1 hour before you serve the crisp.

Apple Strudel

MAKES 8 SERVINGS

½ cup walnuts, chopped
½ cup brown sugar
½ cup golden raisins
2 tablespoons candied ginger, chopped
½ teaspoon cinnamon
¼ teaspoon ground nutmeg
pinch of salt
1½ pounds green apples, peeled, cored, and sliced thinly
½ pound (8 ounces) phyllo dough sheets
½ cup unsalted butter, melted
1 cup plain bread crumbs

Preheat the oven to 350°F. In a baking pan, toast the walnuts for about 10 minutes, stirring often. Set aside to cool.

In a large mixing bowl, stir together the brown sugar, raisins, ginger, cinnamon, nutmeg, and salt. Add the apple slices and toasted walnuts; toss to coat well.

Place 2 large sheets of waxed paper on a work surface. Place one sheet of phyllo dough on the waxed paper and brush gently with melted butter. Sprinkle the butter with a thin layer of bread crumbs. Repeat the process, layering phyllo, butter, then bread crumbs, using one sheet of phyllo at a time until finished.

Mound the apple mixture into the center of the stacked phyllo dough, leaving space around the edges. Fold the long side of the dough over the apple mixture and continue rolling to create a jellyroll. Carefully place the strudel on a parchment paper–lined baking sheet. Brush all over with the remaining melted butter.

Bake 40 to 45 minutes or until the strudel is golden brown. Serve warm.

CHEF JAMIE'S LOW-FAT TIP

Phyllo dough makes great lower-fat desserts; just choose your favorite fruit filling and bake away! The trick is to spray each layer liberally with non-stick cooking spray instead of using melted butter.

PER SERVING					
STANDARD RECIPE:	CALORIES 368	FAT 22G	PROTEIN 4G	CARBOHYDRATES 33G	CHOL 33MG
REDUCED FAT:	CALORIES 220	FAT 10G	PROTEIN 4G	CARBOHYDRATES 33G	CHOL 0MG

Summer Berry Trifle

MAKES 16 SERVINGS

This is the lightest, freshest, most wonderful trifle you have ever tasted! Originally from England, this wonderful dessert was sometimes called a "tipsy pudding" because of the generous amount of cooking sherry used in the recipe.

2 cups heavy cream

4 tablespoons powdered sugar

2 to 3 packages lady fingers *or* 2 (16-ounce) pound cakes

½ cup cream sherry

1 cup seedless raspberry jam

1 quart strawberries, hulled and sliced

1 pint blueberries

½ cup sliced almonds, for garnish

mint sprigs, for garnish

In a medium mixing bowl, beat the cream with the powdered sugar until soft peaks form. Set aside

Line the bottom of a large glass serving bowl or trifle bowl with enough ladyfingers to cover. If using pound cake, cut the pound cake lengthwise into three even pieces, then cut into 1-inch strips. Arrange enough slices to cover the bottom of the bowl. Brush the cake with sherry.

Heat the jam in a small saucepan until just warm and melted. Spread a thin layer of the warm jam over the lady fingers or cake slices. Place a layer of strawberries and blueberries on top of the cake.

Top the fruit with a layer of whipped cream. Repeat the layers, ending with whipped cream.

Decorate the top of the trifle with the almonds and mint sprigs.

CHEF JAMIE'S LOW-FAT TIP

Trifle is a wonderful summer dessert that can be easily prepared in the low-fat fashion. Use non-fat pound cake and low-fat whipped topping (such as Cool Whip) for a light and luscious treat.

	PER SERVING				
STANDARD RECIPE:	CALORIES 212	FAT 16G	PROTEIN 1G	CARBOHYDRATES 19G	CHOL 42MG
REDUCED FAT:	CALORIES 108	FAT 4G	PROTEIN 3G	CARBOHYDRATES 18G	CHOL 0MG

Cherries Jubilee

MAKES 4 SERVINGS

This dessert is a show— igniting the fruit at the table always seems to thrill guests! Serve these sweet and succulent cherries at your next dinner party to keep your guests talking for months.

1 (16-ounce) can pitted sour cherries, with their juice
½ cup sugar
2 tablespoons grated orange zest

1 tablespoon arrowroot or cornstarch
⅓ cup kirsch or cognac
1 pint vanilla ice cream
chocolate shavings, for garnish

Drain the cherries, reserving the juice. Measure the juice and add enough water to measure 1½ cups liquid. Pour the liquid into a small saucepan and add the sugar and orange zest. Bring to a simmer over low heat and simmer, uncovered, for 10 minutes.

Place the arrowroot in a small mixing bowl. Remove 2 tablespoons of the cherry liquid from the pan and add it to the arrowroot. Stir to dissolve. Gradually stir the arrowroot mixture into the liquid in the pan. Simmer, stirring constantly, until thick, about 10 minutes. Add the cherries.

In a small saucepan, warm the kirsch or cognac over medium heat, about 1 minute. Meanwhile scoop the ice cream into 4 dessert bowls. At the table, pour the warm liqueur into the cherry sauce and ignite, using a long match or automatic flame. Gently stir until the flame dies down. Carefully pour the flaming sauce over the ice cream at once, and garnish with the chocolate curls.

CHEF JAMIE'S LOW-FAT TIP

The cherry mixture is fat-free, and dresses up almost anything—low-fat pound cake, cheesecake, and more. Using low-fat frozen yogurt or ice milk creates a wonderfully elegant low-fat dessert.

PER SERVING					
STANDARD RECIPE:	CALORIES 334	FAT 7G	PROTEIN 1.5G	CARBOHYDRATES 47G	CHOL 26MG
REDUCED FAT:	CALORIES 273	FAT 3.5G	PROTEIN 1.5G	CARBOHYDRATES 50G	CHOL 10MG

Warm Gingerbread

MAKES 9 SERVINGS

The fragrance of gingerbread is almost the best part about making it! It is said that this sweet treat dates back to the Middle Ages, when ladies of the court presented the honey-spiced breads as a favor to knights going into battle, thus the "gingerbread man" was born. Dark and spicy, this quick bread makes a great dessert, topped with a dollop of whipped cream or a scoop of vanilla ice cream.

½ cup unsalted butter, at room temperature
1¼ cups sugar
1 large egg
½ cup molasses
2 tablespoons corn syrup
1 teaspoon baking soda

¾ cup hot water
2 cups all-purpose flour
1 teaspoon ground cinnamon
¼ teaspoon ground cloves
2 teaspoons ground ginger
pinch of salt

Preheat the oven to 350°F. Grease an 8-inch-square cake pan.

In a medium mixing bowl, cream together the butter and sugar until light and fluffy. Add the egg, molasses and corn syrup; mix well.

Combine the baking soda and water in a measuring cup.

In a separate bowl, combine the flour, cinnamon, cloves, ginger, and salt.

Add the flour mixture and the baking soda/water mixture, alternately, to the creamed butter mixture, to form a batter. Beat just until the last addition is incorporated.

Pour the batter into the prepared pan. Bake 30 minutes, or until a cake tester inserted in the center of the bread comes out clean. Cool on a wire rack.

CHEF JAMIE'S LOW-FAT TIP

The combination of molasses and corn syrup keeps this bread moist even in its low-fat form. Use ⅓ cup of reduced-fat (50 percent-less-fat) butter or non-diet tub-style margarine and 2 egg whites to lighten the gingerbread.

		PER SERVING			
STANDARD RECIPE:	CALORIES 372	FAT 12G	PROTEIN 4G	CARBOHYDRATES 66G	CHOL 24MG
REDUCED FAT:	CALORIES 324	FAT 6G	PROTEIN 3G	CARBOHYDRATES 66G	CHOL 0MG

The Ultimate Pumpkin Pie
MAKES 8 SERVINGS

Pumpkin pie was introduced to the holiday table at the Pilgrims' second Thanksgiving, in 1623. Still a true comfort food today, I like this American classic with a dollop of slightly sweetened whipped cream and a sprinkle of nutmeg.

For the crust:
1¼ cups all-purpose flour
½ cup powdered sugar
1 stick cold unsalted butter, cut into pieces
3 tablespoons heavy cream

For the filling:
¾ cup sugar
1 tablespoon brown sugar

1 tablespoon cornstarch
2 teaspoons cinnamon
1 teaspoon ground ginger
¼ teaspoon salt
1 (16-ounce) can solid-pack pumpkin
¾ cup heavy cream
½ cup sour cream
3 eggs

To make the crust: In a food processor, blend together the flour, sugar, and butter until it resembles coarse meal. Add the cream and process until moist clumps form. Gather the dough into a ball, then flatten into a disk. Wrap the dough in plastic wrap and refrigerate for 30 minutes.

Preheat the oven to 350°F.

Roll out the chilled dough on a floured surface to a 14-inch round, about ⅛ inch thick. Transfer to a 9-inch pie plate and trim and crimp the edges. Prick the dough all over with a fork, then freeze for 15 minutes. Line the pie shell with aluminum foil and weight with dried beans or pie weights. Bake 15 minutes. Remove the weights and the foil and bake 10 minutes more, or until golden brown.

To make the filling: Reduce the oven temperature to 325°F. Using a whisk, combine the sugars, cornstarch, cinnamon, ginger, and salt in a large mixing bowl until no lumps remain. Blend in the pumpkin, heavy cream, sour cream, and eggs.

Pour the filling into the baked pie crust. Bake 1 hour, until the filling puffs at the edges and the center is almost set. Cool completely, then chill thoroughly.

		PER SERVING			
STANDARD RECIPE:	CALORIES 525	FAT 33G	PROTEIN 4G	CARBOHYDRATES 53G	CHOL 95MG
REDUCED FAT:	CALORIES 370	FAT 12G	PROTEIN 5G	CARBOHYDRATES 52G	CHOL 58MG

Healthy holidays, here we come! This recipe translates beautifully for the "lighter" eaters. For a lower-fat crust, use reduced-fat (50 percent-less-fat) butter, and use 3 egg whites instead of the heavy cream. As for the filling, evaporated skim milk in place of the heavy cream and light sour cream in place of regular do the trick.

HELPFUL HINTS FROM THE WIZARD
- Canned pumpkin should be fresh—when stored for 4 months it loses 50 percent of its flavor.

Classic Apple Pie

MAKES 8 SERVINGS

Pie dough will keep in the refrigerator for up to three days or in the freezer for six months. Thaw frozen dough in the refrigerator, then let it stand at room temperature 30 minutes before rolling it out.

For the crust:
2 ½ cups all-purpose flour
2 teaspoons sugar
1 teaspoon salt
5 tablespoons cold unsalted butter, cut into pieces
¼ cup chilled solid vegetable shortening
9 tablespoons ice water

For the filling:
3 pounds tart green apples (Granny Smith or pippin), peeled, cored and sliced
⅓ cup sugar
2 tablespoons cornstarch
1 teaspoon cinnamon
1 teaspoon grated lemon zest
1 teaspoon lemon juice
½ teaspoon ground ginger
pinch of salt

To make the crust: Sift the flour, sugar, and salt into a large mixing bowl. Using a pastry blender or your fingertips, cut the butter and shortening into the dry ingredients until the mixture resembles coarse crumbs. Stir in enough water, by tablespoons, until the dough holds together. Gather the dough into a ball and divide in half. Flatten each half into a disk. Wrap the disks in plastic wrap and refrigerate for 30 minutes.

Preheat the oven to 450°F. Roll out 1 disk of dough on a floured surface to a 12-inch round. Transfer to a pie plate.

To make the filling: Mix the sugar, cornstarch, cinnamon, lemon zest, lemon juice, ginger, and salt in a large mixing bowl; toss in the apples until well coated. Mound the apple filling in the crust. Roll out the second disc of dough on a floured surface to a 12-inch round. Place the crust atop the pie and crimp the edges together. Cut 5 slits in the crust. Bake 10 minutes, then reduce the oven temperature to 350°F and continue baking 50 minutes longer, or until the apples are tender and the crust is golden.

CHEF JAMIE'S LOW-FAT TIP

Creating a tender-crisp pie crust without a considerable amount of fat is not easy! The recipe on the following page trims away some of the fat without compromising too much taste or texture.

		PER SERVING			
STANDARD RECIPE:	CALORIES 441	FAT 15G	PROTEIN .4G	CARBOHYDRATES 45G	CHOL 21MG
REDUCED FAT:	CALORIES 280	FAT 5G	PROTEIN .3G	CARBOHYDRATES 35G	CHOL 3MG

For Lower-Fat Pie Crust:

1¼ cups all-purpose flour

1 teaspoon sugar

½ teaspoon salt

½ cup plus 2 teaspoons canola oil

2 tablespoons cold 50 percent-less-fat butter

1 tablespoon chilled solid vegetable shortening

4 to 5 tablespoons ice water

Prepare the pie crust according to the directions given opposite, then separate the dough into 2 pieces, using three-quarters of the dough for one piece and the remaining quarter of the dough for the other piece. Roll the larger piece into a thin bottom-crust for the pie. Then roll out the remaining dough and cut it into 1-inch-wide strips. Lay the strips of dough over the filling, before baking, to form a lattice top. Bake the pie on a cookie sheet to catch any drippings! This less-crust pie will lower your fat and calorie intake!

HELPFUL HINTS FROM THE WIZARD

- It's best to use a glass pan when baking fruit pies, since metal tends to react with the acid in the fruit and may cause the fruit to turn brown.

Banana Cream Pie

MAKES 8 SERVINGS

For the crust:
1 cup all-purpose flour
2 tablespoons sugar
¼ teaspoon salt
¼ teaspoon baking powder
4 tablespoons cold unsalted butter
1 large egg

For the filling:
2 tablespoons sugar
5 tablespoons all-purpose flour
¼ teaspoon salt
3 egg yolks

2 cups whole milk
2 tablespoons unsalted butter, cut into small pieces
2 tablespoons dark rum
1 teaspoon vanilla extract
½ cup sugar
1 cup heavy cream
2 tablespoons sugar
1 teaspoon vanilla extract
3 large, ripe bananas, peeled and cut into ¼-inch rounds

To make the crust: Combine the flour, sugar, salt, and baking powder in the bowl of a food processor fitted with a metal blade. Pulse to combine the ingredients. Add the cold butter and pulse, at 1-second intervals, until the mixture resembles coarse crumbs, about 10 pulses in all. Add the egg and pulse until a ball of dough is formed. Remove the dough from the processor and place it on a lightly floured surface. Knead the dough 3 or 4 times until it is smooth and holds together. Press the dough into a disk shape and wrap in plastic wrap. Refrigerate at least 1 hour or until ready to use.

Preheat the oven to 350°F. Roll out the chilled dough on a lightly floured surface to 10 inches in diameter. Place the dough in a 9-inch pie pan and trim and crimp the edges. Refrigerate the pie shell for 20 minutes before baking. Pierce it all over with a fork and line it with wax or parchment paper. Fill the pie pan with pie weights or dried beans. Bake 20 minutes or until the crust is golden brown. Cool completely and remove the pie weights or beans along with the wax paper before filling.

	PER SERVING				
STANDARD RECIPE:	CALORIES 4095	FAT 22G	PROTEIN 6G	CARBOHYDRATES 37G	CHOL 166MG
REDUCED FAT:	CALORIES 358	FAT 15G	PROTEIN 6G	CARBOHYDRATES 39G	CHOL 85MG

To make the filling: Combine the sugar, flour, and salt in a large mixing bowl. Using a large whisk, beat in the egg yolks, one at a time. Heat the milk and 2 tablespoons of the butter in a small saucepan until the butter melts and bubbles form around the edge of the pan. Slowly pour the milk mixture into the mixing bowl, whisking constantly. Add the rum and vanilla; return to the saucepan. Bring to a simmer, reduce heat to low and cook, stirring constantly until thick and smooth. Allow to cool to lukewarm before continuing.

Meanwhile, beat the heavy cream with 2 tablespoons sugar and vanilla until stiff peaks form. Gently fold half of the whipped cream into the cooled custard.

To assemble the pie: Spread ¼ inch of custard on the bottom of the cooked pie shell. Arrange a layer of bananas on top of the custard. Continue layering the pie, finishing with a top layer of bananas. Spread or pipe the remaining whipped cream on the top of the pie in a decorative pattern. Chill for at least 2 hours before serving.

CHEF JAMIE'S LOW-FAT TIP

Prepare a low-fat pie crust (see page 245) or make a low-fat graham cracker crust using 1½ cups low-fat graham cracker crumbs, 3 tablespoons reduced-fat (50 percent-less-fat) butter, melted, and 2 tablespoons of sugar. Combine the ingredients and press onto the bottom of a pie plate coated with non-stick cooking spray. Bake at 325°F for 10 minutes. For the filling, use 1 egg yolk and ¼ cup of liquid egg substitute, along with low-fat milk. Also, in place of the whipped cream, use frozen reduced-calorie whipped topping that has been thawed.

Chef Jamie's Strawberry Pie

MAKES 8 SERVINGS

Here's a delicious dessert dreamed up especially for strawberry season!

For the crust:

2 cups all-purpose flour

2 tablespoon sugar

pinch of salt

½ cup vegetable shortening, chilled

¼ cup unsalted butter, chilled

4 tablespoons cold water

For the filling:

3 ounces cream cheese, at room temperature

½ cup sugar

1 teaspoon vanilla extract

½ cup heavy cream

2 quarts strawberries, hulled and halved

¼ cup red current jelly

To make the crust: In a food processor, pulse the flour, sugar, and salt to combine. Add the shortening and butter, and pulse just until the mixture resembles coarse meal. Add the water by tablespoons, while pulsing, just until the dough begins to form a ball. Remove the dough and gather into a ball. Flatten the dough into a disk shape, wrap in plastic wrap, and chill for 1 hour.

Preheat oven to 375°F.

Roll out the dough on a floured surface to a 13-inch round. Transfer the dough to a 9-inch glass pie dish. Trim and crimp edges. Freeze the dough for 15 minutes. Remove from the freezer and prick the pastry with a fork. Line the dough with foil and fill the pan with dried beans or pie weights. Bake the dough for 8 minutes. Remove the foil and weights and return pastry to the oven. Bake until golden brown, about 10 minutes more. Let cool completely.

To make the filling: In a large mixing bowl, whip the cream cheese with the sugar and vanilla until fluffy. In a separate bowl, whip the cream until soft peaks are formed. Fold the whipped cream into the cream cheese mixture.

Spoon the filling into the cooled crust and spread it evenly. Top the custard with the strawberries.

Heat the jelly in a small saucepan until melted. Using a pastry brush, glaze the tops of the berries with the warm jelly. Place the pie in the refrigerator and chill, uncovered, for 3 hours before serving.

	PER SERVING				
STANDARD RECIPE:	CALORIES 469	FAT 28G	PROTEIN 5G	CARBOHYDRATES 27G	CHOL 49MG
REDUCED FAT:	CALORIES 293	FAT 14G	PROTEIN 4G	CARBOHYDRATES 40G	CHOL 39MG

This pie actually translates quite well to a lower-fat recipe. Use the low-fat pie crust recipe that follows for the base, and be assured that low-fat cream cheese and non-fat whipped topping (such as Cool Whip) work fine in the filling.

JAMIE'S LOWER-FAT PIE CRUST

1¼ cups all-purpose flour

1 teaspoon sugar

½ teaspoon salt

½ teaspoon baking powder

3 tablespoons cold 50 percent-less-
    fat butter, cut into pieces

1 tablespoon chilled solid vegetable
    shortening

4 to 5 tablespoons ice water

To make the crust: In a food processor, pulse the flour, sugar, salt, and baking powder. Add the cold butter and shortening, and pulse at 1-second intervals until the mixture resembles coarse crumbs. Add the water and pulse until the dough forms a ball. Place it on a lightly floured surface. Knead 3 or 4 times until smooth. Press the dough into a disk shape and wrap in plastic wrap. Refrigerate at least 1 hour or until ready to use.

Key Lime Pie

MAKES 8 SERVINGS

Almost nothing compares to a true Key Lime Pie! Developed more than a hundred years ago, the original Key Lime Pie was actually unbaked—the acidity in the lime juice "cooked" the filling. Today we bake the pie to create a perfectly tart, sweet, and scrumptious dessert!

For the crust:
1½ cups graham cracker crumbs
3 tablespoons sugar
½ cup unsalted butter, melted

For the filling:
2 (14-ounce) cans sweetened condensed milk
2 teaspoons fresh lime zest
4 large eggs, separated
¾ cup key lime juice
2 tablespoons cornstarch
pinch of salt
¼ teaspoon cream of tartar
whipped cream, for serving
Preheat the oven to 350°F.

To make the crust: In a mixing bowl, combine the graham cracker crumbs and sugar; stir in the melted butter, and mix until moist. Press into the bottom and sides of a 9-inch pie pan. Bake 8 to 10 minutes. Set aside to cool.

To make the filling: In a mixing bowl, whisk together the condensed milk, lime zest, egg yolks, lime juice, and cornstarch. Blend well.

In a clean bowl with clean beaters, beat the egg whites on low speed until foamy. Add the salt and cream of tartar, and increase the speed to medium-high. Beat the whites until soft peaks form.

Stir ⅓ of the yolk mixture into the egg whites and combine well. In two additions, carefully fold the remaining egg white mixture into the yolk mixture, folding just until combined.

Pour the filling into the prepared crust. Bake 10 minutes. Cool completely, then chill thoroughly before serving. Serve with whipped cream.

CHEF JAMIE'S LOW-FAT TIP

The low-fat version of this classic remains delicious because of the pungent flavor of real key lime juice. You can substitute egg whites for the butter in the crust and use ¼ cup of liquid egg substitute in place of the egg yolks in the filling (still use the egg whites) without noticing much of a difference. Eliminate the whipped cream garnish!

	PER SERVING				
STANDARD RECIPE:	CALORIES 645	FAT 27G	PROTEIN 14G	CARBOHYDRATES 89G	CHOL 179MG
REDUCED FAT:	CALORIES 517	FAT 12G	PROTEIN 12G	CARBOHYDRATES 90G	CHOL 39MG

No-Bake Lemonade Pie

MAKES 8 SERVINGS

A velvety and refreshing treat. . .with no baking involved. So simple you won't believe it!

For the crust:
2 cups graham cracker crumbs
3 tablespoons sugar
½ cup unsalted butter, melted

For the filling:
1 (14-ounce) can sweetened condensed milk
8 ounces cream cheese, softened
1 (12-ounce) container whipped topping (such as Cool Whip)
1 package powdered pink-lemonade drink mix (such as Kool-Aid)

To make the crust: In a bowl, stir the graham cracker crumbs and sugar together, then blend in the butter until moist. Press into a 9-inch pie plate.

To make the filling: In a large mixing bowl, combine the milk and cream cheese. Beat, using an electric mixer, until completely smooth. Add the powdered drink mix and blend well (mixture will be very thick). Add about two-thirds of the whipped topping and continue mixing until combined.

Mound the filling in the center of the prepared crust and smooth with a cake spatula, making sure the middle of the pie is higher than the sides. Refrigerate several hours or overnight.

Before serving, use a pastry bag, filled with the remaining whipped topping, to decorate the pie.

CHEF JAMIE'S LOW-FAT TIP

To make a light lemonade pie, use non-fat cream cheese and non-fat whipped topping in the mix. Also, prepare a homemade low-fat graham cracker crust using egg whites in place of the melted butter.

		PER SERVING			
STANDARD RECIPE:	CALORIES 399	FAT 21G	PROTEIN 7G	CARBOHYDRATES 45G	CHOL 56MG
REDUCED FAT:	CALORIES 276	FAT 7G	PROTEIN 7G	CARBOHYDRATES 45G	CHOL 14MG

Buttermilk Pie

MAKES 8 SERVINGS

This creamy and delicious pie is a true taste of the Old South.

For the crust:
2 cups graham cracker crumbs
3 tablespoons sugar
½ cup unsalted butter, melted

For the filling:
1 cup sugar
⅓ cup unsalted butter, softened

3 large eggs, separated
3 tablespoons all-purpose flour
pinch of salt
1 teaspoon lemon juice
1 teaspoon freshly grated lemon peel
1½ cups buttermilk

Preheat the oven to 450°F.

To make the crust: In a medium mixing bowl, stir the graham cracker crumbs and sugar; blend in the melted butter until moist. Press into the bottom and up the sides of a 9-inch pie pan.

To make the filling: In a large mixing bowl, cream the sugar and butter until light and fluffy. Add the egg yolks; beat 2 minutes. Add the flour, salt, lemon juice, and lemon peel; blend thoroughly. Add the buttermilk; blend just until combined.

In a clean bowl with clean beaters, whip the egg whites until stiff but not dry. Fold the beaten egg whites into the buttermilk mixture.

Pour the filling into the unbaked pie crust and bake 10 minutes. Reduce the heat to 350°F and bake 40 to 50 minutes more, or until just set. (A cake tester should come out not quite clean when inserted in the pie, as the pie will continue to cook after being removed from the oven.)

CHEF JAMIE'S LOW-FAT TIP

Begin by preparing a low-fat graham cracker crust using egg whites in place of the melted butter. Use ¼ cup of liquid egg substitute instead of the egg yolks.

HELPFUL HINTS FROM THE WIZARD

• All buttermilk is low in fat.

		PER SERVING			
STANDARD RECIPE:	CALORIES 413	FAT 19G	PROTEIN 7G	CARBOHYDRATES 52G	CHOL 92MG
REDUCED FAT:	CALORIES 350	FAT 13G	PROTEIN 7G	CARBOHYDRATES 52G	CHOL 2MG

Southern Pecan Pie

MAKES 8 SERVINGS

No dessert seems more opulent or more perfect for holiday entertaining than a deliciously rich Southern pecan pie generously topped with whipped cream. This recipe is said to have come from the wife of a well-known politician, I'm just not sure which politician! All I know is that it makes one of the best pecan pies I have ever tasted. While this recipe is not exactly diet material (desserts like this one keep me working out every day), the low-fat version below features a nice reduction in calories, for those of you who are trying to be good!

1 unbaked pie crust (see page 240)

For the filling:
1 cup dark corn syrup
¾ cup sugar
4 tablespoons unsalted butter

3 large eggs
1 tablespoon bourbon
1 teaspoon vanilla extract
pinch of salt
1½ cups pecan halves

Preheat the oven to 350°F.

Prepare the pie crust according to the recipe on page 240. Roll out to a 14-inch circle and set it in a 9-inch pie plate; trim and crimp edges. Chill until ready to use.

To make the filling: In a small saucepan, without stirring, bring the corn syrup and sugar to a boil. Remove from the heat and add the butter. Allow the butter to melt, then stir to combine.

In a mixing bowl, whisk together the eggs, bourbon, vanilla, and salt. Slowly add the sugar/syrup mixture, stirring just until combined. Allow the filling to cool slightly. Skim off any foam that may form on the top during cooling.

Arrange the pecan halves in the unbaked, chilled pie crust. Pour the filling over the pecans and, using the back of a fork, push the pecans down into the filling so that they are well coated.

Bake the pie 45 minutes, or until the filling is puffed in the center and set. Cool on a rack, then serve warm or at room temperature.

CHEF JAMIE'S LOW-FAT TIP

The good news is that the lighter version of this pie is just as satisfying as the original. Prepare my Light & Flaky Lower-Fat Pie Crust, using the recipe on the following page. For the filling, use only 2 tablespoons of butter or non-diet tub-style margarine, and 1 whole egg plus ½ cup of liquid egg substitute. As for the pecans, use only 1 cup, but use pecan pieces to ensure that every bite gets that great crunch and flavor!

		PER SERVING			
STANDARD RECIPE:	CALORIES 889	FAT 51G	PROTEIN 10G	CARBOHYDRATES 137G	CHOL 129MG
REDUCED FAT:	CALORIES 736	FAT 36G	PROTEIN 8G	CARBOHYDRATES 95G	CHOL 40MG

Southern Pecan Pie (continued)

LIGHT & FLAKY LOWER-FAT PIE CRUST

1⅓ cups all-purpose flour
1 tablespoon sugar
½ teaspoon salt

3 tablespoons chilled solid vegetable
  shortening
3 tablespoons fat-free cream cheese
3 to 4 tablespoons ice water

In a food processor, blend together the flour, sugar, and salt. Add the cream cheese and shortening, and pulse the processor until the mixture resembles coarse meal. Add the ice water and process until moist clumps form. Gather the dough into a ball, then flatten into a disk shape. Wrap the dough in plastic wrap and refrigerate for 30 minutes. Roll out the chilled dough on a floured surface to a 14-inch round, about ⅛ inch thick. Transfer the dough to a 9-inch pie plate, and trim and crimp the edges. Chill until ready to fill.

HELPFUL HINTS FROM THE WIZARD

- If you brush the bottom of the pie crust with egg white, the filling won't make the crust soggy!

Peanut Butter Chocolate Pie

MAKES 10 SERVINGS

This no-bake pie has an intense peanutty flavor. The recipe calls for a peanut butter crust, but if a chocolate crust is more to your liking, substitute an equal amount of chocolate wafer cookie crumbs. Freezing the crust after you press it into the pie plate is the trick to keeping it from getting soggy!

For the crust:
2 cups peanut butter cookie crumbs
2 tablespoons sugar
3 tablespoons (1½ ounces) unsalted butter, melted

For the filling:
12 ounces cream cheese, softened
¾ cup superfine sugar (See *Chef's Note* below)

1 cup smooth peanut butter
1 tablespoon vanilla extract
1½ cups heavy cream

For the topping:
¾ cup semisweet chocolate chips
2 tablespoons heavy cream
½ cup coarsely chopped roasted peanuts

To make the crust: In a large mixing bowl, combine the cookie crumbs and sugar; blend in the butter. Press into the bottom and up the sides of a 9-inch pie plate. Place in the freezer for 1 hour before assembling the pie.

To make the filling: In a large mixing bowl, thoroughly cream the cream cheese and sugar. Add the peanut butter and vanilla and mix well.

In a separate bowl, whip the heavy cream until stiff peaks form. Fold half the whipped cream into the peanut butter mixture and stir to combine, then add the remaining whipped cream and gently combine just until blended.

Spoon the filling into the frozen crust. Refrigerate, uncovered, 2 hours.

To make the topping: Combine the chocolate chips and cream in a microwave-safe bowl. Microwave on high at 30 second intervals, stirring often, until smooth. Drizzle the topping over the chilled pie and sprinkle the peanuts on top. Chill 2 hours more before serving.

Chef's Note: If you don't have superfine sugar, place sugar or sugar cubes in the food processor and pulse until finely ground but not powdery.

PER SERVING

STANDARD RECIPE:	CALORIES 589	FAT 55G	PROTEIN 14G	CARBOHYDRATES 52G	CHOL 92MG
REDUCED FAT:	CALORIES 386	FAT 26G	PROTEIN 14G	CARBOHYDRATES 54G	CHOL 20MG

Peanut Butter Chocolate Pie (continued)

CHEF JAMIE'S LOW-FAT TIP

Substituting frozen reduced-fat whipped topping (thawed), in place of the heavy cream makes an incredible difference in lowering the fat—using light cream cheese helps even more. Low-fat cream cheese easily replaces the regular cream cheese in the filling, and reduced-fat chocolate chips and half & half work great for the topping.

HELPFUL HINTS FROM THE WIZARD

- Do not use all-natural peanut butter in this recipe—the oil will separate.

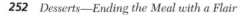

J.G.'s Caramel Candy Pie

MAKES 8 SERVINGS

Using gooey caramel candies makes this pie scrumptious. Use a store-bought chocolate pie crust if you so choose!

For the crust:
1½ cups chocolate wafer cookie crumbs (about 30 cookies)
6 tablespoons unsalted butter, melted

For the filling
40 soft caramel candies
¼ cup water
4 tablespoons (2 ounces) unsalted butter
¾ cup sugar
3 large eggs, beaten
1 teaspoon vanilla extract
pinch of salt
1½ cups pecan halves

Preheat the oven to 350°F.

To make the crust: In a food processor fitted with a metal blade, process the wafers into fine crumbs. Transfer to a bowl and mix in the melted butter until moist. Press into the bottom and up the sides of a 9-inch pie pan.

To make the filling: In the top of a covered double boiler, over hot water, melt the caramels with the water and butter over very low heat, stirring often. When melted, remove from the heat and allow to cool slightly.

In a mixing bowl, whisk together the sugar, eggs, vanilla, and salt. Slowly pour the melted caramel mixture into the egg mixture, stirring constantly with a wooden spoon. Stir to combine well. Add the pecan halves and mix thoroughly.

Pour into the prepared pie shell and bake 45 minutes. Let cool at room temperature.

CHEF JAMIE'S LOW-FAT TIP

Low-fat and fat-free candy is one of the greatest inventions, in my opinion! Fat-free caramels work very well in this pie, significantly lowering your fat intake. For a lighter crust, use 1½ cups of low-fat chocolate graham cracker crumbs, 50 percent-less-fat butter, and 3 egg whites.

		PER SERVING		
STANDARD RECIPE:	CALORIES 750	FAT 46G	PROTEIN 8G	CARBOHYDRATES 74G	CHOL 121MG
REDUCED FAT:	CALORIES 542	FAT 25G	PROTEIN 8G	CARBOHYDRATES 66G	CHOL 96MG

Fudgy Chocolate Brownies

MAKES 12 SERVINGS

The Sears-Roebuck catalog published the first known recipe for brownies in 1897, and they quickly became terrifically popular! Traditional American brownies. . .what could be better?

2 sticks unsalted butter

4 ounces unsweetened chocolate

2 ounces bittersweet chocolate

4 large eggs

1¾ cups sugar

½ cup all-purpose flour

1 teaspoon vanilla extract

⅓ cup chopped walnuts

Preheat the oven to 350°F. Grease a 9 × 13-inch baking pan.

Combine the butter and all of the chocolate (both unsweetened and bittersweet) in the top of a double boiler and place over simmering water; stir often until chocolate is melted. Set aside to cool to room temperature.

In a large mixing bowl, beat the eggs and sugar together until thick and pale yellow. Stir in the vanilla. Fold the chocolate mixture into the egg mixture and mix thoroughly.

Gently fold the flour into the egg mixture just until blended. Fold in the walnuts.

Pour the batter into the prepared pan. Bake 25 minutes, or until the center is just set. Do not over bake.

Allow to cool in the pan for 30 minutes before cutting.

CHEF JAMIE'S LOW-FAT TIP

These lower-fat brownies are scrumptious! Use only 1 stick of reduced-fat (50 percent-less-fat) butter or stick margarine in place of the 2 sticks above. For the eggs, use 1 whole egg and 4 egg whites. Also, add ½ teaspoon of baking powder to the batter to aid in leavening. Be sure to spray the pan well with non-stick cooking spray before pouring the batter in.

PER SERVING

STANDARD RECIPE:	CALORIES 456	FAT 34G	PROTEIN 23G	CARBOHYDRATES 37G	CHOL 115MG
REDUCED FAT:	CALORIES 369	FAT 20G	PROTEIN 14G	CARBOHYDRATES 37G	CHOL 40MG

Chocolate Mint Brownies

MAKES 15 SERVINGS

Another Home & Family Television favorite, these brownies are rich and chocolaty, and minty, too! The secret is to use purchased peppermint patty candies, large or small, for that great, fresh mint flavor and a little extra chocolate!

8 ounces unsweetened chocolate
1 stick (4 ounces) unsalted butter
5 large eggs
3½ cups sugar
2 teaspoons vanilla extract

pinch of salt
1⅓ cups all-purpose flour
2 cups chopped walnuts
2 pounds peppermint patties

Preheat the oven to 425°F. Line a 9 × 13 × 2-inch glass baking dish with aluminum foil. Spray the foil with non-stick cooking spray.

In the top of a double boiler, over hot water, melt the unsweetened chocolate and butter, stirring often, until smooth. Remove from the heat and let cool slightly.

In a large mixing bowl, beat together the eggs, sugar, vanilla, and salt on high speed for 8 to 10 minutes. Turn the mixer to low and add the melted-chocolate mixture. Beat until just combined, then add the flour. Beat on low until just blended. Stir in the walnuts by hand.

To assemble the brownies, pour half the batter into the prepared pan and smooth the top. Place the peppermint patties very close together on top of the chocolate layer. Carefully spread the remaining batter over the candies. Bake 35 minutes.

Lift the edges of the foil, so the brownies come out of the pan in one piece. Cool completely on a wire rack before cutting.

CHEF JAMIE'S LOW-FAT TIP

Did you know that peppermint patties have the least amount of fat of any chocolate candy? To significantly lower the fat in these brownies, use only half the peppermint patties, and remove the walnuts altogether. Use reduced-fat (50 percent-less-fat) butter or non-diet tub margarine and 2 whole eggs, plus ½ cup of liquid egg substitute in place of the 5 eggs.

		PER BROWNIE		
STANDARD RECIPE:	CALORIES 767	FAT 35G	PROTEIN 10G	CARBOHYDRATES 105G	CHOL 87MG
REDUCED FAT:	CALORIES 442	FAT 11G	PROTEIN 2G	CARBOHYDRATES 79G	CHOL 39MG

Homemade Chocolate Pudding
MAKES 6 SERVINGS

There is nothing better than licking the bowl after making homemade chocolate pudding. This recipe is thick and rich and wonderful! And remember, the better the quality of the chocolate you use, the better the pudding will taste!

4 ounces good-quality bittersweet chocolate

3 tablespoons (1½ ounces) unsalted butter

½ cup sugar

2 tablespoons cornstarch

¼ cup unsweetened cocoa powder

2½ cups milk

1 large egg

2 egg yolks

Chef's Note: The trick to preventing a skin from forming on the pudding is to keep the surface from being exposed to the air—follow the instructions below carefully!

In the top of a double boiler, over simmering water, heat the chocolate and butter, stirring often until melted.

In a large mixing bowl, whisk together the cornstarch, cocoa and ½ cup of the sugar. Whisk in ½ cup of milk and combine well. Then whisk in the egg and yolks, one at a time, mixing well after each addition.

In a large saucepan, over medium heat, bring the remaining 2 cups of milk and ¼ cup of sugar to a simmer. When it just begins to simmer, remove from the heat and, while constantly whisking, drizzle the hot liquid into the egg mixture. Return the blended mixture to the saucepan and continue whisking constantly, being sure to scrape the bottom of the pan to avoid scorching, until the mixture thickens and bubbles rise from the bottom. Remove from the heat and strain.

Stir the melted chocolate/butter mixture into the pudding and blend well. Pour into 6 individual serving bowls or 1 large bowl and place a sheet of waxed paper directly on the surface to prevent a skin from forming. Let cool 1 hour, then refrigerate until thoroughly chilled.

PER SERVING

STANDARD RECIPE:	CALORIES 238	FAT 13G	PROTEIN 19G	CARBOHYDRATES 26G	CHOL 84MG
REDUCED FAT:	CALORIES 175	FAT 6G	PROTEIN 19G	CARBOHYDRATES 26G	CHOL 71MG

CHEF JAMIE'S LOW-FAT TIP

To lower the fat in this recipe, eliminate the butter completely and use only 3 ounces of bittersweet chocolate. In addition, use only 1 egg and 1 egg yolk. The pudding will still taste delicious but will be better for you!

Really, Really Easy Chocolate Bread Pudding

MAKES 6 SERVINGS

This bread pudding is a childhood favorite with a new twist.

4 cups day-old bread, cubed
3 cups chocolate milk
3 large eggs

1½ cups sugar
1 tablespoon vanilla extract
1 cup mini chocolate chips

Preheat the oven to 350°F. Grease an 8-inch-square cake pan.

In a large mixing bowl, combine the bread cubes and chocolate milk and let stand for 15 minutes.

In a separate bowl, whisk together the eggs, sugar, and vanilla. Pour the egg mixture into the bread mixture and mix well. Stir in the chocolate chips.

Pour into the prepared pan and bake 1 hour, or until set and golden brown. Serve warm with whipped cream.

CHEF JAMIE'S LOW-FAT TIP

This low-fat version is just as good as the full-of-fat one! To lighten the recipe, use 3 cups of non-fat milk and ¼ cup of unsweetened cocoa powder instead of chocolate milk. Scald the milk, then whisk in the cocoa to dissolve. Let cool slightly, then pour over the bread and let stand for 15 minutes. Use ¾ cup of liquid egg substitute in place of the whole eggs and use ½ cup of *reduced-fat* chocolate chips instead of the real ones.

HELPFUL HINTS FROM THE WIZARD

- Low-fat chocolate milk is also available, and can be used instead of the non-fat milk and cocoa mixture.

	PER SERVING				
STANDARD RECIPE:	CALORIES 450	FAT 14G	PROTEIN 10G	CARBOHYDRATES 109G	CHOL 122MG
REDUCED FAT:	CALORIES 390	FAT 8G	PROTEIN 9G	CARBOHYDRATES 112G	CHOL 34MG

Old-Fashioned Rice Pudding

MAKES 6 SERVINGS

Rice pudding brings back so many wonderful childhood memories . . . and it has a magical way of making you feel better at the first bite! This rice pudding is baked, then served out of the pan.

¾ cup sugar
2 large eggs, beaten
¼ teaspoon salt
2 cups milk
1 teaspoon vanilla extract

1¼ cups cooked white rice
½ cup seedless golden raisins
1 teaspoon cinnamon
dash of nutmeg

Preheat the oven to 325°F. Butter a 1-quart casserole dish.

In a large mixing bowl, whisk together the sugar, eggs, and salt. Stir in the milk, vanilla, rice, raisins, cinnamon, and nutmeg, and blend thoroughly.

Pour into the prepared dish. Place the casserole dish in a shallow pan filled with 1 inch hot water. Bake for 1½ hours, or until set.

Serve warm or cold.

CHEF JAMIE'S LOW-FAT TIP

Low-fat rice pudding is a dream come true. Using low-fat milk in place of whole milk and ½ cup liquid egg substitute in place of the 2 whole eggs will allow you to indulge, guilt free.

		PER SERVING			
STANDARD RECIPE:	CALORIES 279	FAT 5G	PROTEIN 6G	CARBOHYDRATES 56G	CHOL 82MG
REDUCED FAT:	CALORIES 247	FAT 2G	PROTEIN 5G	CARBOHYDRATES 56G	CHOL 9MG

The Perfect Chocolate Soufflé

MAKES 6 SERVINGS

A chocolate lover's dream! In French, "soufflé" means to puff up. The air beaten into the egg whites expands inward from the heat of the oven, making the soufflé light and puffy. When you carry a soufflé to the table, everyone will "oooh" and "ahhh"!

2 tablespoons unsalted butter
3 tablespoons all-purpose flour
1½ cups milk
12 ounces bittersweet chocolate, chopped

½ cup sugar
5 large eggs, separated
1 teaspoon vanilla extract
¼ teaspoon cream of tartar
whipped cream, for garnish

Preheat the oven to 375°F. Butter a 2-quart soufflé dish and dust with sugar.

In a saucepan over medium heat, melt the butter. Stir in the flour until blended. In a separate saucepan, heat the milk until almost boiling. Add the chocolate and ¼ cup of the sugar to the hot milk, and stir until dissolved. Slowly add the milk mixture to the flour mixture, stirring to combine. Set aside to cool slightly.

Beat the egg yolks until very light in color. Add half of the chocolate mixture to the beaten egg yolks and mix well. Pour this mixture into the remaining chocolate mixture and stir constantly over very low heat until slightly thickened. Allow to cool to room temperature. Add the vanilla to the cooled mixture.

Beat the egg whites with the cream of tartar until soft peaks form. Gradually add the remaining ¼ cup sugar and beat until peaks are stiff and glossy. Gently fold the beaten egg whites into the chocolate mixture. Pour into the prepared soufflé dish and bake about 40 minutes, until the soufflé has risen and is firm. Serve immediately with whipped cream.

CHEF JAMIE'S LOW-FAT TIP

For starters, use reduced-fat (50 percent-less-fat) butter and low-fat milk. Use 2 tablespoons of liquid egg substitute plus 2 real egg yolks in place of the 5 egg yolks. The beaten egg whites will ensure the rising of the soufflé, and using a good-quality chocolate will help you forget you ever lowered the fat in the first place.

			PER SERVING		
STANDARD RECIPE:	CALORIES 218	FAT 26G	PROTEIN 9G	CARBOHYDRATES 54G	CHOL 200MG
REDUCED FAT:	CALORIES 136	FAT 19G	PROTEIN 6G	CARBOHYDRATES 54G	CHOL 88MG

Coffee–Almond Baked Alaska

MAKES 8 SERVINGS

An impressive dessert to serve to company, this Baked Alaska is a thing of beauty! In 1867, Chef Charles Ranhofer, of the famous Delmonico's Restaurant in New York City, created a new cake to celebrate the United States' purchase of Alaska. He called it the Alaska-Florida Cake, but the name was soon changed to Baked Alaska!

I have simplified this dramatic dessert so that you can serve it without too much fuss. Completely assembled, it will last in the freezer up to one month, and can simply be browned in the oven before serving. The traditional dessert is made with vanilla ice cream, but I used my favorite ice cream flavor for this recipe. The ice cream and nuts can easily be altered to suit your own taste!

1 quart coffee ice cream, slightly softened
¾ cup sliced almonds, toasted
1 (16-ounce) pound cake
5 egg whites
⅛ teaspoon cream of tartar
pinch of salt
1¼ cups superfine sugar
(see *Chef's Note* on page 251)

Line an 8 × 4-inch loaf pan with plastic wrap, with enough overhang to cover the top. In a large mixing bowl, stir almond slices into the softened ice cream; spread it into the prepared loaf pan, cover with the overhanging plastic wrap, and refreeze until hard.

Cut a ¾-inch-thick slice, horizontally, from the pound cake and place it in the center of an ovenproof platter. Remove the plastic wrap from the loaf of frozen ice cream and place the ice cream on the slice of pound cake.

Slice the remaining cake, horizontally, into 3 even slices. Place one layer of cake on top of the ice cream. Cut the second layer of cake in half lengthwise and press one-half against each lengthwise side of the ice cream. Cut the third layer of cake in half crosswise and place at ends of ice cream, completely enclosing the cake. Trim the ends to fit neatly. Cover and freeze until ready to assemble.

To make the meringue: Beat the egg whites with the cream of tartar and salt until soft peaks form. Gradually beat in the sugar, 2 tablespoons at a time, beating until stiff, glossy peaks form.

Spoon the meringue onto the frozen cake, completely sealing the top and sides of the cake with a 1-inch layer of meringue. Swirl remaining meringue on the top of the cake. Freeze the assembled Alaska, uncovered, until the meringue is hard, then cover tightly with plastic wrap.

		PER SERVING			
STANDARD RECIPE:	CALORIES 431	FAT 23G	PROTEIN 10G	CARBOHYDRATES 65G	CHOL 19MG
REDUCED FAT:	CALORIES 299	FAT 0G	PROTEIN 7G	CARBOHYDRATES 61G	CHOL 17MG

When ready to serve, preheat the broiler to high. Remove the Alaska from the freezer and place about 4 inches away from the heat. Broil until golden all over.

CHEF JAMIE'S LOW-FAT TIP

Create a fat-free Baked Alaska (what a treat!) by using fat-free pound cake (available for purchase in most supermarket bakery aisles), and fat-free ice cream, and by eliminating the nuts. The meringue is fat-free as is!

HELPFUL HINTS FROM THE WIZARD

- If you do a lot of baking that requires egg whites, you might consider buying egg whites in bulk from a bakery supply house, since they freeze well.

Praline Ice Cream

MAKES 2 QUARTS (16 SERVINGS)

I guarantee that the creaminess of the ice cream and the crunch of the praline will tempt you to finish the entire batch in one sitting! The praline itself is delicious over ice cream or when used to flavor icings and cake fillings!

1 cup blanched almonds	6 cups heavy cream
1⅓ cups sugar	¼ teaspoon salt
3 tablespoons water	

Preheat the oven to 350°F. Lightly butter a 9 × 13-inch glass baking pan.

Toast the almonds in the oven until light brown, about 10 to 15 minutes, stirring often.

Stir the sugar and water in a 1-quart saucepan. Cook over medium heat, stirring constantly, until the sugar begins to turn light brown. Remove from the heat when the sugar mixture becomes light to medium brown (it will continue to darken from its own heat). Immediately stir in the nuts. Return the pan to the heat and bring back to a boil. As soon as it comes to a boil, remove from the heat and pour into the prepared glass pan. Allow the praline to cool completely, then break it into pieces and place it in a food processor fitted with a metal blade. Process the chunks to make a crunchy, but not powdery, praline.

Heat two cups of the cream in a heavy saucepan until a shiny film develops on the top of the cream. Remove from the heat and stir in the remaining sugar, the salt, and half the prepared praline. Stir to dissolve the sugar completely. Allow to cool completely before continuing.

Stir the remaining cream into the cooled mixture, then stir in the remaining praline. Pour into an ice cream maker and process according to the manufacturer's instructions.

CHEF JAMIE'S LOW-FAT TIP

The low-fat praline ice cream recipe given below is a good substitute for the full-of-fat recipe above. . . and almost as tasty!

	PER SERVING (½ CUP)				
STANDARD RECIPE:	CALORIES 433	FAT 39G	PROTEIN 4G	CARBOHYDRATES 19G	CHOL 126MG
REDUCED FAT:	CALORIES 54	FAT .6G	PROTEIN 2G	CARBOHYDRATES 10G	CHOL 3MG

CHEF JAMIE'S LOW-FAT ICE CREAM

For low-fat praline ice cream, replace the cream with 4 cups of low-fat milk, substitute 2 teaspoons of vanilla for the almonds, and add 1 (10-ounce) jar of fat-free caramel topping. Combine all of the ingredients in a large bowl. Stir until well blended. Pour into an ice cream maker and freeze according to the manufacturer's instructions. Transfer to a freezer-safe container, cover, and freeze for 1 hour, or until firm. Makes 6 cups of LOW-FAT ICE CREAM!

HELPFUL HINTS FROM THE WIZARD

- When storing ice cream, place a piece of plastic wrap over the top of the ice cream before closing the container's lid to help prevent ice crystals from forming.

Old-Fashioned Fudge

MAKES 5 POUNDS (ABOUT 50 PIECES)

This is one of the easiest candy recipes around! It is unbelievably rich, and makes a lovely holiday or hostess gift.

18 ounces chocolate chips
2 sticks unsalted butter
8 ounces marshmallow cream
2 cups chopped nuts

2 teaspoons vanilla extract
pinch of salt
4 cups sugar
1 (8-ounce) can evaporated milk

Line an 8-inch-square baking pan and a 9 × 13-inch baking pan with aluminum foil.

In a large mixing bowl, stir the chocolate chips, butter, marshmallow cream, nuts, vanilla, and salt. Set aside.

In a 4-quart saucepan, stir the sugar and evaporated milk. Bring to a full rolling boil over medium heat, stirring constantly. Cook 10 minutes, continuing to stir constantly. Pour the hot mixture over the chocolate chip mixture. Stir vigorously until thoroughly mixed. Pour into the prepared pans. Cool completely. Cut into squares and store at room temperature.

CHEF JAMIE'S LOW-FAT TIP

Reduced-fat chocolate chips are a gift from the food gods! Look for them in your local supermarket to make a lower-fat version of this fantasy fudge. Also, low-fat evaporated milk is a great substitute for the full-of-fat kind.

HELPFUL HINTS FROM THE WIZARD

- Evaporated milk will go stale after about 6 months, so it's best to use it while fresh.
- High-quality chocolate chips will make a big difference in the taste of the fudge.

PER PIECE

STANDARD RECIPE:	CALORIES 181	FAT 11G	PROTEIN 3G	CARBOHYDRATES 25G	CHOL 1.5MG
REDUCED FAT:	CALORIES 121	FAT 5G	PROTEIN 3G	CARBOHYDRATES 25G	CHOL 1.4MG

Best Ever Homemade Caramels

MAKES ABOUT 50 CARAMELS

These gooey caramels always please candy lovers. This is one of my most-requested recipes!

2 cups sugar
1 cup brown sugar
1 stick unsalted butter, softened
1 cup whole milk

1 cup heavy cream
1 cup light corn syrup
1 teaspoon vanilla extract

Butter a 9 × 13-inch glass baking dish.

In a heavy 4-quart saucepan, combine the sugar, brown sugar, butter, milk, heavy cream, and corn syrup. Cook over low heat until the sugar is dissolved and the butter has melted, about 20 minutes. Place a candy thermometer in the pan and continue cooking until the candy thermometer reaches 248°F. Do not stir during the cooking process. It should take about 1 to 1½ hours to reach 248°F. When the temperature reaches 230°, watch carefully, because it will rise quickly from that point.

Remove from the heat and stir in the vanilla. Pour into the prepared pan and cool completely at room temperature. Cut into 1-inch squares and wrap individually with wax paper.

CHEF JAMIE'S LOW-FAT TIP

Low-fat caramels (not low-sugar, though) can be made with reduced-fat (50 percent-less-fat) butter, low-fat milk in place of whole milk, and low-fat half & half in place of the heavy cream.

PER CARAMEL

	CALORIES	FAT	PROTEIN	CARBOHYDRATES	CHOL
STANDARD RECIPE:	CALORIES 86	FAT 4G	PROTEIN .3G	CARBOHYDRATES 17G	CHOL 7MG
REDUCED FAT:	CALORIES 66	FAT 2G	PROTEIN .3G	CARBOHYDRATES 17G	CHOL 2MG+

Chapter 12

Old-Fashioned Cookies

Crispy or chewy, studded with chocolate chips or gloriously simple, cookies are everyone's favorite. Consider fresh-baked cookies a portable dessert for a sunny picnic, or settle down with a plateful and a cup of tea for an afternoon treat—whenever and wherever, these sweet morsels are always hard to resist!

Chocolate–Marshmallow Cookies

MAKES ABOUT 40 COOKIES

These tempting cookies, with their gooey marshmallow topping and chocolaty frosting, are truly hard to resist!

For the cookies:

1 cup sugar

½ cup vegetable shortening

2 large eggs

1¾ cups all-purpose flour

½ cup unsweetened cocoa powder

1 teaspoon baking soda

½ teaspoon salt

2 teaspoons vanilla extract

20 large marshmallows, cut in half

For the frosting:

½ cup semisweet chocolate chips

¼ cup whole milk

2 tablespoons unsalted butter

2 cups powdered sugar

To make the cookies: In a large mixing bowl, cream together the sugar and the shortening. Add the eggs, one at a time, beating well after each addition.

In a separate bowl, combine the flour, cocoa, baking soda, and salt. Add the flour mixture to the creamed mixture and beat well. Stir in the vanilla. (Dough will be stiff.) Chill at least 30 minutes before forming cookies.

Preheat the oven to 350°F.

Shape the dough into 1-inch balls and place on greased cookie sheets. Bake 8 minutes. Remove from the oven and place a marshmallow half on top of each cookie. Bake the cookies for 2 more minutes. Cool on wire racks.

To make the frosting: Combine the chocolate chips, milk, and butter in a saucepan. Cook over low heat, stirring constantly, until the chocolate melts. Add the sugar, beating until smooth. Add more milk if necessary for proper spreading consistency. Top each cookie with frosting.

CHEF JAMIE'S LOW-FAT TIP

Did you know that marshmallows are fat-free? That's one less thing in this recipe to lighten! As for the cookies, use ¼ cup of 50 percent-less-fat butter and ¼ cup of light sour cream in place of the shortening. Cream the butter with the sugar and add the sour cream after the eggs. The frosting becomes even lower in fat when you use reduced-fat chocolate chips (a delicious alternative), low-fat milk, and just 1 tablespoon of butter.

		PER COOKIE		
STANDARD RECIPE:	CALORIES 119	FAT 5G	PROTEIN 1G	CARBOHYDRATES 20G	CHOL 11MG
REDUCED FAT:	CALORIES 110	FAT 2G	PROTEIN 1G	CARBOHYDRATES 21G	CHOL 12MG

Thumbprint Cookies

MAKES ABOUT 24

We all remember thumbprint cookies from childhood—keep them in the cookie jar for your children, too!

½ cup vegetable shortening
¼ cup brown sugar
1 large egg, separated
1 teaspoon vanilla extract

1 cup all-purpose flour
pinch of salt
¾ cup pecans, chopped
jam or jelly, for filling

Preheat the oven to 350°F.

In a large mixing bowl, beat together the shortening, brown sugar, egg yolk, and vanilla. In a separate bowl, combine the flour and salt. Add the flour mixture to the creamed mixture; stir to combine well.

Using 1 teaspoon of dough per cookie, form balls of dough. Dip each ball into the lightly beaten egg white, then roll in the chopped nuts.

Place the balls about 1 inch apart on an ungreased baking sheet. Press a thumbprint into the center of each cookie.

Bake 10 minutes, or until lightly golden. Remove from the oven and fill each thumbprint with a small amount of jam or jelly. Return the cookies to the oven and bake 2 minutes more.

CHEF JAMIE'S LOW-FAT TIP

These well-loved cookies slim down quite well with the substitution of 50 percent-less-fat butter for the shortening and a reduction of the pecans to ¼ cup. Their texture changes slightly though, becoming crisper in baking. Be sure not to eliminate the whole egg, as the cookies just won't bake the same.

HELPFUL HINTS FROM THE WIZARD

* To keep cookies moist in a cookie jar, add a slice of bread or half an apple to the jar.

		PER COOKIE		
STANDARD RECIPE:	CALORIES 163	FAT 14G	PROTEIN 2G	CARBOHYDRATES 8G	CHOL 9MG
REDUCED FAT:	CALORIES 112	FAT 7G	PROTEIN 1G	CARBOHYDRATES 8G	CHOL 9MG

Grandma's Rugelach

MAKES 4 DOZEN

Rugelach are small, filled pastries with a rich, flaky dough. After baking, this sour cream dough has a light, flaky texture similar to that of puff pastry.

2 cups all-purpose flour
pinch of salt
2 sticks unsalted butter, cut into small pieces
6 ounces cream cheese, cut into small pieces
⅓ cup sour cream

¾ cup sugar
2 teaspoons cinnamon
1 teaspoon unsweetened cocoa powder
2 cups walnuts, toasted and chopped fine

Preheat the oven to 350°F.

In a food processor, pulse the flour, salt, and butter until it resembles coarse meal. Add the cream cheese and sour cream and pulse the machine again, just until the mixture holds together and begins to form a ball. Turn the dough out onto a floured work surface and form into a ball. Flatten the ball into a disc shape and wrap well in plastic wrap. Refrigerate until thoroughly chilled, several hours or overnight.

In a small mixing bowl, combine the sugar, cinnamon, and cocoa powder. Set aside.

Divide the dough into four pieces and work with only one piece at a time, keeping the remaining dough chilled. Press one of the dough pieces into a round disc shape, then roll it into a 9-inch circle about ⅛ inch thick. Sprinkle one quarter of the sugar mixture over the dough, then sprinkle with ½ cup of the chopped nuts. Using a rolling pin, roll over the filling so the ingredients are pressed slightly into the dough. Cut the circle pie style into 12 wedges. Roll each wedge up tightly, beginning at the wide end. Curve each pastry to a crescent and place, point side down, on a parchment paper–lined cookie sheet. Repeat with the remaining dough, sugar mixture, and nuts.

Bake 20 to 25 minutes or until golden brown. Cool on racks.

Chef's Note: Baked rugelach can be stored in an airtight container for up to 3 days, or can be frozen, baked or unbaked, for several months.

	PER COOKIE				
STANDARD RECIPE:	CALORIES 132	FAT 11G	PROTEIN 3G	CARBOHYDRATES 9G	CHOL 5MG
REDUCED FAT:	CALORIES 108	FAT 8G	PROTEIN 3G	CARBOHYDRATES 9G	CHOL 2MG

Grandma's Rugelach *(continued)*

CHEF JAMIE'S LOW-FAT TIP
Until I tested this recipe in its low-fat form, I would never have believed that rugelach could be tasty without all the richness. The recipe turned out perfectly using light cream cheese, reduced-fat (50 percent-less-fat) butter, and light sour cream.

Old-Fashioned Chocolate Chip Cookies

MAKES 24

These classic chocolate chip cookies are sure to please!

1 stick unsalted butter
⅓ cup sugar
⅓ cup dark brown sugar
½ teaspoon salt
teaspoon vanilla extract

¼ teaspoon cold water
½ teaspoon baking soda
1 cup all-purpose flour
12 ounces semisweet chocolate chips
½ cup chopped pecans

Preheat the oven to 375°F and grease 2 large cookie sheets.

In a large mixing bowl, cream the butter, sugar, brown sugar, salt, vanilla, and water until light and fluffy. Beat in the egg and the baking soda. Add the flour, ¼ cup at a time, until the dough is well combined. By hand, stir in the chocolate chips and the nuts.

With a tablespoon, drop the batter onto the prepared cookie sheets about 1½ inches apart.

Gently pat the tops of the cookies with a spatula, but don't flatten them entirely. Bake 10 to 12 minutes, or until lightly brown.

CHEF JAMIE'S LOW-FAT TIP

For delicious, low-fat cookies, add 1 tablespoon of smooth applesauce to the recipe for added moisture and texture. And, use non-diet stick margarine or reduced-fat (50 percent-less-fat) butter, 2 egg whites, and reduced-fat chocolate baking chips.

		PER COOKIE		
STANDARD RECIPE:	CALORIES 138	FAT 12G	PROTEIN 2G	CARBOHYDRATES 20G	CHOL 9MG
REDUCED FAT:	CALORIES 99	FAT 6G	PROTEIN 2G	CARBOHYDRATES 24G	CHOL 0MG

Lemon Crisps

MAKES ABOUT 7 DOZEN

Lemon zest adds a tangy zip to these delicate cookies. They freeze well, too.

2 sticks unsalted butter
1½ cups sugar
4 egg yolks
juice of 1 lemon

2 teaspoons freshly grated lemon zest
¼ teaspoon lemon extract
3 cups all-purpose flour
½ teaspoon salt

Using an electric mixer, cream together the butter and sugar until light and fluffy. Add the egg yolks, lemon juice, lemon zest, and lemon extract. Continue beating until pale yellow in color.

By hand, mix in the flour and salt, until just blended. Do not over mix. Form 2 cylinders, each 2 inches in diameter. Wrap and chill the dough in the refrigerator until firm, several hours or overnight. (The dough can also be frozen at this point.)

When ready to bake, preheat the oven to 375°F. Grease a cookie sheet. Slice the cookie dough ⅛ inch thick and place slices 1 inch apart on the prepared cookie sheets. Bake 8 to 10 minutes, or until lightly brown around the edges. Remove the cookies to a rack and allow to cool completely. Store the cookies in an airtight container.

CHEF JAMIE'S LOW-FAT TIP

Use just 1½ sticks of butter in the crisps (the recipe still works!), and make it reduced-fat (50 percent-less-fat) butter or non-diet stick margarine to significantly lower your fat consumption. In place of the egg yolks, substitute 2 tablespoons of liquid egg substitute and 2 large egg whites. Bake the low-fat cookies at 350°F to avoid burning.

HELPFUL HINTS FROM THE WIZARD

• Microwaving the lemon for a few seconds before juicing it will cause it to release more juice.

		PER COOKIE		
STANDARD RECIPE:	CALORIES 55	FAT 3G	PROTEIN .6G	CARBOHYDRATES 7G	CHOL 10MG
REDUCED FAT:	CALORIES 42	FAT 1G	PROTEIN .6G	CARBOHYDRATES 7G	CHOL 0MG

Oatmeal Chocolate-Chip Cookies

MAKES ABOUT 2 DOZEN

Growing up, I used to love these cookies fresh out of the oven. Today, to bring the cookies to a whole new level, I like to sandwich vanilla ice cream in between two oversized cookies, refreeze until hard, then enjoy homemade ice cream sandwiches!

1 cup vegetable shortening
¾ cup sugar
¾ cup brown sugar
2 large eggs
1 teaspoon vanilla extract

1½ cups all-purpose flour
1 teaspoon baking soda
1 teaspoon salt
2 cups old-fashioned oats
2 cups semisweet chocolate chips

Preheat the oven to 375°F.

In a large mixing bowl, cream the shortening and the sugars until smooth and fluffy. Add the eggs, one at a time, mixing thoroughly after each addition; stir in the vanilla. Sift together the flour, baking soda, and salt, and add it to the creamed mixture. By hand, stir in the oats and chocolate chips.

Drop the dough by spoonfuls, or roll into small balls, and place on ungreased cookie sheets. Bake 10 to 12 minutes.

CHEF JAMIE'S LOW-FAT TIP

These lighter cookies tend to be a bit crispier, but just as delicious. Substitute reduced-fat (50 percent-less-fat) butter for the shortening, and use 1 whole egg and ¼ cup liquid egg substitute in place of the 2 whole eggs. Reduced-fat chocolate chips work well in place of the real ones, or use raisins instead of the chocolate chips, to lower the fat considerably. Store the cookies in an airtight container, between layers of waxed paper, to prevent sticking.

HELPFUL HINTS FROM THE WIZARD

- Use only high-quality vanilla extract when baking.

		PER COOKIE			
STANDARD RECIPE:	CALORIES 178	FAT 11G	PROTEIN 2G	CARBOHYDRATES 18G	CHOL 18MG
REDUCED FAT:	CALORIES 133	FAT 5G	PROTEIN 2G	CARBOHYDRATES 18G	CHOL 9MG

My Favorite Peanut Butter Cookies

MAKES 4 DOZEN

Chill the dough before baking to firm it slightly—15 minutes is about right. The chilling relaxes the gluten and produces a more tender cookie.

2 sticks (8 ounces) unsalted butter, softened
1 cup chunky peanut butter
1 cup brown sugar
¾ cup sugar

1 teaspoon vanilla extract
2 large eggs, well beaten
2½ cups all-purpose flour
¾ teaspoon baking soda
pinch of salt

In a large mixing bowl, cream the butter, peanut butter, sugars and vanilla until well combined. Add the eggs; mix well.

In a separate bowl, combine the flour, baking soda, and salt. Add the dry ingredients to the butter mixture and blend well.

Roll the cookie dough into a long cylinder and wrap tightly with plastic wrap. Refrigerate at least 15 minutes.

To bake the cookies, preheat the oven to 350°F. Lightly grease a cookie sheet. Cut the cookies about ½ inch thick and place them on the cookie sheet about 1 inch apart. Bake 12 to 15 minutes.

CHEF JAMIE'S LOW-FAT TIP

The invention of reduced-fat peanut butter is a true blessing when it comes to these cookies. Reduced-fat (50 percent-less-fat) butter works well in this recipe also, and ¼ cup liquid egg substitute can be mixed with 1 whole egg to lower your cholesterol!

HELPFUL HINTS FROM THE WIZARD

• Storing brown sugar in the freezer prevents the sugar from clumping up and becoming solid.

		PER COOKIE			
STANDARD RECIPE:	CALORIES 115	FAT 7G	PROTEIN 2G	CARBOHYDRATES 11G	CHOL 9MG
REDUCED FAT:	CALORIES 96	FAT 4G	PROTEIN 2G	CARBOHYDRATES 11G	CHOL 5MG

Molasses Cookies

MAKES 4 DOZEN

This recipe comes from Mississippi, where they know their molasses! These spicy cookies keep very well in an airtight container.

1½ sticks unsalted butter
1 cup sugar
1 large egg
¼ cup molasses
2 cups all-purpose flour

2 teaspoons baking soda
¼ teaspoon salt
2 teaspoons ground allspice
1 teaspoon ground cinnamon
⅛ teaspoon ground black pepper
superfine sugar, for dusting (see
    Chef's Note on page 251)

Preheat the oven to 350°F.

In a large mixing bowl, cream together the butter and sugar. Add the egg and the molasses, and blend to combine well.

In a separate bowl, combine the flour, baking soda, salt, allspice, cinnamon, and black pepper. Add the dry ingredients to the butter mixture and mix well.

Form balls 1 inch in diameter, then roll each ball in superfine sugar to coat. Place the sugar-dusted cookies on an ungreased cookie sheet.

Bake the cookies for 12 to 15 minutes.

CHEF JAMIE'S LOW-FAT TIP

The molasses in the cookies helps keep them moist and allows you to create a lower-fat cookie by cutting the butter in the recipe to only 1 stick and adding an additional 2 tablespoons of molasses. Use 2 egg whites in place of the whole egg for a crispier yet still deliciously robust cookie.

HELPFUL HINTS FROM THE WIZARD

• Blackstrap molasses is the healthiest form of molasses.

		PER COOKIE			
STANDARD RECIPE:	CALORIES 52	FAT 3G	PROTEIN .1G	CARBOHYDRATES 6G	CHOL 4MG
REDUCED FAT:	CALORIES 42	FAT 1G	PROTEIN .1G	CARBOHYDRATES 6G	CHOL 0MG K

Appendix

Roasting Chart

	OVEN TEMPERATURE	ROASTING TIME	INTERNAL TEMPERATURE
Poultry			
Chicken, unstuffed (3 to 3½ pounds)	450°F	13 to 15 minutes per pound (and an additional 15 to 20 minutes if stuffed)	180°F at inner thigh
Chicken, unstuffed (4 to 7 pounds)	350°F	20 minutes per pound (and an additional 20 minutes if stuffed)	180°F at inner thigh
Duckling, unstuffed (4 to 5 pounds)	400°F for 30 minutes; continue roasting at 350°	15 to 18 minutes per pound	180°F at inner thigh
Turkey, stuffed or unstuffed (10 to 24 pounds)	325°F	12 to 15 minutes per pound	180°F at inner thigh
Beef			
Rib eye, boneless— (3 pounds)	350°F	12 to 13 minutes per pound for rare	130°F for rare and 140° for medium
Tenderloin (3 to 3½ pounds)	425°F for 15 minutes; continue at 350°F	11 to 12 minutes per pound for rare	130°F for rare and 140° for medium
Brisket (5 to 6 pounds)	375°F	30 to 35 minutes per pound	
Veal			
Loin, bone in (4 to 6 pounds)	350°F	20 to 25 minutes per pound	165° to 170°F
Breast, stuffed (6½ to 7½ pounds)	350°F	20 to 25 minutes per pound	165° to 170°F
Lamb			
Leg, with bone (6 to 8 pounds)	325°F	20 minutes per pound for rare and 25 minutes per pound for medium	135° to 140°F for rare and 150° to 155°F for medium
Leg, boned, stuffed, and rolled (6 to 8 pounds)	325°F	20 minutes per pound for rare and 25 minutes per pound for medium	135° to 140°F for rare and 150° to 155°F for medium
Pork			
Crown roast (6 to 10 pounds)	350°F	20 to 22 minutes per pound	150° to 160°F
Loin (3 to 5 pounds)	350°F	20 to 22 minutes per pound	150° to 160°F
Ham, fully cooked with bone in (12 to 14 pounds)	350°F	10 to 12 minutes per pound	130° to 140°F

*Note that poultry and meats should rest 15 minutes before carving—the temperature will rise an additional 5° to 10°F as the meat rests.

Metric Conversions

Imperial	Metric
1/4 teaspoon	1 ml
1/2 teaspoon	2 ml
1 teaspoon	5 ml
1 tablespoon	15 ml
2 tablespoons	25 ml
3 tablespoons	50 ml
1/4 cup	50 ml
1/3 cup	75 ml
1/2 cup	125 ml
2/3 cup	150 ml
3/4 cup	175 ml
1 cup	250 ml

TEMPERATURES

Fahrenheit	Celsius
32°	0°
212°	100°
250°	121°
275°	140°
300°	150°
325°	160°
350°	180°
375°	190°
400°	200°
425°	220°
450°	230°
475°	240°

Measuring Equivalents

1 pinch = less than ⅛ teaspoon (dry)
1 dash = 3 drops to ¼ teaspoon (liquid)
3 teaspoons = 1 tablespoon = ½ ounce
2 tablespoons = 1 ounce
4 tablespoons = 2 ounces = ¼ cup

8 tablespoons = 4 ounces = ½ cup
16 tablespoons = 8 ounces = 1 cup = ½ pound
32 tablespoons = 16 ounces = 2 cups = 1 pound
4 cups = 1 quart

Glossary

Baste: To brush or ladle liquid, such as pan drippings, over food as it cooks.

Beat: To stir vigorously with a spoon, wire whisk, beater, or electric mixer.

Blanch: To dip food in boiling water for a brief time to partially cook it or to loosen the skins of fruits or vegetables.

Blend: To mix ingredients together using a spoon, wire whisk, blender, or electric mixer.

Braise: To brown meat and then cook slowly in a small amount of liquid.

Cooling rack: A grid of heavy wire intended for holding baked goods while they cool. Cool cakes for 20 minutes in their pans on the cooling racks, then remove from pans and allow to cool completely on the rack. Remove yeast breads from their pans directly after baking and set them on the cooling rack to prevent the crust from becoming too moist.

Cream: To mix together sugar and fats such as butter until the mixture reaches a creamy consistency.

Crisp-tender: Food, mainly vegetables, that is cooked through but remains a bit crunchy.

Cut in: To blend together cold fats such as butter or shortening with flour or sugar—typically using a pastry blender or two knives in a crosswise motion—so that the resulting mixture resembles coarse crumbs.

Deglaze: To loosen browned bits of food from the bottom and sides of a pan by adding liquid and scraping the pan.

Fold: To mix ingredients gently into another mixture such as a batter.

Julienne: To cut food—mainly fruits and vegetables—into pieces resembling matchsticks.

Knead: To work dough by pressing and folding it repeatedly with the heels of the hands.

Marinate: To saturate food in a seasoned liquid, called a marinade, to tenderize it and/or enhance its flavor.

Poach: To simmer gently in liquid.

Puree: To blend or grind food until it is the consistency of a paste or a thick liquid.

Reduce: To boil liquid in an uncovered pan until much of the liquid evaporates, resulting in more concentrated flavor of the remaining liquid.

Scald: To heat milk to just below its boiling point (when small bubbles begin to form at the sides of the pan).

Sear: To cook meat on high heat on all sides, to seal in juices.

Simmer: To cook in liquid that is just below the boiling point.

Truss: To tie the wings or legs of poultry in such a way that all the pieces are compact.

Whip: To beat ingredients rapidly with a whisk, beater, or electric mixer until the mixture is light and fluffy.

Essentials of Food Safety

GENERAL TIPS

- Wash your hands often while cooking and before serving or eating food.

- Clean kitchen surfaces with hot soapy water, followed by a bleach solution or commercial cleanser.

- Use paper towels when possible, and keep any dish rags or sponges scrupulously clean by washing them in the dishwasher, as they can transmit bacteria to other surfaces.

CHOOSING AND STORING FOODS

- Purchase only those foods that are kept at proper temperatures in the store. Put items that must be kept cold (or hot) last on your list, and take them home immediately. If a package of frozen food appears to have leaked, do not buy it—it may have thawed at an earlier point.

- Do not open cans that are swollen or dented. The food may not be unsafe, but you will not be able to tell by looking at it.

- Wash the lids of canned goods with hot, soapy water before opening.

- Hot foods should be kept hot (above 140°) and cold foods cold (below 40°).

- Store raw meats in the bottom of the refrigerator, in leak-proof containers, so their juice does not drip and contaminate other items.

- Refrigerate cooked food as soon as a meal is finished—definitely within two hours. Mark all leftovers with the date by which they should be used—typically three to five days after it was cooked.

PREPARING FOODS

- Use hot, soapy water to wash your hands and any utensil or surface that has come into contact with raw meat, poultry, or fish. If vegetables or other ingredients touch an unwashed surface, you risk cross-contaminating them with the dangerous bacteria that can reside on uncooked meats, poultry, and fish.

- Wash fruits and vegetables thoroughly under cold running water before using.

- Marinate food in the refrigerator rather than on the countertop, and discard the marinade when you are finished. If you want to use it as a sauce, scoop a bit out of the bowl before you begin to marinate.

- Never set frozen meat or poultry on the counter to thaw; instead thaw it in the refrigerator. Alternatively, thaw it quickly in the microwave oven on the defrost setting.

- Cook foods to their proper temperature (see chart on the inside cover of this book). Use a high-quality meat thermometer to make certain that meats and poultry are cooked thoroughly.

- Cook eggs until all parts of the egg are firm, and avoid preparing foods such as homemade mayonnaise, Caesar salad dressing, or eggnog that require the use of raw eggs. If you want to prepare these foods, consider using pasteurized eggs, which are available in most grocery stores. Note that commercial preparations are safe.

- Before cooking lobsters, crabs, oysters, clams, or mussels, tap their shells to be sure they are alive (they will close up when tapped). Discard any that do not move, or any with cracked shells.

The Well-Stocked Pantry

TO KEEP IN THE KITCHEN CABINET
Beans, variety of dried or canned
Lentils, dried
Spaghetti or other long dried pasta
Penne or other small dried pasta
Egg noodles
Rice, white, brown, wild
Bread crumbs
Dried mushrooms
Beef Broth
Chicken Broth
Vegetable Broth
Canned whole tomatoes
Tomato sauce
Tomato paste
Olives
Canned fruits and vegetables
Extra-virgin olive oil
Vegetable oil
Balsamic vinegar
Red and white wine
Coffee
Tea

TO KEEP IN THE SPICE RACK
Basil
Bay leaves
Cinnamon
Dill
Ginger
Nutmeg
Oregano
Parsley
Pepper
Rosemary
Salt
Thyme

TO KEEP IN THE REFRIGERATOR
Dijon mustard
Parmesan cheese
Variety of cheeses
Unsalted Butter
Eggs
Sour cream
Lemons

TO KEEP IN THE PRODUCE DRAWER
Garlic bulbs
Onions
Potatoes

TO KEEP IN THE BAKING CUPBOARD
Flour
Baking powder
Baking soda
Cornstarch
Brown sugar
Confectioners' sugar
Granulated sugar
Vanilla extract
Chocolate, chips and semisweet blocks
Raisins
Walnuts

Index